WHAT READERS ARE SAYING

"This book completely changed the way I think about spending, saving, and investing ... it's a roadmap for anyone wanting a stronger financial future."

—Harrison, New York, NY

"Landing my first professional job after college, I needed this book. It really helped me UNDERSTAND money management and has dramatically increased my ability to make wise financial choices for myself."

—Claire, Truckee, CA

"If I would have read this book years ago when I was 25, I would have done a lot of things differently."

—Jerry, Boston, MA

"A great manual for handling personal finances. Full of advice on things to do to build wealth, as well as pointing out many common mistakes to avoid."

—Dennis, Hiddenite, NC

"Practical, easy to understand ideas on how to become financially independent from someone who has actually done it."

—David, Charleston, SC

"What a refreshing read of logical common sense! Kurt Reid has done an outstanding job of explaining the areas of personal finances, investing, and wealth building in such a simple manner. This book is an outstanding read for those who want to grow their wealth."

—Mark, Hickory, NC

"After reading the tax-advantaged account chapter, my wife and I immediately increased the amount we are contributing to our 401(k)s."

—Eric, Morganton, NC

"EARN-SAVE-INVEST-REPEAT. A call to action for solid financial planning. This is our investment plan: past, present, and future! Right on target! A good read and great investment advice."

—Tom, Moberly, MO

"My first action item after reading this book was to sign up for an HSA. I had no idea that an HSA could be used as a tax-friendly investment vehicle."

—Nick, St. Louis, MO

"This thorough and well-thought-out book would be helpful to those trying to improve on their money management."

—Gwen, Surf City, NC

"Kurt's approach to producing a net worth statement, income statement, and budget will help many people understand, and improve upon, their financial circumstances."

—Jerry, Tampa, FL

"I had always been told that credit cards were bad so I never had one. After reading the credit card chapter, I got my first card and have been using it wisely to my benefit."

—Wyatt, Raleigh, NC

"I've had money sitting around in the bank for a while and have just never taken the time to figure out how to use it in a future-oriented way. But with this book, I now have a lot of options and the tools to choose wisely. I'm glad I read it!"

—Bob, Omaha, NE

FINANCIAL FREEDOM SIMPLIFIED

A GUIDE FOR BUILDING WEALTH

KURT REID

Reid All About It
PUBLISHING

Financial Freedom Simplified: A Guide for Building Wealth
Published by Reid All About It Publishing, LLC
Morganton, NC

ISBN: 978-0-578-34257-3
BUSINESS & ECONOMICS / Personal Finance / Money Management

Publisher's Cataloging-in-Publication data

Names: Reid, Kurt C., author.
Title: Financial freedom simplified : a guide for building wealth / Kurt Reid. Description: Reid All About It Publishing, 2022. Identifiers: ISBN: 978-0-578-34257-3
Subjects: LCSH Investments. | Finance, Personal. | Retirement income. | BISAC BUSINESS & ECONOMICS / Finance / Wealth Management | BUSINESS & ECONOMICS / Personal Finance / Money Management
Classification: LCC HG4521 .R45 2022 | DDC 332.6--dc23

Cover and Interior design by Victoria Wolf, wolfdesignandmarketing.com. Copyright owned by Kurt Reid

100% of the author's and publisher's profit will be donated to charity.

CONTENTS

PART IV: REPEAT

CONCLUDING THOUGHTS

MISSION STATEMENT

The mission of this book is to assist individuals who want to improve their financial well-being, accumulate wealth, and progress toward financial freedom by providing useful and actionable information relative to personal financial matters.

PREFACE

WHY THIS BOOK ... WHY NOW?

The years 2020 and 2021 will forever be remembered as the era of the coronavirus pandemic, COVID-19. The loss of human life was enormous, and the negative social and economic implications touched all of us. But there could be an ironic positive aspect of the pandemic—sort of a scared straight moment for some people relative to how they handle their personal finances. Stress, fear, and anxiety levels went through the roof for many Americans as the pandemic shut down a huge chunk of our economy and society.

Millions of people with little or no savings and suddenly no job found themselves in a precarious and scary situation. Their primary financial salvation would become a newfound government welfare system of expanded unemployment benefits, government checks for almost everyone, forgivable loans for businesses, rent relief, etc.

Pre-COVID-19, many people had been poor fiduciaries of their finances by choice because they valued other gratifications more than financial security. More candidly, many people choose short-term pleasure at the expense of long-term pain relative to money management.

Many people would like to do better financially, but they just don't know how, or they don't see it as a realistic possibility. Perhaps the mentors in their life have modeled a different behavior for them: You get a job, you pay the bills, you spend, and enjoy what's left. If there's nothing left after paying the bills, you don't buy extra stuff. You wait for the next paycheck. If there is extra money, then you buy and consume more, and live a "better" life. That's what ordinary people are supposed to do, right?

Looking beyond the coronavirus pandemic, maybe there will be an increase in the number of people motivated to do better with their finances going forward. The pandemic was a harsh dose of reality; the economic music stopped, and good luck if you didn't have a financial chair to sit in.

After the pandemic spread across the United States in March 2020, the US Department of Commerce's Bureau of Economic Analysis (bea.gov) reported that the *personal saving rate* hit an all-time high of 32.2% in April 2020, shattering the previous *personal saving rate* record of 17.3% in May 1975. The following month, May 2020, was the second-highest month ever at 23.2%.

In other words, the pandemic very quickly got a lot of people on board with the concept of retaining money for financial security. However, a more effective long-term financial game plan is to save and invest consistently year after year, not wait until a pandemic breaks out to do so.

MY JOURNEY

Since childhood, I have had two major passions: baseball and money. More specifically, the oversight and investment of money. As an adolescent, I was captivated by the wonder of compound earnings. It seemed almost magical to me that your money could make more money for you. As a youngster, I constructed tables filled with handwritten calculations of how long it would take to become a millionaire.

It was fascinating to tinker with the three mathematical variables in those calculations: (1) the amount invested, (2) the rate of return, and (3) the length of time invested. I was particularly inspired when I realized how compounding at a few percent higher rate would get to $1 million so much faster, and if twice as much money were contributed per year, I would get there even sooner!

Little did I know at the time that the financial guiding light for the rest of my life was firmly in place before I even entered high school. Those handwritten compound earning tables from 50 years ago were the genesis of this book and the bedrock for the EARN+SAVE+INVEST+REPEAT formula to accumulate wealth and improve financial well-being. The steps and numbers in the tables virtually screamed at me—the more you EARN, the more you SAVE, the better you INVEST, and the more years you REPEAT it, the more success you will have with the process.

The more you EARN, the more you SAVE, the better you INVEST, and the more years you REPEAT it, the more success you will have at accumulating wealth.

It was intriguing to consider the possibility of how quickly someone's invested money could start making more money than what they were earning at their job, at which point, I rationalized, they wouldn't need to have a job any longer. My handwritten compound tables showed it could certainly be done in much less than a single lifetime. I also noticed that many of the adults I knew didn't seem to particularly love going to work every day; they did so because they had to.

I didn't associate accumulating wealth with a lavish lifestyle or having material possessions like big houses, expensive cars, and certainly not fancy clothes or jewelry. I understood those things are not wealth; they are expenses that actually make wealth accumulation more difficult. Also, I didn't have a desire to grow wealthy to have a social status of appearing *rich*. Material possessions and appearances never meant much to me, and they still don't.

What appealed to me (a lot) was how wealth accumulation equated to freedom. For example, freedom of choice, to do what I wanted to do and live how I wanted to live. It also meant security and safety to be able to handle the unforeseen financial calamities that inevitably occur in life. Once someone had enough wealth that the earnings from their investments could pay for all their expenses with some extra cushion, they would be free to choose how they spent their time—in essence, to decide if they wanted to continue to have a job. I really liked those concepts.

Simply put, at a young age, I associated wealth accumulation with having security and freedom, not with having status and lots of stuff. Consequently, I never viewed having a large income as the ultimate goal. Income is important, very important, as it is the source to start the wealth accumulation process. However, income is yesterday; how much of that income is retained and added to your investments is the future. A large income that is rapidly consumed and spent does nothing to gain security and financial freedom for the future.

A large income that is rapidly consumed and spent does nothing to gain financial security and freedom for the future.

I may not be able to tell you what our family income has been in years past, but I still have our net worth statement for every six months since I got out of college. It's a 39-year quantitative and graphic scorecard for my wife, Ruth, and myself of how we progressed with wealth accumulation. But what it really shows is our trajectory of improving our level of financial well-being over the years.

After wrecking my shoulder in college, the dream of playing big league baseball ended. My focus quickly pivoted to wealth accumulation in a major way. As I neared my college graduation date, I turned down a couple of job offers because they didn't have enough earnings potential for my liking.

I ultimately landed the job I really wanted as a financial advisor (stockbroker). I loved the vocation, and the compensation structure was a perfect match for my ambitions—100% commission and 0% salary. The sky was the limit. My first job out of college put me in a unique position to succeed with step one (EARN) in the wealth accumulation process. (Thank you to my longtime friend, Donald Ray, for urging me to be an investment advisor before I ever considered the possibility.)

Excellent earning potential existed for those who did well as an investment advisor, and I worked extremely hard to build a customer base. I enjoyed interacting with my clients, and I thoroughly appreciated having a job where I was essentially my own boss with great latitude as to how to run the business.

By some standards, it would be fair to say I worked too much in those early years, but it honestly didn't feel like work, as it was extremely satisfying to build a business and see it steadily grow over the months and years. On a more personal level, it was also rewarding to help my clients with their investments and to see them accumulate wealth. My wife and I still live in the same town my office was in, and it's always nice when I run into a former client who tells me how much they appreciate a mutual fund I put them in decades ago that they still own.

My years as an investment advisor were a positive experience for me professionally and personally. I was a diligent worker, but I also enjoyed the process along the way. My employer had wonderful incentive trips a couple of times a year all over the world that Ruth and I never passed up.

Ruth and I did everything we could to make the EARN step successful, and after only seven years in the business, I was the number one producer in the company for a year. Each year, I was consistently near the top of the production rankings of the firm's 1,000 or so financial advisors.

With the full support of my young bride (now wife of 38 years), we lived well below our means as we mastered the SAVE step. Working for a brokerage firm made the INVEST step an easy process, as I put our money primarily in the same investments as my clients. Although I had not yet given any thought to naming the steps, the EARN+SAVE+INVEST+REPEAT process was working well for us. The wonder of compound earnings made accumulating wealth and improving our financial well-being easier and easier over the years.

After 12 years as a financial advisor and a year after having the first of our three children, I left the brokerage business at age 36 and have been a private investor ever since. I have spent my adult life dealing with the care, investing, and management of money for others and myself. Along the way, I have continually learned and broadened my knowledge and awareness of the constantly evolving world of money, finance, and investing. I certainly don't know everything about these topics, and I'm much more of a common-sense generalist than an expert in all things related to the wealth accumulation process.

Do for a while what most people won't so you can live the rest of your life like most people can't.

The central theme of this book is improving financial well-being by following the simple steps of EARN+SAVE+INVEST+REPEAT to accumulate wealth. Nobody explicitly taught or explained this to me, although my dad did a pretty good job of modeling it. My personal journey isn't the typical middle-class story of working at a job for 40 years, but in terms of following the four steps with the support of my wife, we lived it and we nailed it. Taking good care of money seemed as natural and logical to me as exercising, eating right, and getting a good night's sleep does for others. For example, I've never bought a lottery ticket in my life because I know how bad the odds are. It would actually make me feel rather foolish to squander money doing something where the chances are so stacked against me.

Money management, investing, and wealth accumulation have been a keen interest of mine and source of enjoyment for over 50 years now, and I've learned a great deal along the way. Sometimes I've learned a better way by initially choosing a poor way.

Many people don't have the wind at their backs like I did—with so many of my family members and friends serving as positive role models; excellent mentors in the form of coaches, teachers, and business associates; having the opportunity to attend college on an athletic scholarship; and landing my dream job right out of college with an industry-leading company that provided excellent training and support to enable me to succeed.

Ruth and I both grew up in upper-middle-class families, but neither of us has ever inherited money, and we basically began our adult lives as broke newlyweds. Both of us had an innate drive to make our own way financially.

Although we never needed or received monetary help from our families after college, I always felt a deep-rooted sense of security knowing, if I ever really needed help, my parents would have been there for me.

Especially for those people who don't have some of the advantages I have had, I hope that sharing my thoughts and knowledge about the wealth accumulation process can help them improve their financial well-being.

Simply stated, relative to the EARN+SAVE+INVEST+REPEAT process, I envisioned it as a child; my wife and I lived it and succeeded at it as adults; and now I would like to share it with others as an author.

If you find this book helpful, or if you have comments on how it can be improved, I would enjoy hearing from you.

Kurt Reid
kurtreid59@gmail.com

INTRODUCTION

WHAT THIS BOOK *IS*

This book contains information, strategies, and opinions on a wide range of personal money management topics to help readers proceed confidently with the EARN+SAVE+INVEST+REPEAT steps to improve financial well-being, accumulate wealth, and gain financial freedom. This includes positive actions to take as well as specific things to avoid. The book also contains an honest and frank discussion of why so many people have difficulty improving their financial well-being and accumulating wealth.

Most importantly, this book is for YOU! The fact you are taking the time to read this introduction indicates you have interest and desire to learn more about how you can have success in advancing your level of financial well-being. I did it, and chances are, you can too.

WHAT THIS BOOK IS *NOT*

This book does *not* contain information such as "secret tips so you can trade options like the pros" or "how to outsmart Wall Street for only six easy payments of just $39.99." It's not a fountain of investing secrets and untold strategies on how to outperform the market or how to get rich quick. It would be nice if I did have some whiz-bang money-magic advice that would make the wealth accumulation process fast and easy, but I don't.

Pertaining to the investing step of the process, the book primarily focuses on passive investments that do not require ongoing hands-on management. Hence, the book does not cover ownership or management of commercial businesses, or active participation in real estate for investment purposes. Obviously, active business and real estate ventures are viable options for wealth accumulation and investing. However, they generally take a much higher level of time commitment as they are often a full-time vocation rather than a passive investment. Many books have been written about such active types of investing and those topics are beyond the scope of this book.

CONTENT AND FLOW OF THE BOOK

This book is divided into four parts that align with the four sequential steps of EARN+SAVE+INVEST+REPEAT. Step one of the formula, EARN, is covered in Chapter 3 of Part I. Earning money (wages) is as vital to the process as the other three steps. However, this book's primary focus is the handling, management, and investing of money. This is not a career or employment book, or a book about "side hustle" jobs.

In Chapter 3, however, I touch on how being a productive wage earner can impact wealth accumulation, and I offer some general views about employment and personal productivity. But, if in-depth career or job information is what you are seeking, I would refer you to other more appropriate books for those topics.

In Part II (SAVE) and Part III (INVEST), each chapter covers specific topics. For example, there is a chapter specifically on credit cards, another chapter about insurance, another about mutual funds and ETFs, and so on. In essence, most of the chapters are like independent pieces of the personal financial jigsaw puzzle. They fit together nicely, but each piece has its own distinct part.

At the end of 10 different chapters are the stories of various individuals I have personally known who were inspirational to me. Although these stories are not specific to personal finances, I believe each one of them has a powerful message that parallels the effort and discipline to improve financial well-being and succeed with the wealth accumulation process. Hopefully, sharing these stories will encourage readers to persevere and work through challenges relative to their personal financial journey or other aspects of their lives.

SUGGESTIONS ON HOW TO READ THE BOOK

The content of each chapter is generally independent of other chapters. Therefore, you are welcome to go directly to specific chapters of most interest to you. You may have a different level of interest in each of the chapters based on your own level of knowledge and experience with that particular content. Hence, allocate your reading time and focus according to your personal situation. However, I would encourage you to read the Preface first and then the entirety of Part I in sequential order, because these sections provide an appropriate context and introduction for the rest of the book.

PART I

Financial Well-Being
Introduction and Overview

CHAPTER 1

Financial Well-Being and the Case for Wealth Accumulation

THE PROPOSITION

This book's basic proposition is that average Americans can consistently improve their financial well-being, have financial security, and obtain financial freedom by following the simple steps of EARN+SAVE+INVEST+REPEAT to accumulate wealth.

It's easy to understand the straightforward concept of using those four steps to accumulate wealth. However, it's not always easy to do it diligently day by day, month by month, and year after year. Wealth accumulation seldom happens by accident. It happens by being disciplined and consistent while taking specific and intentional actions.

Wealth accumulation seldom happens by accident. It happens by being disciplined and consistent while taking specific and intentional actions.

The process also requires adaptability and continually gaining new knowledge. Wealth accumulation requires more than simply putting a plan in place, as it's not a stagnant process. For most people, enduring success with the process requires continual effort, ongoing learning, adapting to market conditions, planning, diligence, consistency, follow-through, and self-restraint. For many people, including myself, it is an ongoing endeavor that becomes a way of life.

In addition to having the desire and commitment to improve your financial well-being, it also requires the knowledge of how to do so. This is like understanding that one aspect of living healthy is eating a healthy diet, but it also requires some basic and specific knowledge about food and nutrition. Likewise, it's not enough to simply believe in the EARN+SAVE+INVEST+REPEAT formula. It also requires an understanding of specific financial tools, accounts, tax laws, and investment options, as well as numerous other topics, such as specific actions and strategies that can be used.

Being a productive EARNER is a lifetime accomplishment in which most individuals take pride. Being a judicious and thoughtful SAVER of part of the money you earn becomes habit forming. Being a good INVESTOR of the money saved requires ongoing attention and is a constant work in progress. REPEATING the process for many years obviously requires a steadfast focus on each of the first three steps.

The goal is not accumulating wealth just for the sake of being wealthy. First gain financial security and then financial freedom, which is the ultimate objective. Money is simply the way financial well-being and financial freedom are denominated. You are not free if you're always at the mercy of having to make the next paycheck to survive financially. Simply put, wealth *purchases* financial security, financial freedom, and the ability to choose. The accumulation of wealth, which requires the retention of money and growth thereof, provides the freedom to focus on the more important things in life.

The ultimate goal of wealth accumulation is to have financial security and financial freedom.

FOR THE NAYSAYERS

Some people view the entire concept of wealth accumulation as a negative proposition to the current enjoyment of life: "Every dollar I save is a dollar I don't get to enjoy. I don't want to be a penny-pincher, have no fun, and hoard money, so I can die rich." They view saving as a zero-sum game. In reality, it's the other way around! People with poor money management habits are routinely broke because they squandered their disposable income and, therefore, get to do fewer things.

I have wonderful news for those naysayers. It's not about *doing without*; it's about generally *doing better*. Accumulating wealth doesn't mean living like a miser, but rather living wisely and utilizing the various financial opportunities available to continually improve your financial well-being to live your best life. You can still enjoy life while accumulating wealth, but it requires discipline, consistency, perhaps learning some new money management skills, and at times, saying no to unnecessary spending.

Money is like a farmer's seeds. If properly planted (invested) and cared for, money will multiply just like the farmer's crop. Over time, some disciplined saving and investing today can multiply and grow to provide a bountiful crop of money, which in turn can potentially equate to an even more fulfilling and abundant life.

**It's not about doing without. It's about doing better—
living wisely and utilizing financial opportunities to
improve your financial well-being to live your best life.**

THE SUE WATSON STORY

Sue Watson was my extremely capable office administrator when I was a financial advisor (broker). She and I were a team for eight years until I left the company. I used to say, "My job is to sell, and Sue's job is to do everything else."

Sue graduated from a local high school and did not attend college. Her family was working class, and commanding a high income or having significant wealth were not familiar areas to Sue. However, working in an investment advisor's office was eye-opening for her. She witnessed firsthand how other people had accumulated wealth and how it had positively impacted their lives.

Sue was also well aware of the large difference between the wages she made as an office administrator and what I made as a licensed financial advisor. When I left the company, she stayed on and was the administrator for the new advisor, who was my successor.

Ten years later, at age 51, Sue wanted the opportunity to be a financial advisor instead of an office administrator. She also knew such a career change would come with numerous obstacles and challenges.

Her application to be an advisor was accepted by the company. She then had to pass the rigorous licensing exam, followed by months of training in the advisor role. Next, she had to move away from her hometown and her close-knit extended family for the first time to her new office location. Then the real work began, interfacing with investors and earning their business in her new community, overcoming her fear of public speaking, and much more.

Not only did she succeed, but after 16 years, Sue is still going strong in 2022 as a financial advisor. Honestly, I had my doubts if Sue would make it. About 50% of new financial advisors don't last through the first year. Gaining people's confidence so they will invest their hard-earned money with you is not an easy task.

Two expressions come to mind when I think of Sue: "If you believe it, you can achieve it" and "Why not me?" When others doubted her, she didn't back down. Compared to the typical new financial advisor, she was undereducated, under-skilled, under-experienced, and overaged, but none of that stopped her.

The decision to take the risk of going way outside of her comfort zone was life-changing for Sue and her family financially, as well as an accomplishment in which she deservedly takes great pride. As her early mentor in the business, it brings me joy to think I played some role in her successful career.

SUE'S LESSON: The rewards can be enormous for those with the courage and follow-through who dare to take risks to pursue better opportunities.

CHAPTER 2

Levels of Financial Well-Being

Independence, security, and freedom—are terms we often hear in regard to financial well-being. But what do they actually mean? Often, these terms mean different things to different people. However, there is a definable difference between each of them, with independence being the most basic, freedom being the ultimate, and security falling in the middle. Let's take a closer look at each level …

FINANCIAL INDEPENDENCE

Financial independence is the ability to pay for all of your own expenses without assistance. For example, if someone must rely on their parents to pay their rent or help with their car payment, then they are not yet financially independent. Besides the obvious monetary implications of becoming financially independent, there can also be benefits from a psychological and self-esteem perspective. Becoming self-sufficient is a major positive milestone that young adults generally deserve to feel good about.

The term financially independent is sometimes used to describe immensely wealthy people. I use the term in a more basic way by simply meaning not dependent on others financially, but it doesn't necessarily mean someone has accumulated significant wealth yet.

FINANCIAL SECURITY

Financial security means having adequate savings or investments to be able to handle unexpected financial setbacks without having to rely on assistance from others or make substantial lifestyle changes. Monetary reserves equal to at least six months of living expenses is a good starting point to having financial security. Someone who is financially independent but who lives paycheck to paycheck with no money in savings is not financially secure. If they become unemployed or a significant expense arises, they would likely need financial assistance.

FINANCIAL FREEDOM

Financial freedom is acquired when a significant amount of wealth has been accumulated. Having a job becomes optional when investment assets are large enough that a paycheck is no longer needed. Having the financial capacity to easily pay for all planned and unforeseen expenses is another benchmark of financial freedom. The ability to afford significant discretionary expenditures is often associated with financial freedom—such as vacations and travel, second homes, consumer purchases, supporting charities, and assisting others financially.

There is a large gap between the most basic level of financial *security* and obtaining financial *freedom*. The parameters of financial freedom can vary substantially from one person to another. One individual may have a lifestyle in which $1 million in investment assets would provide a comfortable level of financial freedom, whereas an ultra-wealthy individual with an extravagant lifestyle may spend more than that in a month.

THE FINANCIAL WELL-BEING HIERARCHY

Following is a pyramid diagram titled "The Financial Well-Being Hierarchy." In the pyramid, I separate financial well-being into seven separate categories as opposed to just the three discussed at the beginning of this chapter. In reality, there are no sharp dividers separating the various levels of financial well-being.

All of us fit in somewhere on a continual financial spectrum. For example, virtually all young children are at the bottom of the pyramid as they are 100% dependent on others to pay for their financial needs. The Legacy group at the top of the pyramid would generally include the wealthiest individuals. Most people fit in somewhere between those two extremes. There is virtually an endless amount of gradations at each level of the pyramid. Numerous alternative descriptions and titles could be used to describe the various levels as well.

The Financial Well-Being Hierarchy

LEGACY
The transfer of wealth
is paramount.

FINANCIAL FREEDOM
Significant wealth.
Complete freedom of lifestyle.

PRE-FINANCIAL FREEDOM
Aggressively increasing net worth.

FINANCIALLY STABLE
Some financial reserves. Regularly adds to savings. Stable lifestyle.

FINANCIALLY UNSTABLE
Not able to save. Self sufficient, but virtually no financial reserves.

FINANCIALLY DEFICIENT
Unable to take care of all personal expenses. Partially dependent on others financially.

FINANCIALLY DEPENDENT
Completely dependent on others for all financial needs. Has no savings and no income.

CHAPTER 3

The Formula for Wealth Accumulation

There are four distinct steps to the formula for accumulating wealth. The first is EARNING—applying your skills and abilities to being the best wage earner you can be. The second is SAVING—retaining money and not spending everything you make. The third step is INVESTING—wisely positioning the money you save so it multiplies and makes more money for you. The fourth step is REPEATING—doing the first three steps over and over for many years.

Generally, significant wealth accumulation is not instant pudding; typically, it takes years to accomplish. Unless you receive a large inheritance or have extraordinary financial success in some other capacity, it is generally a repetitive process to accumulate wealth. Although each of the steps is uniquely different from each of the other steps, they will ideally all occur simultaneously as you earn, save, invest, and repeat in unison on an ongoing basis.

Succinctly stated, the simple steps to wealth accumulation are:

Step 1: EARN
Step 2: SAVE
Step 3: INVEST
Step 4: REPEAT

It could be said the four steps are all equally important. More accurately stated, they are each important, but their relative importance is seldom equal at any given time. For example, in the early years when someone is just starting the wealth accumulation process, earning and saving money is dramatically more important than the rate of return earned on the relatively small amount of money invested. Conversely, if someone has a large amount invested, the rate of return on their invested money becomes more important than how much additional money they are saving.

Here's a hypothetical example of someone just starting the wealth accumulation process with $2,000 invested: They had great success investing the $2,000, as it grew to $2,600 in the first year, a whopping 30% return! Meanwhile, they paid $100 a month for a gym membership they seldom used, regularly paid late fees on their credit card because they never paid on time, and spent $1,500 during the year on shoes alone. Even though they produced a fantastic rate of return on their $2,000, they would have been thousands of dollars further toward accumulating wealth if their primary focus had been on managing expenses more judiciously. They earned $600 from investing but wasted much more on unnecessary expenses.

The rest of this chapter is devoted to providing a deeper discussion on each of the four steps of the wealth accumulation formula.

STEP 1: EARN

For some individuals, the best way to energize the wealth accumulation process is to earn more in wages.[1] A relatively small increase in wages can result in a huge increase in wealth accumulation if a meaningful portion of those extra wages are saved and invested wisely.

For example, let's assume a young single person is making $50,000 a year working five days a week at their nine-to-five job, and it costs them $47,500 a year to pay all their bills. They diligently save and invest the excess $2,500 in their 401(k) each year in a mix of stock mutual funds. Let's assume their 401(k) grows at an average annual rate of 10%, and after 20 years, they have accumulated $174,000.

But what if they made $55,000 instead of $50,000 per year and were, therefore, able to invest $7,500 a year instead of $2,500? Just a $5,000 increase in wages could triple the amount of their 401(k) contributions, so after 20 years, their 401(k) balance could be $522,000 instead of $174,000.

A relatively small increase in wages has the potential to have an enormous impact on wealth accumulation.

People often toil away working five days a week to pay their bills, but they have no desire to do just a bit more to accumulate wealth and enhance their financial well-being. Here are some possibilities:

$ Be as good as you can be at your job.

$ Make yourself worthy of a raise or a promotion.

$ Prepare yourself to be ready for a more rewarding job opportunity or career change.

---

1   For clarity, "earn" in the context of the wealth accumulation formula is in reference to wages or employment; whereas passive earnings made from money invested is an inherent part of step 3 (INVEST).

$ Improve your skills and education when possible.

$ Be proactive to be aware of opportunities that may be available to you.

$ Be willing to put forth the time and effort to maximize your potential.

$ Take on a *side hustle* opportunity.

Taking on a *side hustle* job could be the difference maker for substantially improving your financial well-being by providing that extra 10% of income. Ideally, pick something you are good at and enjoy. That combination will be beneficial for both your financial health and mental health.

If you love animals, walk dogs for your side hustle. If you are a talented musician, give music lessons. If you are a former athlete, provide lessons in your sport. Teachers or those with academic skills can provide tutoring. A good friend of mine is a school principal, but she's a waitress on the weekends because she loves doing it (and she likes the money). If you enjoy the outdoors and doing physical work, do landscaping or mow a few lawns. A friend of mine teaches Chinese kids how to speak English via video lessons. For some people, making 10% more money could be as simple as working overtime one day a week.

Taking on a *side hustle* doing something you enjoy could have significant benefits financially and mentally.

Be willing to put forth the effort and take actions that can lead to more income. Opportunities abound for those who have the desire and take the initiative to progress.

STEP 2: SAVE

During step one (EARN) of the wealth accumulation formula, **you work for the money**. During step three (INVEST), the **money works for you**. Step two (SAVE) is the necessary bridge between those two steps that allows earners to become investors. Unfortunately, the SAVE step is where many otherwise capable people miss the mark and come up short, resulting in minimal progress toward meaningful wealth accumulation. If every increase in wages is offset by expanded spending, then no improvement is being made in terms of financial well-being, which means no progress toward financial freedom.

Countless studies and surveys have been done over the decades related to how much savings (investments) Americans have. Results vary depending on how the study was conducted, but the general conclusion is that 50% or so of our population have virtually no savings. This means half of us would be in a world of hurt if we didn't get a paycheck for a month.

Why Do So Many Americans Have So Little in Savings?

Some people have very little in savings because they legitimately have tough situations. Their life circumstances make it extremely difficult to just *make ends meet*, let alone save money. The notion of investing for some people in our society is not even on the radar. Until other conditions in their life improve, many aspects of this book will simply not be relevant to them.

However, many people believe they are in this group due to no fault of their own, but in reality, their financial lives could be substantially different if they made different choices in deploying and managing what money comes their way.

Second, it takes time—young folks, you get a pass. However, it is quite possible for many young people (teenagers and up) to save and accumulate money if they're really inspired to do so and know how to do it. But if you're out of school and five years later you're still broke, it's probably your fault. Excuses are aplenty, but at some point, you have to own it.

The third reason such a large percentage of Americans have very little savings is because they lack money management skills and financial knowledge. Many people could be dramatically better at accumulating wealth if they had a better understanding of topics such as tax-advantaged accounts, the power of compound earnings, how to be an investor, wise use of credit cards, and how to purchase insurance wisely. The majority of this book covers a wide array of these various money management issues; therefore, I won't go into further detail here.

Fourth, many people are *spenders*, meaning they have *never seen an income they couldn't outspend.* There are millions of Americans who command the income and have the knowledge to accumulate significant wealth, ultimately capable of becoming millionaires if they make different decisions. But putting it bluntly, they systematically spend money unnecessarily year after year and consequently never get ahead.

If someone has a lifestyle laden with unnecessary expenditures, it will likely be difficult to save money and accumulate wealth. A more accurate adage than "money can't buy happiness" is **"unnecessary spending can't buy happiness."** At some point, many people realize that a lot of frivolous consumption hasn't provided any sustained happiness or fulfillment in their lives.

"Money can't buy happiness" ... true, but a more accurate adage is "unnecessary spending can't buy happiness."

The Brainwashing of the American Consumer

Marketing and advertising are effective. As consumers, we have essentially been brainwashed by commercialism to purchase and consume instinctively. As a matter of lifestyle, many people buy things not because they need them, but because they can afford them, or if they can't afford something, they charge it to a credit card. Shopping long ago replaced sports as America's pastime.

Armed with credit and debit cards, we mindlessly spend. It's payday, so we go out to eat. It's spring, so we need new clothes. I'm on my way to work, so I need a $5 cup of coffee. Marketing messages are enticing. "Studies have proven that our products will make you healthier, happier, and live longer." What kind of idiot wouldn't buy that? "Our stuff is faster, cheaper, and more reliable." Well, heck yes, sign me up!

We've been made to believe that truly patriotic Americans have an obligation to shop and spend. We've grown up hearing feel-good phrases like *shop local* and *buy American-made.* It makes you feel like you are some type of selfish SOB if you're not buying stuff with all your money—as if the burden is on you personally to keep the economy going.

There is a certain irony in the way so many Americans routinely end every two-week pay period in the same way—with a depleted bank account and heavily dependent on the next paycheck. Yet many of those same people would say there's nothing they value more in this country than their freedom and independence. But when you're broke, you are not financially free, and you certainly are not independent.

The obvious conclusion is that unnecessary or frivolous spending is the enemy of wealth accumulation. If you want financial freedom, if you want the liberty to focus more on those things that are most important to you, then a careful review of how you are spending your money may not be a bad idea. If you don't retain any of the money you receive and accumulate wealth, then your ability to make choices in the future is substantially diminished. You become trapped in the ongoing cycle of working to subsist. You unwittingly relinquish the independence to choose what, when, where, and how to do things.

Frivolous spending is the enemy of wealth accumulation

Pay Yourself First

Pay yourself first is a strategy financial advisors frequently champion. This simply means to save and invest a portion of your income first and foremost, then make sure your expenditures don't exceed your remaining disposable income. An effective way for many wage earners to accomplish this is by having a fixed percentage of their wages deducted from their paycheck and invested in a retirement account, such as a 401(k). The belief is that if you never receive the money, you won't miss it. I think this is an excellent strategy for most wage earners.

For those readers who would like to work on reducing their expenditures, Chapter 19, titled "Personal Financial Documents" may be helpful as it covers personal budgeting and monitoring of expenses. Other chapters that can help with certain spending decisions include "Credit and Debit Cards" (Chapter 5), "Insurance: What You Need, What You Don't" (Chapter 6), "Home Ownership and Mortgage Loans" (Chapter 7), and "Myths and Misconceptions That Could Cost You Money" (Chapter 22).

STEP 3: INVEST

Investing, which is the next step in the wealth accumulation formula after earning and saving, can be a daunting task, particularly for inexperienced investors. Who can I trust? Where do I go? What do I invest in? Can I lose my money? How much can I make? Is it really worth all the effort to be an *investor*?

As previously mentioned, one of the reasons many people never become meaningful investors is because they lack money management knowledge. Unfortunately, the education system in America has historically had very little emphasis on teaching students about investing and financial affairs. Unless someone receives guidance from family members, they often have little understanding of money management and investing when they enter the workforce.

When they do accumulate some savings to invest, they often don't understand the difference between an investment and an expense, or an asset vs. a liability. They think buying a home is a great investment, when in reality it is an ongoing expense with an extremely low rate of return once all the costs are considered. They think buying a car is an asset, when it's actually a liability. They haven't yet learned the difference between prudent investing and high-risk speculating, and therefore may become disenchanted with the process if they lose money on overly aggressive attempts at what they thought was investing.

Perhaps the most fundamental reason many people are not proactive about investing is they simply don't understand the math of compound earnings. They don't realize how earning just a few percentage points higher return per year can be an absolute game changer when compounded year after year. Compounding is discussed in detail in the next section of this chapter.

In well under a decade, the earnings from an investment portfolio can far exceed the amount originally invested. When invested wisely, money has the potential to multiply many times over during an investor's lifetime. Especially for those who start investing at a young age, it is quite possible the earnings on their investments will eventually exceed the wages they earn from employment.

Time is on the side of the young wage earner, but only if they take advantage of it by saving and investing early. For example, a simple strategy of owning and consistently adding to a tax-advantaged retirement account invested in mutual funds that own high-quality stocks has been an effective and simple time-tested way to accumulate wealth. Many young wage earners could be virtually set for life financially by the time they are age 35 to 40 if they started in their early 20s being judicious savers and wise investors.

When invested wisely, money has the potential to multiply many times over during an investor's lifetime.

Sometimes, people in their 40s or 50s believe they have already missed their opportunity to do well financially. They think it is too late in life for them to worry about saving and investing. Hence, they become content with the rhythm of earning and spending, as the notion of wealth accumulation seems hopeless and out of reach for them.

Many people in this situation are actually in much better financial shape than they realize. The "high-expense era" is coming to an end as they are finishing up paying their home mortgages and raising their kids. For years, they have been paying into the social security system, which will produce a significant monthly income in retirement. Additionally, they are probably in their highest wage-earning years.

The home stretch is in sight with retirement ahead, and finally, the wind is at their back financially—low expenses for the first time in decades and their highest income ever. It is the perfect time to pivot financially and start focusing on wealth accumulation and investing. Readers who are at a similar point in their life will find Chapter 8 of interest as it describes an action plan for a 45-year-old couple with these same circumstances.

Part III (Chapters 9 through 18) is devoted to sharing information about the various investment choices that are available and related issues. Information is provided about the different types of investments, tax considerations, retirement accounts, risk factors, companies and professionals that offer investment services, and much more.

STEP 4: REPEAT

Step 4 (REPEAT) of the wealth accumulation formula is simply continuing with the first three steps on an ongoing basis. It's easy to understand the straightforward concept of EARN+SAVE+INVEST+REPEAT to accumulate wealth. However, being able to consistently follow the formula over the years can be quite challenging.

Oftentimes, the circumstances of life can make the REPEAT step the most challenging of the four. A common scenario is when someone with a good job is saving and investing a nice portion of their earnings each month, and then they need a new car—there goes $600 a month. They buy a house and then discover all the additional costs of home ownership. And maybe they have a child, etc. Before you know it, saving and investing have given way to the expenses of living.

Doing a personal budget can be a valuable tool to help with the REPEAT step to ensure that you continue to save and invest along with earning and spending. The budget and review process identifies exactly how money is being spent, which is helpful for making positive changes. Chapter 19 covers how to do a budget as well as a net worth statement.

The Paperboy Epiphany

Circa 1968, when I was an eight-year-old boy, my brother Billy and I had a paper route. Initially, we were just storing our cash earnings in our bedroom until one day mom had a conversation with us that went something like this:

Mom: "Now that you boys are saving up money from this paper route, you need to set up a savings account at the bank to put your money in."

Boys: "Huh? Why do we need to do that?"

Mom: "It's safe that way. You shouldn't leave money loose in your room. You could lose it."

Boys: "How much does the bank charge to look after our money?"

Mom: "Nothing! They pay you interest on your money."

Boys: "What do you mean by pay 'interest' on our money?"

Mom then did her best to explain what *interest* meant. I was in total amazement that the bank would actually pay me to safeguard my money. I don't think Mom understood it well enough herself to explain how banks profit by charging borrowers a higher rate than they are paying their depositors, but her comments certainly grabbed my attention.

At age eight, this was a seminal moment for me that would profoundly impact the rest of my life. I can still remember the conversation with Mom, and I can remember walking into the institution to open the account. But what I really remember is how fascinated I was with the notion that my money could make more money for me ... the possibilities ... WOW! What a concept!

The revelation that money could make more money had a profound and lasting impact on me when I was a youngster.

I like the old TV commercial where a man is scolding his money. The money is sitting in a big pile on his bed, and he says something like, "I'm tired of you just lying around all the time while I work every day. Starting today, you're going to work!" Then the tagline says, "Don't let your money just lie around while you do all the work. Invest with blah blah blah." Unfortunately, a lot of people do let their money lollygag.

Compound Earnings: The Eighth Wonder of the World

Albert Einstein called compound interest the eighth wonder of the world. However, in the broader context of investing and wealth accumulation, I prefer the term *compound annual growth rate* (CAGR). They mean the same thing mathematically, but CAGR isn't limited specifically to just interest-producing investments. CAGR could also be derived from dividends, capital appreciation, rent, or other types of earnings or gains besides just *interest*. Interest is the annual percent paid on a deposit account or the rate a borrower pays on a loan.

The key word is *compound*, which means to earn on your earnings, or earn interest on your interest. The following is an example of what CAGR means: If $1,000 is invested at the beginning of the year and that investment is worth $1,100 at the end of the year, then it produces a 10% annual rate of return ($100 earnings divided by the $1,000 investment = 10%).

If that investment produced a CAGR of 10% for each of the next two years, it would have earned an increasing amount of gains each year due to compounding. At the beginning of year two, the account had grown to $1,100. $1,100 x 10% = $110 in earnings in year two ($10 more than in year one) because you also earned 10% in year two on the earnings from year one. So, at the end of the second year, the account would be worth $1,210. At the end of year three, the account would be worth $1,331, and so on. This is assuming the account grew at a CAGR of exactly 10% each year.

What Einstein was alluding to captivated my attention when I was a youngster. The enormous difference in total growth that occurs by just a few higher percentage points of CAGR truly is a wondrous thing. For example, the difference in total wealth accumulation between earning 8% vs. 4% for many years is not just twice as much. In time, it will be three times as much, four times as much, or six times as much, depending on how many years it compounds. The spread in terms of dollars becomes exponential the longer it is invested.

The twin engines of this eighth wonder of the world are **time** and the **CAGR**. The longer the time invested and the higher the CAGR, the more exponential the absolute growth of wealth will be. And by the way, these numbers are not specific to money; it's just math. Bunny rabbits, oak trees, bad habits, money, whatever you want to examine will grow identically as long as time and the CAGR are the same.

A third engine, and also very important, is your contribution (how much you save and invest). Even a great CAGR for many years won't do much good if you spend virtually all of your money and invest only a paltry amount.

The following is a table similar to those I created on paper as a young-ster when I initially discovered the wonder of compounding. It shows how a onetime, single investment of $10,000 would grow at various CAGRs for various numbers of years. Comments are provided below the table.

Compound Growth Table for $10,000						
Compound Annual Growth Rate (CAGR)						
Years	**2%**	**4%**	**6%**	**8%**	**10%**	**12%**
0	$10,000	$10,000	$10,000	$10,000	$10,000	$10,000
1	$10,200	$10,400	$10,600	$10,800	$11,000	$11,200
10	$12,190	$14,802	$17,908	$21,589	$25,937	$31,058
20	$14,859	$21,911	$32,071	$46,610	$67,275	$96,463
30	$18,114	$32,434	$57,435	$100,627	$174,494	$299,599
40	$22,080	$48,010	$102,857	$217,245	$452,593	$930,510
50	$26,916	$71,067	$184,202	$469,016	$1,173,909	$2,890,022

Table 3.1

Comments on the Table Above

The table assumes a constant rate of return (CAGR) for each column over a 50-year period. For example, the 2% column assumes the account grew at exactly 2% each year, compounded annually.

Look at the staggering difference between the increase in values over the years in the 10% or 12% CAGR columns vs. the 2% or 4% columns. These numbers graphically demonstrate how impactful it is to repeat the compound-ing for many years. It also shows how important investing wisely can be to wealth accumulation. In other words, there is more to wealth accumulation than simply being a good saver and not wastefully spending money. Selecting investments that produce superior long-term results is a big deal.

The table emphatically illustrates all four of the wealth accumulation steps discussed at the beginning of this chapter: **EARN+SAVE+INVEST+REPEAT**. It is easy to see how time and CAGR impact results by looking at the various columns. However, if someone would have earned less money, or spent half of the $10,000 and only invested $5,000, then every number in the table would be reduced by 50%.

The table does not take into consideration any taxation of gains.

Chapter 21 is devoted entirely to providing compound earning examples for various hypothetical investors. The examples graphically show how the wealth accumulation process is impacted by the three variables of (1) the amount invested, (2) the rate of earnings, and (3) the number of years invested (time).

THE GRANDPA REID STORY

William M. Reid, Grandpa Reid to me, was my father's father. Born in 1900 in Richmond, Missouri, he was the son of a Scottish immigrant. While in high school, he began working as a clerk at Mr. Duval's clothing store in Richmond. Retail clothing was a thriving industry in those days, as three-piece suits and top hats were customary daily attire for many.

By age 27, he had thoroughly learned the business and was, by then, Mr. Duval's assistant manager. Young William was smitten with the idea of owning and running his own men's clothing store, but he didn't have the necessary savings to make it happen. Mr. Duval agreed to provide the financial backing for Grandpa to establish a clothing store in another town, so it wouldn't compete with his Richmond store.

In 1928, Grandpa moved to Moberly, Missouri, and launched a new business—Duval & Reid Clothing Company. For the ensuing 87 years, the business was owned by my grandfather, then by my father, and finally by my brother until it was destroyed by arson in 2015.

Only over the past few years have I reflected deeply on the historical period that Grandpa endured after opening his new business. There was an indelible trickle-down impact that his experiences in those early years had on me. In fact, I believe the philosophical bedrock of this book was inspired by my grandfather: diligence, enduring focus, conservative lifestyle, attention to money management, etc. Grandpa was the living embodiment of the EARN+SAVE+INVEST+REPEAT formula for wealth accumulation.

The inception of his new business in 1928 was precisely one year before the epic stock market crash of 1929 and the beginning of the Great Depression that lasted for a decade, which was immediately followed by the onset of World War II. For his first 17 years in business, Grandpa was either running a brand-new enterprise, struggling to stay in business throughout a devastating economic drought, or operating under the uncertainty of whether our country would win or lose the largest war the world has ever experienced.

Those uncertain and challenging times, in part, shaped Grandpa into a frugal, hardworking, and conservative businessman who ran his shop six days a week. Not a grandiose business, but it was successful enough to survive the most difficult period in the last 150 years. He was, in fact, an EARNER, he was a SAVER, he was an INVESTOR, and he REPEATED the process through both the difficult times and the better times that followed.

Grandpa's core values, conservative ways, and prudent money management were clearly learned and absorbed by my dad and, in turn, were taught to my brother and me. Perhaps, in some small way, a part of his legacy will be transferred to those who read this book.

GRANDPA'S LESSON: Simply surviving difficult periods can be a victory in itself and can have rippling benefits far into the future in ways impossible to see during those challenging times.

CHAPTER 4

Author's Letter to a Young Adult

This chapter is a hypothetical letter from the author written to a young adult just entering the workforce and eager to start the wealth accumulation process. Young readers who are in a similar phase in life may find the suggestions in the letter beneficial in dealing with their personal finances.

Dear Young Adult,

Congratulations on landing your first job as a young professional!! Look at you now, out on your own with your own income and now responsible for all of your expenses too. I'm glad you reached out asking for my thoughts on how to accumulate wealth in the decades ahead, so you can live and ultimately retire with financial freedom. You are to be commended for being proactive about focusing on your financial well-being so early in your adult life.

There are four basic steps to accumulating wealth:

STEP ONE: Earn money
STEP TWO: Save money
STEP THREE: Invest the money you save profitably
STEP FOUR: Repeat steps one, two, and three for many years.

Maybe this could be your mantra:

EARN+SAVE+INVEST+REPEAT

The more you do of any one of the four steps, the less you need of the other three to reach your goal, and of course, the more you do of all four, the more effective you will be at obtaining financial security and financial freedom. The following are some specific key action points that should be helpful. Some are things to do, and just as importantly, some are things to *not* do.

Things to do related to step one (Earning)

Be good at your job. Always do your best. Take advantage of opportunities to improve your skills, experience, and education. Make yourself worthy of a promotion, a pay raise, or a positive career change. Also, utilizing a special skill or passion in the form of a side hustle job in your spare time can be a powerful wealth-building tool. One of the simplest ways to accumulate more wealth is to command a higher wage.

Things to do related to step two (Saving)

Live modestly. One of the main reasons people fail to accumulate wealth is they get in the habit of spending money unnecessarily. Don't fall into the lifestyle creep pattern, where you greet every increase in pay with an increase in your spending. Wealth accumulation is about what you retain, not what you earn.

Budget. Do a personal budget and income statement for at least each of the next few years. This will be a valuable tool to make you aware of exactly how you are spending your money. The budget is your plan for what you anticipate to earn, spend, save, and invest.

Net worth statement (NWS). Do a NWS every six or twelve months forever. The NWS will be your ongoing report card that shows you exactly how you are progressing in the wealth accumulation process.

Pay yourself first. If you do nothing other than contribute 10% of your wages in a retirement account every year and avoid consumer debt, you will probably be in solid financial shape.

Things to do related to step three (Investing)

Fund an emergency account and maintain it at about two months' worth of expenses. This serves as a reserve fund that is immediately accessible to take care of unforeseen expenses.

Contribute to a tax-advantaged retirement account every year. If your employer has a 401(k), particularly with a match, do that. If not, set up an IRA or a Roth with an investment company.

Invest in stock mutual funds in your retirement accounts. Stocks have historically outperformed bonds and money markets by a wide margin. It's good to spread the money out over several stock funds (for example, some in *growth, value, large cap, small cap,* etc).

Educate yourself about investing and finance. Start with learning the basics of understanding the exponential wonder of compound earnings. Earning 10% annually will produce cumulative earnings considerably more than twice as much as 5% will when compounded for many years.

Things to do related to step four (Time/Repetition)

Time is on your side, so take advantage of it. The sooner you get started, the easier it will be in the years ahead to reach financial freedom. Getting started young is beneficial.

Start investing now. The following are two examples of how valuable it can be to start investing when you are young.

Let's assume you invest $6,000 a year each of your first three years on the job ($18,000 total) in a retirement account, and the account grows at an annual rate of 11% a year. That initial $18,000 would be worth $949,000 in 40 years.

Let's assume you want to have $2 million in your 401(k) at age 65 and assume the account will grow at 9% compounded annually. If you start at age 25, you will have to contribute about $5,450 per year to have $2 million at age 65; however, if you wait until age 35 to start contributing, you will have to invest about $13,450 a year to reach the same goal. *Time in* the market is much more important than *timing* the market. Start investing ASAP!

Things to watch out for

Credit card usage: Get rid of your credit cards if you tend to use them unwisely. The convenience of having access to a credit card has gotten many people into financial problems.

Spending as a reward: Don't get in the habit of spending money as a personal reward system. Routinely enjoying a free hike or a day outdoors rather than a shopping spree will be good for your physical and financial health.

Car purchases: Trading cars frequently and owning expensive cars are a major drag on wealth accumulation. Take care of your car and get a new one when you *need* it, not just because you *want* it.

Home purchases: Home ownership is an expense, not a wealth-building asset. Buying more house than you need will hamper the wealth accumulation process month after month. Home ownership costs are ongoing, and they tend to increase over time. Don't be in a hurry to buy a home just because you can afford it.

Unnecessary spending: Excessive material possessions have little correlation to happiness and quality of life. Enjoy life within the constraints of a well-planned budget.

Stay the course: Wealth accumulation is a lifelong journey. Look for opportunities and be willing to assume some calculated risks, but don't take excessive risks hoping to get rich quick.

In summary, do well in your profession, don't spend money unnecessarily, invest regularly in stock funds in a tax-advantaged retirement account, and do so for many years. **EARN+SAVE+INVEST+REPEAT.**

Thanks again for reaching out,
Kurt

PART II

SAVE

CHAPTER 5

Credit and Debit Cards

Clint Eastwood's 1967 classic Western *The Good, the Bad, and the Ugly* needs a sequel. Instead of desperados wielding pistols in pursuit of buried gold, it will be moms, dads, and kids wielding gold credit cards as they bury themselves in debt.

In reality, a lot of good can come with credit cards (when used wisely), some bad with them, and, unfortunately, when credit cards turn ugly for people, it can get *really* ugly.

For many years, my wife and I have done almost all of our consumer spending by credit card rather than cash, and we have never used a debit card. For us, there are many good features that make using credit cards our preferred payment method. The bad points are actually just minor inconveniences, and we have never experienced anything close to ugly with credit cards (and I don't plan to). The following are my thoughts on various considerations for credit and debit card use.

WARNING: Easy credit is a temptation that has caused significant financial harm for many people. If you find it difficult or impossible to avoid using credit cards imprudently, then I would strongly urge you to not possess them. Either destroy your cards or put them in the control of someone who can be trusted to ensure they are used wisely on your behalf.

THE GOOD ABOUT CREDIT CARDS

Following is an overview of the numerous attractive features associated with having a credit card.

Fraud Protection

The main feature that makes me quite comfortable using credit cards is fraud protection. By federal law (The Fair Credit Billing Act of 1974), cardholders are not responsible for fraudulent charges if their card number is stolen. If the physical card is stolen, you could be liable for at most $50 in fraudulent charges; however, most card issuers won't hold you responsible for any amount. By law, if you notify the issuer your card was stolen before any fraudulent charges occur, you owe nothing. However, if fraudulent charges do appear on your account, you must promptly notify the card company within 60 days, or you may be responsible.

My wife, Ruthie, has always been diligent about promptly reviewing our credit card statements. On several occasions over the years, she discovered fraudulent charges on our bill. Each time, we immediately notified the card company, and after we completed the required forms, the charges were removed from our bill. Obviously, the card company generally doesn't know if a particular charge is fraudulent or in error, so the burden is on the cardholder to notify the company.

Monthly Report

The monthly credit card bill provides a graphic summary of exactly when, where, and how much money was spent. It can be a valuable tool for monitoring your spending habits. Before making the monthly payment, always review the bill to check for any fraudulent charges or errors.

No Cost

By paying off the balance each month, there are no finance charges, and many credit cards have no annual fee as well. Essentially, a credit card provides free credit (a loan with no interest) as long as you pay off the balance each month.

Cash Back

Some credit cards will give cash back to the cardholder as a percentage of the amount charged. The card I personally use pays us 3% back on gasoline purchases and 2% on all other charges. Upon the cardholder's request, they will either mail a check for the cash back or credit the amount against charges. However, not all cards offer cash back, and often a good credit score is required to get a cash back card.

Award Points

Another popular perk frequently offered by credit card issuers is various types of *award points*, where each dollar you charge on the card you earn points toward airline tickets, hotels, restaurants, etc. I've never seen a card offer both cash back and award points—you receive one or the other, not both.

Personally, I detest award programs. I dislike everything about them for the same reasons I dislike frequent flyer miles with airlines. I don't want more clutter in my life, I want less. Just give me cash back on my purchases, and I will buy my own plane ticket. I find it annoying to keep track of what, where, and with whom we have points, the restrictions and limitations on the usage of the points, and the time and aggravation to cash in the points.

Building Credit History

Particularly for young people, using a credit card can help establish a credit history as opposed to spending cash or using a debit card, which generally do not impact your credit history. But it is important to make your monthly card payment on time, so you are establishing a good credit history.

Convenient and Safe

The modern retail economy has made credit card usage much more convenient than paying by cash. Card readers, embedded chips in the card, online purchases, and unmanned payment kiosks are now ubiquitous, which makes credit cards very convenient. I don't normally even bother carrying a wallet anymore. If you carry cash and lose it, well, you lost it. If you carry a credit card and lose it, just call the card company to cancel the card, and they will mail you a new card for free.

Line of Credit

Most credit cards have a *cash advance* feature which can serve the purpose of an emergency line of credit. Typically, the cash advance limit is less than the overall credit limit. For example, the overall limit (for purchases) might be $10,000, with a cash advance limit of $5,000. There are usually multiple ways to access a cash advance, such as writing a check, ATM withdrawal, or by electronic funds transfer (EFT) to a bank account. However, there is usually a 3% or 4% fee (not cheap) of the advance amount, *plus* you will pay interest on the outstanding balance from the day of the advance. Due to those high costs, I hope you never have to make such a cash advance, but it is nice to know that in a worst-case scenario, the money is available if needed.

Lock or Freeze Feature

Many credit cards (and debit cards) allow you to freeze or lock the card by using a mobile app or on their website. This feature temporarily deactivates the card so it can't be used. Then you can unlock the card at your discretion. This is a nice feature if you temporarily misplace your card, or if you want to ensure nobody uses the card for a certain time period.

Travel Insurance Benefits

Besides cash back and award points, many credit cards have additional perks for travelers. Common travel insurance benefits include the following: rental car protection, trip cancellation or interruption insurance, accident insurance, emergency medical transportation, luggage protection, and trip delay insurance.

Make sure you understand the specific details of what your card covers, as benefits and requirements can vary substantially for different cards. Most cards have a maximum dollar limit per trip or occurrence for each type of coverage. Generally, travel protection is provided only if you used the credit card to pay for some or all of the trip. Just having the card in itself likely doesn't provide any protection.

> When used wisely, credit cards can be a great financial tool as they have numerous beneficial features.

THE BAD ABOUT CREDIT CARDS

There are also a number of potentially negative aspects of credit cards users need to be aware of. However, most of the negatives are self-inflicted situations that can be avoided.

Makes Unnecessary Spending Easy

There's something about whipping out the credit card that doesn't feel as costly as handing over green money for a dubious purchase. Some people have a really hard time controlling their credit card usage.

Very High Interest Rates

Generally, you are only required to pay 2% or 3% of your balance each month. On the amount you don't pay off, they charge you interest … a lot of interest! Even with a good credit score, the interest rate charged will likely be

10% or higher, and with a poor credit rating, your annual rate may be in excess of 20%. A simple philosophy that could keep many people out of credit card problems is to never charge more than you can pay off at the end of the month. That way, you will never incur interest charges.

Late Fees

In addition to charging interest on the unpaid balance, card companies also charge late fees for every month you don't at least pay the required minimum on time. A $28 to $39 fee is typical.

Annual Card Fee

Some issuers charge an annual fee of up to $100 just to have the card.

Fraud

As previously discussed, cardholders are generally not responsible for fraudulent charges, but it is an inconvenience to have to deal with fraud if it shows up on your account. Even worse, you could be responsible for the fraudulent charges if you fail to review your monthly statement, don't realize the fraud occurred, and therefore fail to notify the card company promptly.

Protect the secrecy of your passwords, PINs, card CVV numbers, and all other personal data. Most credit card theft occurs when fraudsters obtain your personal data, not from actually stealing the physical card.

Monthly Payment

Using a credit card will add one more chore to your monthly list, as you will need to take the time to review the statement and pay the bill every month. Due to the possibility that fraudulent charges or errors could occur, I would never put a credit card on automatic payment where the company is authorized to debit your bank account for the amount due. You could find yourself in the unattractive position of having money automatically taken out of your account for fraudulent charges, and not having access to the money until you retrieve it back from the card company.

Replacing Compromised Cards

If you report your card is lost or you report the card has been compromised due to fraud, the company will immediately deactivate your card and issue new replacement cards to you with a new card number. This can be a bit of a hassle. First, you won't have access to the credit until you receive the new card, and second, if you have set up automatic payments to your credit card, you will need to contact all those companies and provide the new card information for the automatic payments.

I generally take two different credit cards with me when traveling. If one card is compromised, I have a backup card. Another good precaution is to call your credit card company in advance of traveling and tell them where you are going. I have been inconvenienced several times when my card issuer froze my card because I was using it out of state, which triggered a fraud alert in their system. They unfroze the card when I called and explained the situation, but it would have been an even bigger inconvenience if I didn't have a second card.

Bad Credit

If you have a poor credit history, you may not be able to get a credit card at all, and if you can, you may have higher fees, higher interest rates, fewer benefit features, and lower credit limits.

On the other hand, if you initially have a good credit history and then you tarnish your credit file due to poor personal management of your credit card, you may be negatively impacted in numerous ways, such as denial of loan requests for a home or car, being charged higher interest rates on loans, insurance companies charging you higher premiums, landlords refusing to rent to you, not getting hired by a potential employer, and more onerous terms with utility companies. In other words, when you apply for a job, a loan, housing, etc., your credit history may be considered, and a poor credit history may lead to a negative outcome for you.

The most important factor influencing your credit score is your loan payment history, which includes your credit card payment history. Therefore, always try to make your payments on time and for at least the minimum required amount.

THE UGLY ABOUT CREDIT CARDS

Most adults "have a friend," or know of a friend of a friend, who has experienced the ugly downside of credit card usage. That person on a modest income that went from $0 to $10,000 in debt on a credit card in no time flat, then turned around and got another card and did the same thing again! They put themselves in that position, so they could enjoy a wonderful vacation, have nice new clothes, buy jewelry they always wanted, shower friends and family with Christmas gifts, impress their friends, etc. The resulting aftermath was monthly interest charges they could barely afford, let alone pay back the principal.

I won't attempt to dissect the various reasons that compel people to misuse credit cards and put themselves in such difficult financial situations. I'll just say there are some people who should not have a credit card, or the card should be controlled by a trusted person who can help prevent unwise use.

The price of short-term pleasure is often long-term pain.

Another large group of credit card users are those who don't get themselves into serious financial trouble, but they consistently use the card to consume all their disposable income. They sort of have a balancing act of how much money they make, what their regular monthly bills are, and then however much is left over is the amount they can spend. The credit card is the easiest, most convenient way to ensure that by the end of the month, their income has been consumed.

It's really not the credit card's fault; it could just as easily be a debit card, a checkbook, cash, or the ATM that is consistently exploited. But the convenience and availability of credit cards has been a factor contributing to many Americans' failure to save and invest consistently and ultimately their failure to accumulate wealth.

DEBIT CARDS

With a credit card, the card company is loaning you money that you prom-ise to pay them back, whereas a debit card simply provides access to your own money. Debit cards are basically high-tech versions of a checkbook. If you try to use your debit card and there is not enough money in your bank account, the transaction will be denied. With a credit card, transactions will be approved until you reach the card's limit, whether you have the money to pay back the loan or not.

Debit cards may be a viable alternative for people who find it difficult to use credit cards responsibly. Having easy access to borrowed money via a credit card is a temptation some people have a difficult time resisting. As a mechanism to prevent self-inflicted financial harm, the debit card is ideal in that if you don't have the money, then you can't spend the money.

Following is information about some of the unique aspects of debit cards.

Fraud Risk

Fraud can potentially be much more of a problem for a debit card account than a credit card account, and for this reason alone, I have never had a debit card. If fraudsters make charges on your credit card account, you simply don't pay the charges and notify the credit card company immediately, but the fraud-sters don't have your money; they have the lender's money (the credit card issuer).

If fraud occurs on your debit card account, the money will come out of YOUR account. Consequently, if the fraudsters get the last $1,000 out of your debit account, you may (or may not) get it back eventually, but until you retrieve the money, you won't have access to the funds. Additionally, if you had written checks on the same account that had not yet cleared, they may bounce, poten-tially resulting in bank fees and other problems. There are laws providing debit card users with fraud protection, but there is still risk.

Effectively Managing a Debit Card

By using strategic limitations and managing their usage, debit cards can be ideal for some situations and for some people.

Example #1: Let's say you are the parent of a high school or college student who has difficulty managing their expenses, or they have not yet proven their money management skills. You could give them a credit card with a low limit of, say, $500, but that is still a lot of money that could be misused, and once they hit the limit, the card is temporarily unusable. With a debit card, the parent can conveniently transfer money from another account to the debit card account as desired. For example, if you want to provide your child $50 a week, you transfer the funds into their account weekly, and that's all they have access to. If an emergency comes up and your child needs a larger amount ASAP, with a few clicks on the computer or on the phone, funds can be transferred to their account.

Example #2: If someone decides they prefer using a debit card instead of a credit card on a consistent basis, I would strongly suggest setting up two bank accounts to be used in tandem—one account having the debit card with it, and the other account with no debit card. The second account acts as the *feeder* account to the debit account.

Have paychecks and all deposits going into the feeder account, and only transfer smaller amounts to the debit account as needed for expenses. That way, if fraud occurs on the debit card, only a relatively small amount is compromised. The *big* money is in the other account, whereas if all the money was in the debit card account, it could be temporarily wiped out by fraud.

Our children have effectively used this technique in their lives as students and young adults. They have proven themselves to be responsible, and they manage the movement of their own funds between the accounts using their phones. The nature of their transient lifestyles made a debit card more prudent sometimes than credit cards. Now that they are out of school and are employed, I have encouraged them to switch over to credit cards so they can receive the cash back benefits as well as building a positive credit history.

A debit card may be a wise choice for young people when parental assistance is appropriate to monitor and manage spending.

Daily Purchase Limits and ATM Limits

To protect the cardholders and the bank from fraudsters, banks set daily limits on how much can be purchased with the debit card and how much cash can be withdrawn on the card at an ATM. The amounts vary substantially from one bank to another, so be sure to understand the daily limits for your bank account. ATM limits are usually smaller than the debit purchase limit.

For example, a common daily limit is around $500 for ATM withdrawals and $2,000 for debit purchases. So, if a fraudster gained control of your debit card and you didn't realize it for three days, they could drain $6,000 out of your account ($2,000 per day for three days). Although you may be reimbursed for the fraud eventually, you will likely be without access to that money for at least a few days or weeks.

Cash Back and Rewards for Debit Cards

Some debit cards actually pay cash back as a percentage of your debit purchases and have award programs based on usage. Those amounts are generally not as generous as those for credit cards because the banks are not loaning you money and therefore, banks don't have the opportunity to make money charging you interest. However, they do make money by charging merchants a fee when you make purchases on the card.

10 BEST PRACTICES FOR USING CREDIT AND DEBIT CARDS

If used prudently, credit and debit cards can both be convenient and positive financial tools for consumers. The following is a summary of some best practices to keep in mind.

1. Don't have credit or debit cards at all if they will likely lead to unwise or excessive spending.
2. Pay off credit card balances each month to avoid interest charges.
3. Never be late paying your bill, as doing so may negatively affect your credit rating and you will incur late payment fees.
4. Promptly review your monthly statements and immediately notify the card company if there are any errors or fraudulent charges listed.
5. Ideally, have a card with no annual fee.
6. Try to get a card that has attractive cash back features.
7. Understand any travel insurance protection your card provides, particularly if you frequently travel.
8. Debit card accounts are a good choice for young people when parents need to manage and monitor a child's spending.
9. If you are using a debit card account, keep small amounts in the debit account, and transfer money from another account into the debit account as needed. That way, if fraudsters do access the debit account, it will not be for a large amount.
10. Protect the secrecy of all numbers and data related to your cards and your personal information. The majority of card fraud occurs when someone obtains your data, not your physical card.

The ultimate objective of using credit and debit cards is not to spend more money but simply to make your spending more convenient, safer, and hopefully save you some money. Cards are just one aspect of effectively managing personal finances and improving financial well-being on the road to wealth accumulation and financial freedom.

HOW CREDIT CARD ISSUERS MAKE MONEY

Interest Charges: Card issuers generally charge interest on any account balance that is not paid off every month. The annual interest rate is commonly in the teens or in excess of 20%. Interest income is the largest source of revenue for credit card companies.

Merchant Fees: Card companies charge merchants a percentage of each charge the merchant's customers make. The fee is usually about 3% on the high end and considerably lower for large merchants who can negotiate a lower fee.

Annual Fees: Some cards charge an annual fee simply to have the card, regardless of usage.

Late Fees: If you don't make your monthly payment on time, an additional fee is charged.

Cash Advance Fees: Issuers typically charge between 2% and 5% on cash advances, which could be from an ATM, a physical check, or an electronic transfer.

Balance Transfer Fees: Issuers frequently try to take customers away from other card companies by offering cardholders a lower interest rate if they move their outstanding account balance to the new card company, and, of course, they charge a fee to do so, which is usually in the range of 3% to 5% of the amount transferred.

SUMMARY

We've all seen the book cover or article showing someone cutting up their credit card with scissors. The overarching message is … "credit cards are bad—wise people who are good with money matters don't have them."

In reality, credit cards are commonly the preferred and wise payment method of people who use them to their advantage and exercise prudent judgment. They have numerous features that generally make them more convenient and safer than paying with cash or checks. Additionally, many cards actually pay users *cash back* as a percentage of their purchase amounts. One tenet of using credit cards wisely is paying the entire balance off each month to avoid being charged interest because card companies generally charge extremely high interest rates (often 20% annual rate or higher).

Unfortunately, there are some credit card holders who should get the scissors out. Due to their convenience, credit cards are easy to misuse and have resulted in many users getting themselves into problematic levels of debt. Oftentimes, the burdensome high interest rate cardholders must pay becomes as onerous as the original amount of the purchases charged. For these reasons, debit cards may be a better option than credit cards for some individuals.

Credit cards are a useful tool when used wisely but can lead to serious financial problems when used unwisely.

THE KROSS ROBINSON STORY

After his junior season on the Patton High School baseball team in 2015, Kross Robinson had seen far more action keeping the score book for the team rather than actually playing in games. At that point, Kross was still physically small at 5'7" and generally not very athletic with a "skill set" that included slow running speed, a weak throwing arm, well below average hitting ability, and no defensive position he was well suited for.

The majority of young players facing similar circumstances would have "retired" from baseball and found other more appealing high school pursuits, but not Kross. He continued to practice hard and keep the scorebook, as well as maintain a good attitude.

In my role as part-time assistant coach, Kross and I had many sessions together in the batting cage. I genuinely felt bad for him; he was such a nice kid, and he tried and worked so hard, but he just wasn't developing as a hitter or as a pitcher.

Then a wonderful thing happened; Kross had a growth spurt. By the time his senior season started, he had grown six inches and gained 25 pounds. He started developing what I call man muscles as his overall strength and coordination accelerated rapidly. His fastball velocity increased to a respectable 82 mph, and the now 6'1" former scorekeeper not only got his first opportunity to play regularly in the games, but he became the #2 starting pitcher on the team and had a fantastic senior season!

As of spring 2022, Kross is now 6'4" and 200 pounds with consistent velocity on his fastball in the 91 to 93 mph range as he pitches regularly for the University of North Carolina at Greensboro Spartans. He hopes to pitch professionally after his collegiate career.

There's not a player I ever coached who I admire more than Kross Robinson in terms of not giving up, continuing to work hard for years despite slow progress, and ultimately developing himself to a level of play that few people would have thought possible.

Kross' story is not about money or building wealth per se, but rather the testimony of a young man's resilience and determination that can be extrapolated profoundly to the business world, careers, and life, in general, as well as the entire wealth accumulation process. As Kross can attest, success sometimes requires patience. Work and dedication come first, then come results.

Kross's Lesson: Hone your skills and prepare yourself today so you are positioned to take advantage of opportunities tomorrow.

CHAPTER 6

Insurance: What You Need and What You Don't

The cost of buying unneeded insurance can negatively impact your ability to accumulate wealth on an ongoing basis. Consumers are consistently presented with a barrage of warranties and insurance protection they can purchase for various products, services, and risks. Almost everyone needs certain types of insurance, but the premiums paid for some coverages are often money not well spent.

INSURANCE YOU PROBABLY *DO* NEED

If your answer is **yes** to any of the three questions below, then you should probably buy the insurance:

1. Is the insurance **required**?
2. Would it be a **financial hardship** if you did not have the insurance and a loss occurred?
3. Is the cost of the insurance vs. the likelihood of a claim **in your favor**?

The following are some examples of each of the three reasons to buy insurance.

#1: When Insurance Is Required

Some agreements, contracts, loans, or licenses require that certain insurance be kept in place to protect the financial interests of others that could suffer financial damages, such as counterparties. Some examples include the following:

Home Loans: Mortgage lenders generally require home insurance during the life of the loan.

Auto Loans: Auto lenders generally require collision and comprehensive insurance during the life of the loan to protect their financial interests.

Vehicle Licensing: Most states require auto liability insurance before they will license a vehicle.

Renters Insurance: Many landlords require tenants to have renters insurance.

Studying Abroad: Health insurance is legally required to obtain a student visa in many countries.

#2: Financial Hardship if a Loss Occurred

There are several types of insurance that are generally wise to have because the negative financial consequences of being uninsured are too risky to assume. Although the odds of the insured event occurring may be low, the size of the financial risk is too large to not have the insurance, sort of like a reverse lottery situation—you don't want to be the unlucky winner.

Homeowners Insurance: Homeowners policies insure both the dwelling and personal contents, and most policies have some liability coverage as well. For most homeowners, it would be a devastating financial setback to be uninsured and have their home and belongings destroyed.

Health Insurance: Everyone needs health insurance for obvious reasons. Even the mega-wealthy who could easily afford to pay major medical bills should probably have health insurance. Insurance companies negotiate huge discounts with health-care providers that uninsured/self-insured patients don't receive; therefore, uninsured individuals are routinely billed much higher amounts than insurance patients pay. Also, studies have shown insured patients receive better care than the uninsured.

Life Insurance: If losing a deceased person's income would create a financial hardship for the surviving dependents, then life insurance is probably a good idea. The classic young couple with two kids and the stay-at-home spouse clearly needs life insurance on the working spouse's life, and probably on the other spouse as well. Conversely, once someone has accumulated adequate net worth, they may not need any life insurance.

The primary purpose of life insurance is usually to replace the earning power of the deceased and/or pay off debts of the deceased, or debts of the beneficiary. Paying funeral expenses and related costs are also a consideration. Therefore, an important issue is to determine the appropriate amount of insurance to replace the earnings the deceased was producing as well as how much is needed to retire debts. Life insurance proceeds are generally not subject to income tax.

Auto Insurance: There are several basic parts to auto insurance, and you don't have to purchase all of them. *Liability* coverage is required by law in most states, and it pays other parties if you are at fault. *Collision* coverage pays for damages to your vehicle from a collision (auto accident). *Comprehensive* coverage is for damage to your vehicle from things other than a collision, such as hail, theft, vandalism, etc. There is often optional coverage for personal injury and medical. Coverage is also available for when you are in an accident with another vehicle in which the other driver is underinsured or uninsured.

It would be wise for many people to have collision and comprehensive coverage, even if the car is paid for, as it could create a financial hardship otherwise. For example, if a tree fell on your car without comprehensive coverage, you wouldn't be covered. If someone has adequate net worth so they can comfortably pay for a total loss of their vehicle, collision and comprehensive coverage may not be necessary, as the most they would lose is the value of the vehicle.

Disability Insurance: The basic concept of disability insurance is that if the insured becomes disabled, then the insurance company provides some financial consideration to the insured. There are numerous types of and aspects of disability insurance, such as how much it pays, how long it pays, the definition of disabled, and how much it costs.

If the primary family wage earner becomes disabled and can't work, it could create a real family hardship without disability insurance. However, there are some unique considerations relating to disability. For example, the disabled person may qualify for Social Security disability payments, or they may qualify for workers' compensation. Depending on how they became disabled, they may receive a lump-sum cash settlement or a lifetime monthly payment. Similar to life insurance, once someone has an adequate net worth to provide for themselves and their dependents, then disability insurance may not be needed.

#3: When the Cost of Insurance Is in Your Favor

The cost of insurance or warranties being in the consumer's favor is generally a rare event. Companies set their insurance and warranty pricing with the expectation they will be able to pay claims for losses, pay their sales and administrative expenses, and still make a profit.

Situations when buying coverages that are in the consumer's favor are usually due to unique personal situations. For example, buying phone insurance if the user is prone to losing or breaking personal items may be wise.

THREE GOOD REASONS TO BUY INSURANCE

If the insurance is required.

When it would be a financial hardship if you did not have insurance and a loss occurred.

When the cost of the insurance versus the likelihood of a claim is in your favor.

INSURANCE YOU PROBABLY *DON'T* NEED

The previous section covered the three major reasons when insurance is a good idea or is compulsory. If you can't say yes to one of those three scenarios, then you probably don't need the insurance. People frequently purchase insurance for protection from relatively small losses because at the point of sale, they have the illusion that the small cost of the insurance vs. the coverage protection is in their favor. In reality, that is seldom the case; if it were, the underwriters and actuaries who determine the premiums might be looking for a new job soon thereafter. The following are some examples of when insurance is unneeded, not cost-effective, or both.

Life Insurance for Children

It's a tragedy when a child dies, but unless the child was a TikTok star or the family breadwinner, it is generally not a financial hardship. Parents sometimes buy life insurance for kids because it's much cheaper due to their young age. Of course, it's cheaper—the insurance company knows a child will likely live another 60+ years.

Note that a relatively small amount of life insurance on a child's life may be appropriate to pay for a potential funeral and related costs—particularly if those costs would likely create a financial hardship for the family.

Life Insurance when You Have No Dependents

A single person with no dependents or a couple with no kids where each spouse is employed with adequate income to meet expenses on their own may not need life insurance. If the surviving spouse would have difficulty living on their single income, then life insurance is probably a good idea.

Once again, having a relatively small amount of life insurance may be appropriate to pay for a potential funeral and related costs if not having the insurance would create a financial hardship.

Life Insurance when You Have Adequate Net Worth

You may not need a $1 million life insurance policy if you have a $5 million net worth already. The primary reasons to buy life insurance are generally to replace the income the deceased was producing, to pay off debts and expenses, and to ensure that beneficiaries have adequate money for their future needs. At some point, life insurance may be unnecessary if adequate wealth has been accumulated to cover all the financial considerations.

Of course, the appropriate amount of wealth to conclude that life insurance is not needed depends on multiple factors such as the age and number of dependents, whether the spouse works and their age, lifestyle and expenses, debts owed, the type of assets owned, and the liquidity of those assets.

Rental Car Insurance

Maybe the most oversold and unneeded insurance is for rental cars. Most personal auto policies cover rental cars. For most insured drivers, it is a complete waste of money to buy coverage again when renting a car. Check with your insurance agent to confirm what your policy covers for rentals.

Extended Auto Warranties

Extended auto warranties are recognized as a nice profit center for those offering the warranty and expensive for the auto owner. In the aggregate, consumers lose money on extended auto warranties. However, for those on a tight budget and limited financial resources, not having such coverage could result in a real hardship if there is a car failure, particularly if it occurs with a car loan still outstanding.

Cell Phone Insurance

Most responsible adults don't need cell phone insurance. However, taking into consideration their level of maturity and lifestyle, it may make sense for some teenagers and young adults. Be aware that many cell phone policies have a deductible of $200 or more, and filing a claim could get you dropped by the phone carrier. The combination of the cost to buy the insurance and the deductible could easily be half as much as the phone would cost.

Hotel and Flight Insurance

Insurance offerings for canceling hotel stays and flights are generally not worth the cost. Be sure to read the terms and conditions if you are considering this type of coverage, since the circumstances under which it pays is generally limited to specific reasons such as illness, job loss, jury duty, etc.

Extended Warranties on Small-Cost Consumer Items

Extended warranties are offered on all sorts of low-cost consumer items. I never purchase such warranties for several reasons. First, the cost of the warranty is in the company's favor, not mine; otherwise, the company wouldn't offer it. Second, it's not going to be a financial hardship if my toaster or leaf-blower fails. Third, for such small items, it's generally more hassle than it's worth to deal with it. Fourth, many products have a free manufacturer's warranty for a certain time period anyway.

If your checkbook *can* easily take care of the issue, it's an expense. If your checkbook *can't* handle it, then you have a problem. Don't waste money buying insurance to protect from an expense. Buy insurance to protect from losses that would create a problem.

INSURANCE THAT SOME PEOPLE NEED AND SOME PEOPLE DON'T

Some types of insurance make sense for certain people, yet the same coverage may be unnecessary for someone else. Usually, the determining factor in such scenarios is if not having the coverage and suffering a loss would create a financial problem—a minor expense for one person could be a major financial problem for someone else.

Extended Warranties on Big-Ticket Consumer Items

If someone is living paycheck to paycheck with little in savings, then it may be a good idea to get an extended warranty on big-ticket consumer items such as HVAC systems, computers, autos, household appliances, and even TVs. It could be a problem if your heating unit fails in the middle of a cold winter and you don't have the money to buy a new unit.

Supplemental Health Insurance

There are various types of supplemental health policies that are designed to pay health-related expenses that primary health insurance policies typically don't cover, such as dental and vision care, paying deductibles, copayments, coinsurance, and numerous other potential benefits such as a lump-sum payment directly to the insured if certain illnesses, diseases, or injuries occur.

Depending on what someone's primary health insurance will pay and the individual's financial resources (or lack thereof), not having a supplemental health policy could cause a financial hardship, depending on the injury or illness and the resulting circumstances.

Supplemental health policies and extended warranties present the same basic dilemma for consumers, which is whether they have adequate savings to self-insure and assume the risk themselves rather than paying for insurance protection. For most people, once they have adequate savings to easily assume those risks, it is generally not financially beneficial to buy such policies.

Renters Insurance

If renters insurance is not required by the landlord, the deciding factor may be the value of your insured personal property. If you are a college student with $2,000 worth of insurable items, you may be less inclined to get coverage, whereas someone with $200,000 worth of personal belongings is in a different situation. However, renters insurance often has some liability coverage included, so therefore, it may be wise to have coverage even if the value of the renter's personal property is small.

Personal Umbrella Policy

Excess liability policies—commonly referred to as *umbrella* policies—provide excess (additional) liability coverage over and above another policy such as a homeowners, auto, or watercraft policy. It can also provide coverage for certain types of claims that are not covered at all by another policy.

For example, if your auto policy provided for a maximum liability claim of $200,000 and you were found liable for $300,000 as a result of an auto accident, then an umbrella policy could cover the excess $100,000 you owe. Another example is if someone was injured on your property and you were found liable for an amount in excess of your homeowners policy limit, then an umbrella policy could cover the additional amount owed. Umbrella policies typically cover other liabilities that most auto and homeowners policies don't, such as slander and libel, and personal liability associated with owning housing rentals.

Umbrella policies cover liabilities you may owe to others. They do not provide coverage to pay for the replacement of or damage to your personal property or assets. For example, if your fishing boat sinks, an umbrella policy won't pay you for the value of the boat. But if your buddy drowned when the boat sank, the policy may pay if you were found liable for his death in an amount in excess of the coverage provided by your homeowners or watercraft policy. Most umbrella policies require that you have an underlying homeowners, auto, and/or watercraft policy in place in which the umbrella policy provides excess coverage beyond the limits of those underlying policies.

Excess liability policies are a logical choice for both high-income and high-net-worth individuals because those two groups have assets worth protecting, and they are more apt to be sued because they have assets to go after. An umbrella policy with $1 million in coverage typically has an annual premium of $100 to $300; hence it is relatively inexpensive for the amount of coverage. The premium also gets incrementally cheaper as the coverage amount purchased increases—$5 million of coverage doesn't cost five times as much as $1 million of coverage.

Miscellaneous

Is insurance needed on a $5 million home? Maybe not if you have a liquid net worth of $50 million, but yes, if your net worth is $6 million. Not having a particular coverage may be a major risk for someone, while merely being a minor expense to someone else. Always consider the risk vs. reward of any insurance plan or warranty in light of your personal circumstances and financial situation.

My insurance agent thought I was crazy when I dropped collision insurance on our autos. My wife and I are both safe drivers, and the financial risk was not that significant for us, although I joked that it would sting a bit if Ruthie and I had a head-on collision in the driveway and totaled both cars. However, when our three kids started driving, I added collision coverage again, since the risk/ reward profile changed considerably at that point.

Every dollar spent unwisely on insurance premiums is a dollar that doesn't get invested to accumulate wealth

---

SUMMARY

The concept of insurance and warranties is where a consumer makes premium payments to the insurer, and in return, the insurer pays the consumer if an insured event/loss occurs. Insurers endeavor to set the premiums so they will be able to pay all expenses and make a profit. So, the nature of an insurance model is for the insurance company to profit, and, therefore, consumers, on average, pay more in premiums than they receive back from claims. However, consumers generally need certain types of insurance because the risk is simply too great not to have coverage.

With the exception of those large risks or when insurance is required, consumers would generally be well-advised to self-insure and not pay for insurance or warranties on smaller items. In an effort to be prudent and conservative, some people end up *insurance poor*. This happens because they buy unneeded product warranties for everything they can and buy excessive amounts of coverage for the policies they actually do need.

One of my favorite sayings is, "Don't mistake an expense for a problem." Relative to insurance, that concept means don't waste money buying insurance to protect from minor expenses. Buy insurance for protection against losses that would create a financial problem.

THE RALPH KETNER STORY

In 1957, Ralph Ketner opened his first grocery store, Food Town, in Salisbury, North Carolina. Over the following 34 years, Ralph led the company now known as Food Lion to phenomenal growth, as they had more than 500 stores by the time he retired in 1991.

After his retirement, Food Lion hosted several annual casual meetings for nearby investment advisors with my brokerage company. They told us all the good things they were doing and answered our questions, as most of us had numerous clients who owned Food Lion stock. The highlight of the gatherings was always when they turned it over to Ralph for 30 minutes of storytelling about his adventures leading Food Lion through that remarkable period of growth.

At one such event, Ralph told the story of calling random people in the local phone book to ask them to buy stock in his new company, so they could open the first store. One person who considered buying stock ultimately used the money to buy a new lawn mower instead. As the company grew and Food Lion's stock price soared, Ralph began referring to the man's million-dollar lawnmower because the money he spent on the mower would have grown to in excess of $1 million if he would have bought the stock instead!

It was clear Ralph was a tough, determined, hard-charging, risk-taking businessman. A huge turning point in the company's success was when he decided to reduce the price on all of their items so dramatically that it would require a 50% increase in sales just to break even. The gambit worked; Food Lion's sales soared, and the rest is history, as the saying goes. His strategy, in part, revolutionized the entire grocery industry.

Ralph said when he contemplated aggressive and innovative ideas for Food Lion, other company executives or board members would often say things like, "You can't do that, Ralph," "That won't work," or "That's too risky." He told us that his response to those naysayers was, "Don't tell me what I can't do—I'll show you what I can do!" and "Just because you say it's so, doesn't make it so."

Those profound statements from Ralph served as a source of reinforcement and conviction for me over the years, as I occasionally dealt with conflicts or people who doubted me. Ralph said he told his attorneys, "I don't pay you to *keep* me out of trouble. I pay you to *get* me out of trouble!" I'm glad I've never had to employ that line, yet.

Few of us will ever have accomplishments that reach the magnitude of Ralph's. However, I think all of us can benefit in some way from emulating his toughness, drive, and determination in our own endeavors. My brief interactions with Ralph definitely impacted me.

RALPH'S LESSON: From humble beginnings, great things can happen when combined with hard work, determination, and vision.

CHAPTER 7

Home Ownership and Mortgage Loans

Chapter Abbreviations

ARM:	Adjustable-Rate Mortgage
HELOC:	Home Equity Line of Credit
LTV:	Loan to Value
PMI:	Private Mortgage Insurance
Refi:	Refinance

Buying a home is the largest purchase most people will ever make, and it can dramatically impact the owner's finances in various ways—both positively and negatively.

RENT OR OWN?

The decision whether to rent or purchase a residence should be predicated more on personal circumstances than strictly on money and the financial ability to purchase. Before the implosion of the housing bubble around 2008, politicians and others frequently asserted home ownership was a major part of the American dream. Subliminally, the message was that until you own a home, you haven't truly succeeded. Encouraging unnecessary home ownership was a disservice to some people whose situation made renting a much better choice.

The common wisdom is that when you rent, you are not *building equity* like when you're a homeowner; therefore, you are wasting money if you rent. If the total costs of home ownership were the same as the total costs of renting, I would readily agree. Unfortunately, that is usually not the case after all the costs of home ownership are considered. If you have a lower overall housing cost because you rent rather than own, you can invest the money you saved by renting to "build equity."

Obviously, it is generally unwise to buy a home until you have adequate financial stability, both in the form of savings to pay for the costs of purchasing the home, and also income or cash flow to meet the costs of ongoing home ownership.

Renting may be a logical choice for people whose careers or lifestyles are likely to cause them to relocate in the near future. The typical real estate commission to sell a house is 6% of the sales price, which would be $12,000 for a $200,000 sale. So, obviously, buying a home if you don't plan to live there for at least a couple of years or longer is probably a losing proposition compared to renting.

If someone has adequate financial resources and they plan to stay in the same area for at least a couple of years, the decision whether to buy should be based on other personal considerations, such as the following:

$ Family size and makeup: A single person may be less inclined to want or need to own a home vs. renting, whereas a family of four may be more interested in a house and yard to enjoy. The size of your family may determine your need/desire for things like a two-car garage, a basement, extra bedrooms, being able to make permanent changes to the property to suit your needs, etc.

$ Your interest or ability to maintain a home—do you want to maintain the grounds and be responsible for repairs?

$ Cost to rent vs. home prices (and the resulting monthly loan amount).

$ Availability of appealing rental units vs. homes on the market.

A positive financial consideration that makes owning attractive vs. renting is that if you take out a fixed-rate mortgage, your payments are fixed for the life of the loan, whereas rent payments tend to rise over time. For example, if a rental rate increased only 2% a year, the rent would be 48% higher after 20 years. Fixed-rate home loans also have the advantageous feature that the homeowner can refinance if rates go down and thereby actually lower the cost of housing. However, although the loan payment may be fixed, all other costs of home ownership will likely increase over time, just like rent payments.

The decision whether to rent or own should be made after careful consideration of financial and personal factors.

Another point that makes home ownership appealing is the low current interest rate levels. As of March 2022, fixed mortgage interest rates are in the 4% range, which is extremely low by historical standards. This has the practical effect of reducing the true cost of the home. Having such low rates available is a game changer for some potential homebuyers compared to years past when rates were much higher.

For example, let's compare $200,000, 30-year, fixed-rate loans at today's 4% rate vs. 6% and 9% in previous decades.

$ At 4% the monthly payment is $955, and total payments over 30 years is $344,102.

$ At 6% the monthly payment is $1,199, and total payments over 30 years is $431,676.

$ At 9% the monthly payment is $1,609, and total payments over 30 years is $579,330.

With home mortgage rates currently at such historically low levels, it has the benefit of making a home at a particular price point much more affordable today than it was when interest rates were at higher levels.

Here's another way of looking at the impact of lower rates. The monthly payment on a 30-year loan for $200,000 at 6% would be $1,199.10. If you made the same payment of $1,199.10 per month, but the interest rate was 4%, you would have the $200,000 loan paid off in just over 20 years and four months. Poof! Almost 10 years of payments, amounting to more than $139,000, were completely eliminated due to the lower interest rate. Now don't get me started about where you would be if you invested the savings in a diversified stock portfolio. Ha!

ARE HOMES GOOD INVESTMENTS?

It can be a costly financial trap to purchase a home on the basis of it being an attractive financial investment. Sure, some housing markets provide excellent rates of return during some periods of time for homeowners. And some time periods, such as 2020 and 2021, saw home prices appreciate substantially in almost every market nationwide. However, when all the costs are considered, home ownership generally resembles an expense more than an investment asset over longer time periods.

First and foremost, the home ownership decision should be based on *housing* needs and desires. Particularly, buying a larger home than you actually need based on the notion that it is a great investment opportunity can be a financially crippling decision. Homes are generally not great investments, they are great places to live and raise families.

Fully loading all the costs of ownership, homes fall in the middle between a pure expense and a pure investment asset. At one extreme, a pure expense item is purchased for the utility it provides with no expectation of residual value, such as food, toilet paper, phone service, and gasoline. On the other extreme, a pure investment provides no utility value and its sole purpose is financial rewards (earnings).

In 2020, my mom sold her home for $140,000, which is more than four times the $33,000 my parents paid for it in 1970. But considering that they owned it for 50 years, the compounded growth rate was about 3% a year. Located in a thriving neighborhood and just the right size for us, it was a good home for our family for five decades. It was money well spent for our family's housing needs, but certainly not a great investment from a financial perspective.

The rate of return is near zero (or negative) after factoring in 50 years of property taxes and insurance, the cost of a couple new roofs, of repaving the driveway twice, exterior and interior painting a few times, new garage doors, renovating the bathroom, tree removal, sunroom and exterior deck additions, new kitchen cabinets, various electrical and HVAC maintenance, and other costs I forgot or am unaware of.

One of the most ill-advised perspectives I ever heard related to home ownership came from a wealth-building book that has sold over 1.5 million copies. In the book, the author describes home ownership as a great investment. He supports his *opinion* (he calls it a *fact*) by pointing out that studies have shown homeowners have an average net worth many times greater than renters.

In essence, the author concludes homes must be good investments simply because homeowners are worth more than renters. In reality, home ownership is a benefit of having wealth, but it's not generally an efficient way to create wealth. A parallel to that author's conclusion would be "studies show people who own expensive cars have an average net worth substantially greater than people who don't own a car, so buy an expensive car if you want to be wealthy."

IS BIGGER BETTER?

What if my parents had decided in the spring of 1970 to spend $66,000 instead of $33,000 to buy a house twice as big, just because they could afford it? First, we didn't need a bigger house for the four of us to live comfortably, and I don't think a bigger house would have added to our quality of life or made us any happier.

Spending twice the money on a house twice as big would have done the following: doubled the amount of property taxes every year for 50 years, doubled the cost of furniture and fixtures for Mom to trick the house out initially and keep up with it over the years, nearly doubled the monthly utility bills and cost of insurance, increased the roof size and the subsequent cost to replace the roof twice, doubled the cost for each painting, doubled the cost for each change of floor and wallcovering over the years, and likely a significant increase or burden to clean and maintain the inside of the house and the exterior grounds.

It's fair to assume that the bigger house would have sold for twice as much, such that the appreciation of the value of the house was more or less equal to the additional expenses of the bigger house. So, the net effect would have been an additional $33,000 tied up in the house, producing a rate of return of zero.[2]

I'm not suggesting that home ownership is a bad idea. Whether you rent or own, everyone needs a place to live. However, the proper way to view housing is that it is a cost of living, not an investment. Many people have made the expensive mistake of purchasing more house than they need simply because their income or assets indicate they can afford the house payment. Based at least partially on the faulty notion that homes are good *investments*, people figure that a bigger home makes for an even better investment.

Home price indexes show that home values have increased only about 1% more than the inflation rate on a long-term basis, which is far less than the long-term appreciation on common stocks, for example. Of course, the change in home values can vary dramatically from one market to another.

The true cost of oversized house purchases is the negative impact it makes on those homeowners' ability to otherwise accumulate wealth. Month by month, year by year, money that could have been invested and growing is instead consumed by the ongoing additional cost of maintaining a larger home.

---

2   By the way, $33,000 invested at a compounded after-tax annual growth rate of 5% (all earnings reinvested) would be worth $378,000 after 50 years. At 6%, it would be worth $607,000, and at 8%, it would be worth $1,547,000.

Buying a larger home than needed as an investment strategy can be a costly mistake.

THE 15-YEAR VS. 30-YEAR MORTGAGE DILEMMA

Many financial gurus and advisors say never get a 30-year mortgage. They insist a 15-year mortgage is better because you will save tens of thousands of dollars in interest, you will build equity in your home faster, and you will pay off your house in half the time and therefore be that much closer to being able to retire.

Yes, of course, if you make larger payments and pay off a debt in half the time, you are going to save interest. Using that logic, it would be wise to pay cash for your home and have zero interest cost. The primary reason these experts advise to pay off home loans as quickly as possible is the view that most people lack the sustained discipline to simultaneously pay off a 30-year mortgage and consistently save additional money for retirement.

For example, currently, on a $200,000 mortgage, the monthly payment on a 30-year loan would be about $500 less than the payment on a 15-year loan, so the 15-year mortgage is like a forced savings account to the tune of $500 per month.

The reasoning behind the idea that 30-year mortgages are terrible is this: if you can afford the higher monthly payment of the 15-year loan, but instead you take a 30-year loan with the idea that you will invest the extra $500 each month, it won't happen. You will blow the money on fancier cars, more clothes, better vacations, more frivolous expenditures, etc. People lack the discipline to keep their spending in check—this is the basic premise of these advisors.

Conversely, if you take out a 15-year loan, you will have the external discipline imposed on you by the mortgage company that you must pay $500 more each month on the loan. After 15 years, you will own your home free and clear, and hopefully, you will have developed the discipline to continue to save and invest the money that was formerly going to home loan payments.

Sadly, for perhaps half (or more) of American homeowners, the assumptions above are probably accurate—that the lower monthly mortgage payment that comes with a 30-year mortgage will only lead to more unnecessary consumer spending, and not to any consistent additions to their investment accounts. But, for the half or so of the population that do have the discipline to save and invest systematically, there may be another option worth considering, as detailed in the next section.

KEEP THE MORTGAGE AND KEEP INVESTING!

Let's consider a few facts about home mortgages:

1. Interest on a loan for a primary residence is tax deductible on the federal income tax return for those who itemize.
2. Earnings for a Roth IRA account are tax free (if left in the Roth for the required time).
3. As of March 2022, mortgage rates are near their lowest levels ever, with 30-year fixed mortgage rates hovering around 4.25% and 15-year rates near 3.5%.
4. The compounded return on broadly diversified equity (common stock) investments has averaged in excess of 9% per year, going back well over a century.

In sum, we can currently borrow at unprecedented low levels and possibly deduct the interest, invest in stocks with a long-term track record in excess of 9%, and possibly do it in an account (Roth IRA) in which the earnings are tax free. Hmm. Something about that sounds good to me, but yet "experts" say, "pay off that tax-deductible 3% or 4% mortgage as fast as you can!"

Personally, I have one debt outstanding: a fixed-rate home mortgage of about $250,000 at 2%. I could easily pay it off tomorrow, but I have no intention of doing so because I would prefer to pay $5,000 a year in tax-deductible interest and invest the money in a diversified portfolio of stocks, which has historically produced earnings in excess of $22,000 a year on a $250,000 investment.

Conceptually, there is good conservative logic to paying off loans as quickly as possible and being debt free. If mortgage rates were currently at levels like those in the '70s, '80s, '90s, and 2000s, when rates were at times more than 10% or even 6%, I would pay off my home loan and not take the risk. But with rates at such historically low levels, I like my chances that I will make more investing than my cost of funds at 2.00%.

Let me be clear on a few points. Obviously, there is no guarantee what the rate of return will be on equity investments in the future. The stock market has always had volatility, and it always will. The rate of return the stock market produces can vary substantially over time, and it has had many periods with negative returns; therefore, a long-term approach is paramount to having success investing in stocks.

THE NO-BRAINER: REFINANCING

Home loans with fixed interest rates are one of the few transactions between a consumer and a lender in which the consumer holds the upper hand. Mortgage loans can almost always be paid off early without any penalty. If rates go down, the homeowner can refinance (refi) their home, which simply means replacing their existing loan with a new loan at the new lower prevailing rates.

On the other hand, if interest rates rise, homeowners can sit tight on their fixed-rate loan and enjoy the lower interest rate for the life of the loan. It's truly a "heads, you win; tails, they lose" situation in the homeowner's favor. The only negative to refinancing is it often costs about 1.5% of the loan amount in fees to do so.

However, it is not uncommon for there to be no out-of-pocket expenses when refinancing. Many lenders will allow borrowers to *roll the fees* into the new loan, meaning they are just added to the principal amount, and the fees are amortized as a part of the new loan. This is an attractive option and worth taking the time to shop around with different lenders to ensure you are getting the best terms available. Another added benefit is it can make you feel really smart to say, "There was zero out-of-pocket cost for my sweet mortgage refi because I rolled all the fees into the loan, and I reduced my monthly payment a boatload because I got this sick totally lit crazy-low new interest rate." Ha!

A Refinance Example

Let's assume someone bought a home in the year 2000 with a $200,000, fixed-rate, 30-year home loan at 8%, which was the prevailing rate at the time. The monthly payment for principal and interest would be $1,467.53, for a total of $528,311 in payments over the 30-year life of the loan.

Three years later, in 2003, 30-year fixed rates had declined to 6%. So, to compare apples to apples, let's assume this astute owner refinanced at 6% for a 27-year loan, so the term of the new loan is identical to that of the original loan. Just like that, the owner's monthly payment instantly dropped to $1,199.10, or a decrease of $268.43 a month, times the 324 remaining months on the loan equals a whopping $86,971 reduction in their payments over the remaining life of the loan! Oh, I forgot they'll have to pay approximately $3,000 in fees to do the refi—not a bad trade-off, $3,000 in fees for $86,971 less in payments.

It gets even better. Eight years after they refinanced down to 6% in 2003, fixed rates had dropped to 4% in 2011. So, once again, to keep the comparisons equal, let's assume they refinanced at 4% for a 19-year loan. On this new loan, their monthly payments would decrease to $954.83, for an additional decrease of $244.27 per month, or $55,694 additional total savings over the 19 remaining years on the loan. Of course, we have to remember the refi costs, again assumed at $3,000.

So, if the homeowner had kept their original mortgage at 8%, they would have to make total payments of $528,311 over the 30-year life of the loan. But, by wisely taking advantage of the decline in new mortgage rates and refinancing twice, they would have decreased their total loan payments to $385,646, which is a total reduction of $142,665 (less $6,000 or so in fees).

This is not just a hypothetical situation that few people have utilized—millions of homeowners have taken advantage of this strategy. Since purchasing our home in 1991, I have refinanced four times, with the last refi getting our rate down to 2% in October 2021.

The general rule of thumb is if you can reduce your interest rate by 2% or more, then refinancing is a good idea, assuming you're planning to keep the home for at least a couple more years so you will be able to experience enough lower payments to recoup any refi fees.

Refinancing a high-interest home loan can permanently
reduce your monthly mortgage payment and serve as the
catalyst to begin consistently accumulating wealth.

REFINANCE AND INVEST THE SAVINGS

The example above detailed how a homeowner could save $142,665 in monthly payments by refinancing twice. Let's further assume each time the owner refinanced their loan, they invested the savings every month. That is, on the first refi, their monthly payment decreased from $1,467 to $1,199. So, every month thereafter, they invested $268, which was the reduction in their monthly loan payment.

The second time the homeowner refinanced, their payment was further reduced to $954, for a total decrease of $513 from the original monthly payment amount. So, after the second refi, they invested $513 monthly. Let's further assume they put the monthly investments into a Roth IRA account, which means the earnings will be tax free when withdrawn if left in the Roth for the required time period. Let's also reduce the amount that goes into the Roth by the assumed $6,000 in refi costs.

And lastly, let's assume that in the Roth IRA, the homeowner invested in a diversified portfolio of high-quality common stocks. If their average compounded annual growth rate was 6%, which is well below what common stocks have averaged over the long haul, that Roth IRA would be worth $297,117 at the end of the 27 years since the first refinancing.

If the homeowner averaged a 9% growth rate, the account would be worth $467,042 at the end of the 27 years. So after the two refinancings, their total loan payments over 30 years was $391,646 (including $6,000 in refinancing fees). This means that at the time of their last loan payment, their Roth account would be worth more than the total of all their payments, simply by investing the reductions in their payments from the refinancings. Now that is a beautiful thing.

ADJUSTABLE-RATE MORTGAGES (ARMs)

In 1980, the first variable interest rate home loans were offered. These types of loans are most commonly referred to as adjustable-rate mortgages (ARMs). ARMs were extremely popular throughout the 1980s, 1990s, and 2000s, when interest rates were substantially higher than they are currently.

The basic concept of an ARM is that the loan interest rate is adjusted periodically based on where market interest rates are at the time of the adjustment. From the borrower's perspective, ARMs have the appeal that their interest rate is automatically adjusted downward if rates decline, rather than having to go through the expense and effort of refinancing their loan to get the lower rate. A second benefit of ARMs was that historically, the initial interest rate for an ARM was typically about one-half of 1% lower than the rate for prevailing fixed-rate loans.

A negative characteristic of ARMs is that if interest rates rise, then the mortgage rate may increase in the future. Therefore, the fundamental dilemma of whether to go with a fixed interest rate loan vs. an ARM is a judgment call as to whether interest rates are most likely to increase or decrease in the future.

With fixed mortgage rates currently near their all-time low levels, I find very little appeal to ARMs at this time for most homeowners. However, an ARM could be an attractive option if a homebuyer knows with a high degree of certainty that they will be moving within a relatively short time period. For example, if someone is confident they will be moving within five years, then it is worth considering an ARM in which the first interest rate adjustment occurs no sooner than in five years. Hence, if the five-year ARM rate is better than the rate on longer-term, traditional, fixed-rate loans, then the ARM may be the best loan for such a homebuyer.

Even with interest rates near historically low levels, an ARM may still be an attractive alternative if the homebuyer is confident they will be moving close to or sooner than when the first interest rate adjustment occurs.

There are several important contractual aspects of ARMs that will be detailed in the loan document, such as the initial interest rate, when the first rate adjustment may occur, when subsequent rate adjustments may occur, what the interest rate index is, what the interest rate margin is, and whether there is a limit (cap) on how much the interest rate can change. Borrowers should understand the specifics of each of those details relative to their loan before committing to the loan.

The following is an explanation of some of those key ARM terms borrowers should understand:

Initial Interest Rate

ARMs have a stipulated initial interest rate that remains constant until the first rate adjustment. Sometimes, lenders will offer an extremely low initial rate, referred to as a teaser rate, to catch the attention of borrowers. Then, when the first adjustment occurs, the borrower may experience a substantial increase in their interest rate and, therefore, an unexpected increase in their monthly payment.

Initial Rate Lock Period

The initial interest rate will remain constant for an initial period of time, which could be as short as just one month or as long as 10 years, or even longer. Common periods are one, three, five, or seven years, but the initial rate could be fixed for whatever time period the lender and borrower agree to. How long the initial rate is fixed for is an extremely important detail for a borrower to understand. Generally, an ARM with a low initial rate, say of 3%, that adjusts after the first year wouldn't be nearly as appealing as a 3% ARM with no rate adjustment until after the fifth year.

Frequency of Subsequent Rate Adjustments

After the initial interest lock period, the loan agreement will also stipulate how frequently the loan will adjust thereafter. Most ARMs adjust annually after the first adjustment. For example, a 30-year ARM that has a fixed rate for the first three years, and then adjusts annually for the remaining 27 years thereafter, is called a 3/1 ARM. A 5/3 ARM has a fixed interest rate for the first five years, and then the rate is adjusted every three years thereafter. The first number always indicates the number of years for the initial rate lock period, and the second number indicates how frequently the rate is adjusted thereafter.

Interest Rate Index and Margin

When interest rate adjustments occur, the new rate is determined by a precise formula with two distinct parts: the *index* and the *margin*. The index is a measure of current market interest rates, and the margin is an additional percentage amount added to the index to determine the new rate. The index + the margin = the new interest rate.

Common indexes lenders use include the prime interest rate, 1-year Treasury rates, or any one of the other various Cost of Funds Indexes (COFI). The loan document will specify the index that is used. Unfortunately, for most homebuyers, these various indexes are unfamiliar topics and mean very little to them. However, the impact of one index vs. another can equate to tens of thousands of dollars in interest over the life of the loan.

For example, as of March 2022, the prime interest rate is 3.50% and the 1-year Treasury rate is 1.35%. So, if the interest rate was up for adjustment now for an ARM with a margin of 3% using the prime rate as the index, the new rate would be 6.50% (3.50% prime rate + 3% margin = 6.50%).

If another ARM was due for a rate adjustment now with the same 3% margin, but it uses the 1-year Treasury rate as the index, the new rate would be 4.35% (1.35% 1-year Treasury + 3% margin = 4.35%). It may be helpful to conduct a simple internet search to look at historical charts for different indexes being used when considering various ARMs.

Teaser Rates

A good question to ask the lender when considering an ARM is, "Based on the index and margin for this ARM, what would the interest rate be if it were adjusted today, and what would my monthly payment be after the adjustment?" If the interest rate and monthly payment would increase substantially after this hypothetical adjustment, as compared to the initial rate and payment being offered, then you are being offered a teaser rate. A teaser rate doesn't necessarily mean it is an unattractive loan; it just means the payments will likely rise after the first adjustment, and the borrower needs to be aware of that.

Loan Term

Just like fixed-rate mortgages, ARMs can be for various terms, the most common being either 15-year or 30-year loans.

Periodic and Lifetime Interest Rate Adjustment Limits

Most ARMs will have a cap (a maximum limit) on how much the interest rate can change for any single rate adjustment and for the life of the loan. For example, if an ARM had an initial rate of 4% and a 2% limit per rate change, then the most the rate could increase to at the first adjustment would be 6%; then, it could increase at most 2% more at the second rate change to 8%, and so on. The maximum interest rate for the life of the loan could be stated either as a percentage above the initial rate, or as a specific number such as 10% or 12%.

Fixed-rate home loans are much less complex and simpler to understand than ARMs. For those reasons, borrowers should be sure to understand all the details before they commit to an ARM. What may seem like an irrelevant point at first glance could have a major impact on the amount of future loan payments.

KNOW THESE ARM DETAILS BEFORE COMMITTING

- $ What the initial interest rate is
- $ How long the initial rate remains fixed
- $ What the index and margin are
- $ If there are limits on how much the interest rate can change
- $ How often the rate may be adjusted after the initial period

---

PRIVATE MORTGAGE INSURANCE (PMI) AND DOWN PAYMENTS

An important consideration when borrowing to purchase a home is the down payment amount. Most lenders require the borrower to pay for a specific type of insurance policy referred to as private mortgage insurance (PMI) if the loan amount exceeds 80% of the appraised value of the home.

A PMI policy is entirely different and separate from a homeowners policy, which protects against fires, damage from weather, etc. PMI is a policy to provide financial protection for the lender (not the borrower) in the event the borrower defaults on the loan.

From a planning perspective, if a prospective homeowner can make at least a 20% down payment, it will likely save them many thousands of dollars by avoiding the requirement to purchase PMI. For example, to avoid PMI, the buyer of a $200,000 home would typically need to make a $40,000 down payment at purchase. The following is some additional information about PMI.

How Much Does PMI Cost?

The insurance company providing the PMI policy determines the premium amount (cost) based on a number of risk factors. The higher the perceived risks, the higher the premium. The annual premium cost generally ranges on the low end at about 0.2% of the loan amount, up to 2.5% or more on the high end. For example, a $200,000 loan with a 1% annual premium would cost the homeowner $2,000 per year.

Why Is PMI Required?

By industry standards, lenders generally have adequate protection in the event of a default if the initial loan to value (LTV) ratio is no greater than 80%. In theory, if the borrower defaulted and the lender had to foreclose and sell the property to get repaid, the cushion provided by the down payment would be enough to pay expenses and fees and mitigate a potential decline in the value of the home.

Obviously, the lender's risk of losing money on a default is correspondingly greater as the down payment amount decreases. PMI is simply a financial tool that allows for the purchase of a property with a lower down payment while still providing adequate financial protection to the lender.

What Risk Factors Determine the PMI Premiums?

Insurers consider a number of factors to determine the premium amount for a particular loan. The combination of these factors and the corresponding perceived level of risk ultimately determine the premium charged to the borrower. The following are some of those risk factors.

The borrower's credit worthiness: The cost of PMI for someone with a credit score below 630 could be as much as four times the amount of someone with a 760 credit score.

The LTV ratio: The higher the LTV, the more PMI will cost. For example, PMI will be more expensive if the loan is 95% of the appraised value of the home vs. a loan that has an LTV of 82%.

The mortgage time period: A 15-year mortgage would have a lower premium than a 30-year mortgage. The shorter the mortgage period, the more quickly the principal is paid off.

Primary residence: The premium would be lower for a loan on your primary residence vs. a second home or rental property. Loans on primary residences have a lower default rate than on other types of property.

Size of the loan: Larger loans, referred to as jumbo loans, are generally charged a higher percentage than non-jumbo loans.

Loan type: An adjustable-rate loan may have a higher PMI premium than a fixed-rate loan because there is a higher risk in the event the adjustable rate increases substantially.

Cash-out refinance loans: The premium will likely increase if the borrower is refinancing the property and receiving cash from the lender (cash out).

When Is the PMI Premium Paid?

PMI is generally paid monthly, and the cost is rolled into (added to) the monthly mortgage payment. The mortgage servicer then pays the PMI provider.

Cancellation of PMI

Generally, PMI is no longer required, and the policy is automatically canceled when the loan is paid down to 78% of the original appraised value. However, PMI may continue to be required if there is another lien on the property or if the borrower is not current on payments.

Borrowers who make at least a 20% down payment can avoid the expense of obtaining private mortgage insurance (PMI).

HOME EQUITY LINE OF CREDIT (HELOC)

A home equity line of credit, or HELOC (pronounced he-lock), is an innovative type of home loan that in many respects resembles a credit card. Like credit cards, HELOCs can be a convenient, cost-effective financial instrument when used wisely. Also, like credit cards, HELOCs can be a quick and easy way for people to impulsively borrow money and get themselves into financial trouble.

The general concept of a HELOC is when a lender provides a *revolving* line of credit to a homeowner based on the equity in the home. The term revolving means the credit line can be accessed and paid off repeatedly, much like a credit card. The term *equity* means the value of the home, less any outstanding mortgages or liens on the home. Most HELOCs are put in place as a *second* mortgage subordinate to the homeowner's primary amortized first mortgage. For many people, a HELOC is like an insurance policy—they're glad they have it but hope they never need to access it.

A HELOC Hypothetical Example

Let's assume you purchased a house years ago for $200,000. You made a $40,000 down payment and took out a conventional amortized mortgage loan for $160,000 to purchase the home. Hence, your original LTV ratio was 80% ($160,000 loan divided by the $200,000 home value).

Today, your mortgage balance is $90,000, and your home has appreciated in value to $300,000. Hence, you now have $210,000 of equity in your home ($300,000 value less the $90,000 remaining mortgage balance = $210,000 equity), which means your LTV is now only 30% ($90,000 loan divided by the $300,000 home value).

You have had some unfortunate personal expenses and a few instances of poor judgment, and you now have $20,000 in credit card debt on which you're paying 20% annual interest. Additionally, you have a $15,000 car loan with a 9% interest rate and, two months from now, you need $10,000 for your child's college tuition payment.

Your lender approves you for a second mortgage HELOC at 80% LTV. The home appraises for $300,000 x 80% = $240,000, less the $90,000 outstanding on the first mortgage = a $150,000 limit on the HELOC.

Your lender offers HELOC customers with excellent credit a floating interest rate of prime (currently 3.50%) +1% = 4.50%. However, due to your high credit card balances and several late loan payments, you have a lower credit score; therefore, the lender charges you prime (3.50%) + 3% = 6.50%.

You immediately take a $35,000 draw once the HELOC is in place and pay off your $20,000 credit card balances and your $15,000 car loan. By paying off these higher interest rate debts with the HELOC, it will save you over $3,000 in interest in the first year alone. When the college tuition is due, you will take another advance of $10,000.

By using the HELOC, you haven't reduced your overall debt, but you have shifted the debt to a much lower interest rate and a substantial reduction in your monthly payment. In theory, this should allow you to pay off the debt at a much lower overall cost.

HELOC Loan Maximums

Lenders will generally offer HELOCs with an LTV ratio up to at least 80%. Some lenders will offer HELOCs up to 90% LTV, but they may increase the interest rate to do so. Likewise, the rate may be reduced for a substantially lower LTV of say 50%. A higher LTV increases the risk a lender could lose money if they had to foreclose due to default; therefore, they price the loan based on the perceived risk.

Consider your current and future borrowing needs when deciding on the appropriate HELOC amount. In other words, there may be no benefit in agreeing to a higher loan limit that comes with a correspondingly higher interest rate if you are unlikely to ever borrow the additional amount.

HELOC Fees

Since HELOCs are based on the home's value, a current appraisal is usually necessary. However, some lenders will agree to pay for the appraisal and all other costs as an inducement for your business. Some HELOCs come with an annual fee of $100 or so.

Accessing the Line

HELOCs are revolving lines of credit with a specific maximum borrowing amount that can be accessed and paid off at the discretion of the borrower. For example, if you are approved for a $100,000 HELOC, you may go for months or years and never take an advance (borrow) on the line. Then, you may borrow $12,000 to remodel the house, and a month later, borrow $20,000 to buy a car. HELOCs often come with a book of checks, whereby accessing the line is as easy as writing a check.

HELOCs can provide peace-of-mind knowing money is available if needed. However, they can also be a source of easy credit that results in burdensome debt.

Payment Requirements and Interest Charges

Once you access the line of credit, you are generally required to make interest-only payments monthly, with no required principal payments. For example, if you have an outstanding balance of $30,000 and your interest rate is currently 6%, then your required monthly payment would be approximately $150 for interest only.

Floating Interest Rate

Just like personal and commercial lines of credit, HELOC interest rates are usually floating rates, most often based on the current prime interest rate.[3] Any time the prime rate changes, the rate on the HELOC immediately changes. This is different from ARMs, where the interest rate usually adjusts only once a year or longer. HELOCs will frequently have stated minimum and maximum interest rates for the life of the loan.

First or Second Mortgage

Traditionally, most HELOCs are put in place as a *second* mortgage, meaning the homeowner still has another mortgage (the *first*) in place. This is an important distinction from the lender's perspective because a second mortgage is subordinate to the first. This means that if the home is foreclosed on and sold to satisfy the loans, the first mortgage must be paid off completely before the second is paid.

Consequently, a second mortgage is considerably higher risk than a first. For that reason, banks may charge 2%, 3%, or more, higher interest rates for a second mortgage HELOC than the same borrower would be able to get with a first mortgage.

Tax Deductibility of Interest

Prior to 2018, one of the attractive features of HELOCs was that the interest was tax deductible if you itemized, regardless of what the loan proceeds were used for. Beginning in 2018, federal law no longer allows HELOC interest to be tax deductible unless the loan was specifically used to "buy, build, or substantially improve the taxpayer's home that secures the loan." In other words, the interest is no longer deductible if the loan proceeds were to take a vacation, buy a car, pay tuition, etc.

---

3   Prime is a stated benchmark interest rate that banks declare; it is the interest rate banks charge their most creditworthy borrowers.

The Ugly Side of HELOCs

A friend of mine, Jerry, was a federal bank regulator in the 80s and 90s. As Jerry went about his job examining banks and reviewing their problem loans, he witnessed firsthand the ugly side of easy credit after HELOC loans were invented and gained widespread popularity.

The alarming trend Jerry saw was related to homeowners who had gotten themselves into trouble with high credit card debt and other consumer loans. The newfound HELOC loans came along and made it enticingly convenient for struggling homeowners to replace all of their consumer debt with a lower-interest-rate loan. Additionally, the novel HELOCs had no mandatory principal payments.

At first glance, it appeared to be a great financial tool to help people out of a hole. In theory, since the HELOC lowered their interest payments, the homeowners would be in a much better position to pay off their debt and manage their overall finances.

Unfortunately, for many of the troubled loans Jerry reviewed, rather than helping people gain control of their finances, HELOCs did just the opposite. After paying off their consumer debts with the HELOC loans, many of the borrowers immediately ran their credit balances up again, and found themselves in a financial double bind! All the HELOC did was allow them to continue to overspend, resulting in an even more daunting total sum of debts to pay off.

The vast majority of HELOC borrowers didn't have such unfortunate outcomes. However, it does underscore the need for caution when credit is easily available. Much like some people having a difficult time controlling their spending with credit cards, a set of HELOC checks can be very tempting.

Housing decisions can significantly impact the wealth accumulation process, positively and negatively.

SUMMARY

Buying a home on the basis of it being an attractive investment can be a costly mistake. Homes generally appreciate in value over time, but after all the costs of home ownership are considered, they are generally not a great way to accumulate wealth.

Home ownership is ideal for many people and families, while renting is a much better choice for others. The decision whether to buy a home rather than rent should be predicated on personal considerations as well as financial considerations. Being able to afford the upfront cost to buy a home is one issue, but just as important are the ongoing costs—such as insurance, taxes, maintenance, and repairs.

The belief that renting is unwise simply because you are not *building equity* would be true if the all-in cost of home ownership was no greater than the cost to rent—unfortunately, that is seldom the case. Renters can effectively *build equity* by wisely investing the money they saved by renting.

When buying a home, carefully consider which loan is best for you. Shop around for the best rates and fees, and consider the term (number of years) and whether a fixed or variable rate loan suits you best. Refinancing an existing mortgage is worth considering any time you can reduce your loan rate by 1.5% or so. A home equity line of credit (HELOC) is a convenient and flexible way for a homeowner to access the equity in their home to meet financial expenses. Having a HELOC in place can also provide comfort and peace of mind, knowing money is readily available if a financial emergency arises.

CHAPTER 8

Author's Letter to a 45-Year-Old Couple

This chapter contains a hypothetical letter from the author written to a middle-aged couple who want to improve their financial situation. They realize they need to make changes in regard to their money management to have an adequate nest egg to be able to comfortably retire in their 60s. Many people will be able to identify with this common scenario. Hopefully, some readers will find the letter beneficial in dealing with their own finances.

Dear 45-Year-Old Couple,

It was so nice to hear from you after all these years, and it was most helpful that we were able to spend a couple of hours together. The following is my summary of your current financial situation as you explained it to me, followed by an action plan on how I believe you can dramatically improve your finances and be on schedule to retire in your 60s with adequate income and assets to enjoy your golden years.

You have taken a huge step toward improving your financial situation by acknowledging you are not where you want to be financially. It is important that both of you are willing to make sacrifices and changes relative to your spending and investing. It is also vital for the two of you to share the same vision and commitment for your future.

As we discussed, it is not a trivial task to turn your finances around. You will need to spend some time assessing your current financial status, as described below, then you will also need to devote time to making an action plan for the future. Then the real work will begin—living the plan day by day and repeating the process for the next 20 years. Changing familiar habits and sticking to those changes will be a challenging and ongoing task.

SUMMARY OF CURRENT SITUATION

1. **Wages**: You have combined family wages of $150,000.
2. **401(k)**: Both of your employers offer 401(k) plans with a 50% match on up to 6% of your wages; however, neither of you have contributed to your 401(k).
3. **Savings**: $5,000 in a checking account is the extent of your savings. In your words, "if we had excess money, we had no problem figuring out ways to spend it."
4. **Credit card debt**: You have $15,000 in credit card debt on which you're paying 20% annual interest.
5. **Autos**: You own two cars that are paid for.
6. **Home loan**: In three more years, your home loan will be paid off. Your monthly payment is $2,000.
7. **Children**: Your two sons will graduate from high school in three years and five years, respectively, and you think both of them will go to college; however, you have no money set aside to pay for college costs.
8. **Budgeting**: You have never done a budget, an income statement, or a net worth statement.

KEY ACTION POINTS

The driving force to improving your financial picture will be your sustained ability to substantially reduce your spending. If you're able to reduce your expenses, you'll then be able to contribute to your 401(k) plans over the next 20 years to accumulate wealth. The following are some specific steps I would suggest.

Complete an income statement (IS) and a budget: The IS shows what your expenses and income were last year, and the budget shows what you plan for them to be next year. This will take some time and effort, but it needs to be done. The IS will detail exactly where all of your money went over the last 12 months. Since you primarily use credit cards, checks, or electronic payments, it will be very easy to go back over each of your last 12 monthly statements to construct the IS.

Use the IS to develop a budget and look for every opportunity possible to reduce expenses. Each month in the future, you will then input your expenditures to show what you actually spent and compare it to your budget. This is a powerful tool to ensure you are following through with the expense reductions you have planned to make, as well as proving whether or not your budget is realistic. Chapter 19, in the copy of my book that I gave you, is devoted to personal financial statements. That chapter provides considerable detail on how to construct and use an IS, a budget, and a net worth statement.

The following are just a few examples of specific options to consider putting in the budget to reduce expenses.

- $ **Eating out**: Limit the number of times you eat out to once per week.
- $ **Lawn services**: Cancel your lawn service and have the boys do the mowing.
- $ **Golf club membership**: Since you seldom golf anymore and your boys are not golfers, cancel your membership.
- $ **Alcohol consumption**: You stated that both of you would like to reduce the amount of alcohol you consume; doing so will have both physical and financial benefits.
- $ **Vacations**: Since everyone in the family enjoys hiking and the wilderness, make your next vacations low-cost outdoor adventures instead of the expensive resort destination vacations you have traditionally taken.

$ **Clothing purchases**: You acknowledged your closets are full, and you could probably go several years without actually needing another article of clothing.

$ **Electric bill**: Contact your utility provider to do an energy efficiency review of your entire home and be conscious of thermostat settings, turning off lights and appliances when not in use, etc.

Expense reduction goal: Eliminating $15,000 a year in expenses is a very modest and achievable goal based on your spending. By questioning every expense, a $25,000 annual reduction is quite possible for you.

Contribute to 401(k)s: Since each of your employers offers a 50% match on contributions up to 6% of your wages, both of you should start immediately contributing 6% to your 401(k) plan—no more and no less than 6% to start with. Taking advantage of the employer match is like getting an automatic 50% rate of return the first year on all contributions. Based on your $150,000 in wages, 6% is $9,000 that you will contribute the first year, and with the employer match of $4,500, total contributions will be $13,500. Since contributions are pre-tax, you will only see your take-home pay decrease by about $7,000. I recommend you invest in a mix of stock funds in the 401(k).

Pay off credit card debt: Since you are paying a burdensome interest rate of 20% on your $15,000 outstanding credit card balances, try to get them paid off as quickly as possible. If you can budget for about $20,000 in expense reductions, you can retire the credit card debt and contribute 6% to your 401(k) in the first year. Paying off this debt will save you $3,000 a year in future interest payments.

College costs: Unfortunately, paying for your boys to attend an expensive private college will make it more difficult to achieve your retirement goals. Ways to keep college costs low include the boys attending the local community college for two years and then transferring to a state university. You should seek out all available grants, and the boys can work to pay part of their costs. If need be, student loans could also be part of the solution.

Home loan: Your final home mortgage payment is in three years, which will then free up an extra $2,000 per month when those payments end. That $24,000 a year will be an integral part of growing your 401(k) accounts thereafter. If necessary, part of that could be used for potential college expenses.

HYPOTHETICAL 20-YEAR PLAN

Here is a simplified overview of what a 20-year game plan might look like for you:

Year One

$ Within one month, complete an income statement and a budget for the next year.

$ Immediately reduce expenses as much as possible (even before completing the budget).

$ Start contributing 6% of your wages to each of your 401(k) plans immediately.

$ Use expense reductions to pay off your $15,000 credit card debt within 12 months.

$ **401(k) balance end of year one:** $14,100. $9,000 employee contributions, $4,500 employer match, and accumulated earnings.

Years Two and Three

$ Continue doing a budget each year and stay vigilant to minimize expenses.

$ By the end of year one, or shortly thereafter, you will have paid off all credit card debt, which will allow you to increase your 401(k) contributions substantially at the start of year two. I am assuming you will be able to contribute a total of $2,000 a month to your 401(k)s at this point.

$ You should also start saving more in your checking account to have at least $10,000 as an emergency fund.

$ **401(k) balance end of year three, age 48:** $79,000. $24,000 annual employee contributions, $4,500 annual employer match, and accumulated earnings.

Years Four through Nine

$ Your cash flow will increase by $2,000 a month when your home loan is paid off in three years. However, you may start incurring expenses for your oldest son's college costs at this point, and two years later, your other son may be going to college as well.

$ At some point, you will need new autos for each of you and possibly the boys.

$ To be conservative, let's assume you only increase your 401(k) contributions from $2,000 to $2,500 a month. Earmark the other $1,500 a month from the retired mortgage for college or auto expenses.

$ Of course, you will have become experts by now at doing the annual budget and eliminating unnecessary expenses; continue budgeting annually.

$ **401(k) balance end of year nine, age 54:** $403,700. $30,000 annual employee contributions, $4,500 annual employer match, and accumulated earnings.

Years 10 through 20

$ Nine years from now, college expenses will hopefully be behind you. The two of you will be 54 years of age and on the home stretch toward retiring in good financial condition.

$ Let's assume you work until age 65, and beginning in year 10 you are able to contribute $3,500 a month to your 401(k) plans.

$ **401(k) balance end of year 20, age 65:** $1,895,100. Over the entire 20-year time period, you will have contributed a total of $699,000 to your 401(k)s, your employers will have contributed $90,000, and you will have amassed $1,106,100 in earnings. Obviously, your actual 401(k) balance will depend on several variables, such as how much you contribute and the actual rate of return achieved.

CLOSING THOUGHTS

The estimate of your 401(k) balances going forward assumes your employers continue to do a 50% match on up to 6% of your wages and the accounts grow at an average annual compound rate of 9%, which is slightly below the rate of return on stocks over the last century. Although I left the employer matching contribution constant at $4,500 per year over the 20 years, it will likely increase to correspond to any future pay raises you receive.

$ I assumed increases in your expenses and your income will likely offset each other going forward; therefore, I didn't make any adjustments to either in the years ahead.

$ To take advantage of the tax benefits, I am assuming all of your future investments go into your 401(k) plans. If you need to access funds for college expenses, car purchases, or other expenses, you have multiple ways to provide liquidity, such as borrowing from your 401(k)s, establishing a home equity line of credit, temporarily suspending 401(k) contributions, and temporary use of your credit cards.

$ In current dollars, the Social Security Administration estimates the two of you combined will be able to draw about $5,000 a month in Social Security at age 65. If your 401(k) grows according to my projections and you start drawing out only 4% annually of your 401(k) balance at age 65, you will be able to receive over $6,000 a month from your 401(k) accounts. Combined with your Social Security, your total income would be a comfortable $11,000 per month in retirement.

There are many moving parts to your financial situation over the next 20 years. Unforeseen things will occur, but if the two of you hold each other accountable and both of you remain committed to adhering to your annual budgets as much as possible, you should be able to live comfortably while improving your financial well-being as you accumulate a sizable 401(k) balance by the time you retire.

You should be proud of yourselves for addressing your financial issues and your willingness to make a commitment to do better going forward. Please say hi to the boys for me.

Your friend, Kurt

PART III

INVEST

CHAPTER 9

Trading and Speculating ... Difficult and Unnecessary

The four-step mantra of EARN+SAVE+INVEST+REPEAT is the formula for wealth accumulation. Three of those four steps are intuitively easy to comprehend. EARN obviously relates to having a job and getting paid wages or producing earnings. SAVE means to not spend all the wages you earned. REPEAT means to do these steps again and again for many years.

But what exactly does INVEST mean? Is a bank account an investment? Is buying cryptocurrency an investment? Is buying a lottery ticket every week an investment? It depends on your definition of investing.

THE CONTINUUM OF RISK

In a broad, all-encompassing sense, *investing* is **deploying money to make money.** Using that definition, there is an enormous range of investment options. In the context of trying to guide yourself to appropriate and wise investments to meet your long-term financial goals, it may be helpful to contemplate investing as a continuum relative to risk—with *risk* meaning **the odds/probability of losing part or all of your money.**

When more precisely categorized by risk, the options to deploy money to make money can be differentiated as gambling, speculating, or investing, with gambling having the most risk, investing the least risk, and speculating in the middle.

Gambling

Wagering and risking money on an event with very uncertain outcomes or playing games of random chance, often with no intellectual judgment required. Losing the entire wager or winning twice the amount risked or more is common when gambling. The timeframe for gambling is often just seconds, minutes, or hours.

Speculating

Aggressively deploying capital with a perceived opportunity for a high rate of return and a corresponding high risk of a partial loss (sometimes complete loss) of the money deployed. Speculative investments normally seek capital appreciation rather than dividends or interest income. Intellectual judgment is a major factor, but there is often a high degree of uncertainty and unpredictability. The time frame is commonly hours, days, or weeks but can sometimes be months or years.

Trading or *day trading* are common types of speculative and aggressive activities where the focus is often on making relatively small gains on each trade but doing so quickly and repetitively by buying and selling assets as they fluctuate in price. Such speculators often open and close trades (buy and sell) within the same day, hence the term *day traders.*

It is important to understand the difference between investing vs. gambling, speculating, and trading.

Investing

Deploying money with the expectation of receiving income and/or capital appreciation. Most investments assume some fluctuation in value, but a complete loss of capital is rare. Preservation of capital is a much greater consideration for investors than for speculators or gamblers. Investments can range from very conservative to very aggressive in terms of both potential risk and reward. The holding period for investments is typically years or at least months.

Hopefully, the preceding tutorial on the difference between gambling, speculating (trading), and investing provides some perspective on what approach makes the most sense for you personally. Obviously, the theme of this entire book promotes the idea of being a long-term investor, not a speculator, not a trader, and certainly not a gambler.

Difficulties with Being a Trader

I'm going to elaborate a bit on trading, not because I think it is generally profitable or beneficial for most people, but rather because young adults are one of the primary groups I hope to impact positively with this book, and it is young adult males who seem to find trading or speculating appealing most frequently. Often, it is a relatively short-lived and unrewarding foray that doesn't end well.

Over the years, I've had numerous young men ask me about some type of trading they have recently been involved with or are about to venture into. The following are typical conversations:

$ "Hey Kurt, my cousin said he's been killing it trading options."
$ "What do you think of XYZ stock? I've made some good money trading it in the last two weeks."
$ "I really like Robinhood. I can trade on my phone any time, and there's no commissions."
$ "I've been doing really well with binary options."

When I see them six months later and ask how the trading is going, the typical response is, "Oh, I'm not messing with that anymore."

Trading "careers" are often short-lived and end badly because trading is difficult. It's not easy to make money consistently as a trader. Being a successful trader requires time and expertise/ability. Unlike a successful long-term investor who owns mutual funds, which take relatively little ongoing time and scrutiny, trading is a demanding and never-ending task. When traders have positions open, they're constantly reviewing the status to stay on top of any indication of when it's time to close the position.

When the average person decides they want to trade, they're often going up against professionals who work for the most savvy and sophisticated financial firms in the world. These pros make a living by trading all day, every day. They have significant resources and capital (money) supporting them. It's like a novice sitting down at a poker table with the best players in the world.

Trading is particularly treacherous when dealing with options and futures contracts because the very nature of the contract is a zero-sum game. This means for every dollar you make, someone else loses a dollar. Much like a poker player, the only way they win is if someone else loses. The fundamental tenet of such speculators is that they are better/smarter than the other person.

Long stock traders (buyers) at least have a little wind at their back in that stocks, in general, go up in value more often than they go down, so in theory, everybody can win trading during a rising stock market. But when you enter into an options trade, there is always a counterparty taking the opposite side of the trade; often, that counterparty is an experienced professional.

Unlike commission-free trading on stocks, the norm is still for commissions to be charged on every options trade, which of course makes profitable trading that much more difficult. An additional cost of trading is the wages not earned at some other job because the individual was trading instead of being employed elsewhere.

Short-term trading profits during a rising stock market can be alluring. Over the long haul, trading is usually a difficult way to make money.

I'm not saying it is impossible for the average person to be successful as a trader. Simply be aware it mandates close attention, is time-consuming, and the odds are usually not good for amateurs when trading against pros.

Over time, for nonprofessional traders, the entire process tends to wear people out. The typical life cycle begins when they hear of a friend who is having success in some type of trading. They're enticed to give it a try. Often, with a minimal amount of knowledge, they place a small trade or two. They make a little money, and the visions of grandeur set in—"This is pretty cool. I made x dollars in one day. This could just be the way I get rich and prove what a smart guy I really am."

Then it consumes hours of their time, and the size of their trades increase as the dopamine kicks in and the adrenaline flows. But then a few larger trades go the wrong way, and the Venus flytrap begins to close. Ego gets in the way of good judgment as they don't want to sell at a loss, which turns into a bigger loss, and now a *trade* turns into an *investment* as they hold on simply because they are down in value. The process can become consuming, stressful, and not much fun. Ultimately, six months after inception, it becomes "Oh, I'm not messing with that anymore."

I get it. I sound like a grumpy old man, but I've seen it too many times. In my first silver trade back in college, I lost 50% of my savings. As a broker, I saw long-term investors do well and saw short-term novice traders consistently not do well. A personal friend started a day trading company with many traders, and it failed miserably. Years ago, I paid for an expensive stock quote service with scant profits to show for it. A stock club with 12 of my broker buddies was started back in the day in which each club member got to select their favorite stock—after a few years, the club disbanded because our results sucked. I've never met a nonprofessional who had enduring success as a trader. In the short term, traders frequently mistake a raging bull market for trading prowess, but over the long haul, it is a difficult and time-consuming way to make money.[4]

---

4   A period when stock prices are generally rising is referred to as a bull market. Conversely, a bear market is a period when stock prices are declining.

A famous businessman said that he became
successful *by making good decisions.*
He explained that he learned to make good
decisions *by making bad decisions.*
Experience is sometimes the best, and only, way to learn.

MARGIN LOANS

Perhaps the easiest way to make trading riskier is to do so with borrowed money. When a broker loans a customer money to buy securities, it is called a *margin loan.* By Regulation T (Reg T), the most a broker may loan a customer to buy stock is 50% of the transaction.

Risk takers use margin loans to leverage their equity to make larger profits. For example, if a customer has $10,000 to invest, they could borrow another $10,000 from the broker with a margin loan and buy $20,000 worth of stock, thus doubling their potential profit; less the interest owed on the margin loan.

Likewise, if the stock goes down in value, it amplifies the loss. Continuing with the example above, if the stock decreased 50% in value from $20,000 to $10,000, the investor would lose all of their money, since the entire remaining $10,000 would be needed to pay off the margin loan.

As a stock declines in value, brokers are required to give *margin calls* to their clients if they don't have adequate equity in their account to meet the Reg T requirement. In other words, as a stock goes down in value, margin traders must be prepared to put up more equity (cash or securities), or their position will be sold by the broker to meet the margin call. Likewise, if a stock increases in value, a customer can borrow more due to the increased equity.

At most, Reg T permits the equity to drop as low as 25% before a margin call must be issued, but most brokers impose more restrictive standards, issuing margin calls at 35% or 40% equity levels.

If all that sounds a bit scary and confusing to you, good! Hopefully, it will prevent you from ever trading on margin. Short-term trading is risky enough; trading on margin magnifies the risk even more.

TRADER VS. INVESTOR

The terms *trader* and *investor* are commonly used to differentiate a short-term (trader) or a long-term (investor) approach. Trading is more speculative in nature and often based on short-term trends relative to price momentum, share volume, and other *technical* factors. Traders are also frequently motivated to buy or sell based on recent news events or in anticipation of upcoming news. Traders often flip back and forth from being buyers to sellers very quickly.

$ **Technicals:** The analysis of price and volume (shares traded) trends to make buy/sell decisions is key to *technical* analysis. For example, common technicals include price trend lines, moving averages, resistance and support levels, relative strength index, and share volume. Pure technicians are not concerned with *fundamentals* or what the asset is. They could use their charts and tools to make buy/sell decisions without knowing if they're trading IBM, Bitcoin, or soybeans.

Since investors take a longer-term approach, they're much less concerned with short-term price fluctuations than traders are. Instead of relying heavily on technical analysis like traders, investors are much more concerned with the long-term *fundamentals* of a company or the economy to guide their investment positions.

$ **Fundamentals:** Analyzing a company's past performance and assessing their business prospects for the future are key to fundamental analysis. Some examples include profitability, market share growth, customer growth, quality of the management team, competition in the industry, new product development, balance sheet information, dividends paid, brand recognition, and stock price relative to earnings (P/E ratio).

Most professional investors will have some consideration for both fundamental and technical information. Frequently, fundamental analysis may dictate which stocks they do or don't want to own, and technical analysis will aid in their decision-making process in terms of the timing and speed of getting in or out of a position.

The INVEST step doesn't need to include aggressive speculation, short-term trading, borrowing, or gambling.

SUMMARY

It is understandable that the allure of quick and large profits can entice people into taking undue risks on speculative ventures, particularly when they hear of others doing so profitably. Every lottery has a winner, but on average, the odds are stacked heavily against everyone who buys a ticket. Speculative trading has a similar profile. Yes, some speculators will do well as a career endeavor, and others will do well for a relatively short time period. For the vast majority, however, speculative trading is not an effective way to accumulate wealth.

THE FLOYD RILEY STORY

Floyd Riley is the most dynamic, multitalented person I have ever known—a lifetime entrepreneur with incredible drive and energy. His quick wit and extremely likeable personality made him an extraordinary salesman and promoter of his many ventures. He was the consummate work hard, play hard, always on the go, wheeling and dealing, risk-taking businessman with an insatiable appetite for the next deal.

One of Floyd's first business ventures was around age 10 at the local country club, where he contracted with the members to clean their clubs and shoes for the season for a fee paid in advance. One day, when a customer complained his items hadn't been cleaned lately, Floyd responded, "I sold that business to [another boy], you need to talk to him!"

In high school, Floyd had a thriving business booking live bands in the area for dances at fraternities, sororities, and town halls. In his early 20s, he had a beer distributorship. By his mid-20s, he had an industrial tire business and an oil distribution company. Before he was 30, he owned a bank and was a high-end genetic cattle breeder owning huge tracts of land where he also had a catfish and lobster farming operation. Floyd's biggest venture was a coal strip-mining operation, which I worked in one summer during college.

By his early 30s, he was a self-made high-flying multimillionaire with helicopters and a Learjet. His annual Brangus cattle sale was the biggest event in town and featured entertainers such as Gloria Estefan and Lee Greenwood.

Unfortunately, Floyd was somewhat like the mythological Greek god whose wings melted when he soared too close to the sun. Moderation and conservatism were not in Floyd's vocabulary. Regrettable business decisions ultimately not only bankrupted Floyd, but also landed him in federal prison for a while.

Mom and Dad taught me right from wrong, hard work, and honesty. Witnessing Floyd's many positive and exceptional traits in my youth impacted me in an enduring and profound way, and taught me different skills that I truly believe helped prepare me to tackle some of the biggest challenges of my life.

Particularly when I was a young man faced with difficult circumstances, I would sometimes draw on my remembrances of Floyd for inner encouragement: "What would Floyd do?" The answer was always the same: "Take your best shot. You didn't get this far to quit or back down. Make it happen. Let's go!"

FLOYD'S LESSON: People with exceptional talent often have exceptional accomplishments, but that doesn't make them invincible. Don't soar so high that your wings melt.

CHAPTER 10

Types of Investments

ASSET CATEGORIES (CLASSES)

In the language of the investment world, types or categories of assets are referred to as *asset classes*. A class is a group of assets or investments that share similar characteristics or features. Experts have differing opinions on how many unique classes there should be. I am going to separate them into the following seven classes:

1. Stocks
2. Bonds
3. Cash
4. Real Estate
5. Tangibles
6. Derivatives
7. Alternative Investments

Virtually everyone agrees stocks, bonds, and cash should each have a separate class designation. After those three, it often varies. For example, some experts have a separate class for real estate while others include it in the tangibles class, as it's certainly a tangible asset in a strict sense. However, I put real estate in a class by itself because it's such a large category in terms of total value and is significantly different in many ways from other tangible assets.

Some assets are a blend of more than one class, and therefore it is debatable as to which class they belong. For example, gold and oil are tangible assets but are frequently traded as derivatives in the form of futures contracts. Short term (90-day term or less), safe, and highly liquid debt instruments are viewed as cash assets. As the maturity lengthens, the safety decreases, or liquidity diminishes, the asset more appropriately belongs in the bond class instead of the cash class.

There are practical reasons for individuals to understand how their personal investments are allocated relative to *asset classes*. Assets in the same class tend to share common attributes and often respond to market conditions in the same manner. For example, stocks often tend to rise and fall as a group. Cash assets are very liquid and have virtually no fluctuation in value, while the real estate class is much less liquid. The bond class offers greater predictability but with historically lower returns than stocks. By understanding how your personal assets are diversified based on these classes can help ensure that you own appropriate investments based on your circumstances and objectives.

In this chapter, there's no discussion of mutual funds, ETFs, IRAs, Roths, 401(k)s, etc., because they're not specific types or classes of investments. They are all simply types of accounts or conduits in which investments are owned within. For example, within an IRA, you can own stocks, bonds, money market funds, etc. Those various account types are often appropriate and advantageous ways individuals can invest; therefore, an entire chapter is devoted to both mutual funds (Chapter 12) and tax-advantaged retirement accounts (Chapter 14).

OWN OR LOAN

In the simplest terms of investing, there are only two things you can do with your money: (1) own something or (2) loan it. Own = stock and loan =

bond. When publicly owned corporations need more long-term capital to operate or grow, they typically sell stock and/or bonds to do so. Everyone has heard of stocks and bonds and they are often mentally lumped together, but they are completely different types of investments in terms of their potential risks and rewards.

When you buy stock in a company, you're literally becoming a partial owner of the company. Usually, a very small owner, but an owner, nonetheless. You're not guaranteed to get your money back, but you are entitled to your pro rata share of the upside of the company. When you buy a bond, you're loaning your money to that entity in return for usually a set interest rate and for repayment of that loan at a stated date in the future. However, you're not entitled to share in the future upside performance of the company beyond the stated interest rate.

Historically, the *own* (stocks) category has far outperformed the *loan* (bonds) group. The own group tends to be more volatile and less predictable, but over the long haul, *owning* shares of companies has been far more profitable than *loaning* money to those same companies.

Some other types of *ownership* investments besides stocks include real estate, precious metals, collectibles, commodities, and the relatively new cryptocurrency category. The main concept to understand is that with all of those investments, you own something that has the opportunity to appreciate in value beyond what you paid for it, but also, there is no guarantee of getting any certain amount of money back at any certain time in the future. Likewise, there are other types of *loan* investments besides bonds, primarily deposit accounts with financial institutions such as banks, credit unions, and savings and loans.

(1) STOCKS

Stocks are also referred to as equities. Owning stock means you're a part owner of that company. *Publicly owned* companies are those that have sold shares to the general public at some point in the past—typically via an *initial public offering* (IPO). Since they are publicly owned, anyone may buy shares in the open market. Historically, owning stock in publicly traded companies has been one of the most effective ways for investors to accumulate wealth.

Shareholders may benefit financially by receiving cash dividends from the company as well as from appreciation in the price of the stock.

Shares of *privately* owned companies are not available to the general public. All the shares of private corporations may be owned by only one person or entity, or there may be multiple owners. Generally speaking, the larger a company is, the more likely it is to be publicly traded. However, there are some enormous companies that are privately owned. Likewise, there are many relatively small companies that are publicly owned.

Chapter 11 is devoted entirely to stocks, therefore, I won't go into further detail here.

(2) BONDS

Bonds are also referred to as debt or fixed income. They are loans or indebtedness whereby the issuer of the bond is borrowing from the purchaser (investor) of the bond. Bonds have a stated maturity date when the face amount (the principal) of the bond is to be repaid to the bondholder. Most bonds have a fixed interest rate for the life of the bond, whereby the interest is paid at regular intervals (for example, monthly, quarterly, or semiannually) to the bondholder.

Bonds often appeal to investors seeking income, predictability, and safety. However, the total return from owning stocks has consistently outpaced bond returns over long periods. Chapter 16 is devoted to bonds since they are such ubiquitous investments; therefore, I won't go into further detail here.

(3) CASH

Cash is also referred to as *cash equivalents*. Money market funds and bank deposits are the most common types of cash equivalents used by individual investors. The main features of this class are liquidity, safety, and little or no fluctuation in the principal value. In the investment world, cash doesn't mean green money like it does in an everyday sense, as in, "Hey dude, you have any cash on ya? I need twenty bucks." Cash means safe and quickly available. The downside of safe and available is a low rate of return. In fact, for a number of years now, the going rate on cash has been between zero and 1%.

Everyone should ideally have some amount in cash as a reserve, an operating cushion to pay the monthly bills, unforeseen emergencies, etc. Also, investors sometimes hold large sums in cash if they don't think it's a good time to invest in other areas. Other types of cash investments that are generally the domain of institutional investors include commercial paper, overnight paper, short-term treasuries, and others.

In the investment world, *cash* doesn't mean green money. It means deposit or debt instruments that are extremely liquid, very short term, and very safe with virtually no fluctuation in principal value.

---

(4) REAL ESTATE

There are four major subgroups of real estate: (1) residences (your home), (2) undeveloped land (raw land), (3) residential rental property (for example, apartments), and (4) commercial property (property occupied by businesses).

Many fortunes have been made via *active* investing in various types of real estate. However, most individuals are not well suited to being *active* real estate investors for various reasons, including lack of expertise, ongoing management and time requirements, lack of economies of scale, capital requirements, geographic limitations, and the illiquid nature of real estate, to name a few. Stocks and bonds are *passive* investments, meaning the investor is not involved with actively managing the enterprise; that's not the case with most real estate investments. Besides owning their residences, most individuals don't own other real estate. Chapter 7 covers home ownership vs. renting, as well as related topics such as home mortgages; therefore, we won't go into further detail here.

(5) TANGIBLE ASSETS

Tangible means something you can touch, which is precisely the items that belong in this category. With real estate separated into its own category, other types of tangible assets include precious metals (gold, silver, etc.), collectible art, precious stones (for example, diamonds and emeralds); and various collectibles (for example, stamps, wines, cars, rare books, sports trading cards, toys, and antiques).

When I was a rookie investment broker in 1983, it was not uncommon for investment advisors to recommend that everyone have somewhere between 2% and 5% of their net worth in gold. They viewed it as a "hedge against inflation." The 1970s was a decade when inflation and gold prices soared, so it seemed like prudent advice at the time. Unfortunately, owning gold has not been a good long-term method to accumulate wealth unless you were extremely good at timing gold's high and low prices to know when to get in and out.

Purely as an investment, I don't believe investors need to own tangibles as a hedge against inflation or for the sake of having a diversified portfolio. There are multiple reasons that may make this class of assets a poor choice for most investors, such as: lack of liquidity (markets for sellers can at times virtually disappear); lack of convenient markets to sell in (many tangible assets require that you personally find a buyer); frequent large spreads between the price at which you can sell vs. the price at which you can buy; lack of income during the ownership period (no interest, dividends, or rent); cost and risk of storage (either the cost of insuring items or the risk of physical damage); some tangible assets are fad-like and subject to sharp price declines if appeal wanes; the risk of counterfeit or inauthentic items; and, in general, investors buying tangibles would be well-advised to have personal expertise related to the assets they're purchasing.

If someone has specialized expertise in a certain asset, it logically becomes a better potential investment for that person. For example, a jeweler who thoroughly understands the precious stones market and has the opportunity to purchase at wholesale prices would probably do much better than the average person investing in stones. A professional antique dealer would be in a much better position to take advantage of that market compared to someone not in the antique business.

Commodities such as oil, agricultural products, and livestock could also be in this category, but many of these are more often traded as derivative contracts, so they could also go in the derivatives class.

INVESTOR ALERT: The final two categories below, derivatives and alternative investments, include a wide range of exotic, sophisticated, often confusing, and often very-risky instruments. For those reasons, these categories are generally unsuitable for most investors. However, I think it is educational to at least provide a brief overview of these classes.

(6) DERIVATIVES

This is a complex category in which new and original contract structures are routinely being created. The term derivative simply means an instrument/product/investment that is derived from or based on some other asset, such as futures contracts. Derivatives are primarily the domain of large institutions rather than individuals.

Using the word "investments" for this group would be generous as it relates to individual investors, as many of these products are more accurately described as highly leveraged speculations or gambles. However, when used cautiously and prudently, some derivative products can actually reduce overall risk and be an excellent tool in certain circumstances. It is beyond the scope of this book to attempt to discuss derivatives in detail; entire books are devoted to individual subsets of this category. The following are a few simple examples of how derivatives might be used:

Stock Options

Options are one of the OGs (Original Gangsters) of derivatives. They have been in existence for many decades in their current form and are still going strong today. *Puts* and *calls* are the two basic stock options.

$ *Call* options give the owner the *option* to buy shares of a specific stock at a specific price (the strike price) for a specific time period. Investors buy calls when they think a stock's price is going to increase.

$ *Put* options are basically the opposite of a call option in that the put owner has the option to sell rather than buy shares at a specific price. A put owner benefits when the price of the stock declines.

Agriculture and Livestock Futures Contracts

These contracts were originally conceived to allow farmers to lock in prices in advance of delivering their crop or livestock to the buyer. For example, if a farmer intends to deliver their corn crop to the grain elevator in August, they may sell an August futures contract months prior, thereby locking in the price for their crop. Investors and speculators trade these commodity contracts in hopes of taking advantage of price swings, not as a hedge for a farming operation.

Other Derivatives

Derivatives are also based on precious metals, currencies, interest rates, stock market indexes, bonds, and many other financial instruments.

FAILURE OF A LOCAL SAVINGS & LOAN

Surety S&L was located across the street from my brokerage office in Morganton, North Carolina. The week before I first arrived in town in 1983, it was disclosed that Surety's treasurer had lost more than $14 million in unauthorized trading of interest rate futures contracts in the S&L's account. This ultimately wiped out all of this small institution's equity, and resulted in its closure.

The treasurer's trading activities were supposed to be limited to hedging the S&L's mortgage loan portfolio. As small losses apparently turned into bigger losses, he took incrementally larger speculative positions in hopes to make back the money he had lost. Unfortunately, the losses only snowballed, and in a relatively short time period the results were devastating.

When the news broke, there was an immediate old fashioned run on the bank, as the line of customers wanting to withdraw their money went out the front door and down the block.

(7) ALTERNATIVE INVESTMENTS

Perhaps most accurately, alternative investments should be called the class containing everything that doesn't belong in one of the other six classes. Much like the derivatives category, these assets are generally the domain of sophisticated investors with large amounts of capital and a corresponding tolerance for risk. The following are examples of this class:

Hedge Funds

These are pooled funds for high net worth investors where the managers can invest in an array of products based on the funds' criteria. Hedge funds often take long (buy) and short (sell) positions in marketable securities, as well as trade-in derivatives and leveraged products. Some hedge funds have made extraordinary returns for their investors, but there have also been significant failures. *Hedge* means to take a position that reduces the risk or exposure to some other position. Decades ago, hedge funds were conceived as a way investors could be protected against declining asset prices. Today, the term is often a misnomer, as these funds frequently take positions that have little to do with hedging.

Venture Capital and Private Equity

This is what the popular TV show *Shark Tank* is all about. Investors inject money into private companies for an ownership percentage or some other financial incentive.

Cryptocurrencies

These are digital assets that have gained increasing levels of recognition and acceptance in the last few years from investors, businesses, financial institutions, and government entities. There are now more than 10,000 different cryptocurrencies available to investors. Bitcoin, which was started in 2009, is generally considered the first cryptocurrency and is also by far the most widely owned by investors. Bitcoin's total market value has exceeded $1 trillion. Although the price of Bitcoin (and most other cryptos) has generally been much more volatile than the stock market, it has appreciated at a rate substantially greater than stocks over its relatively short existence. The size, role, and acceptance Bitcoin and other cryptos will ultimately have in global finance, economics, and investing are widely debated and likely won't fully play out for many years to come.

At one extreme, naysayers think cryptos, including Bitcoin, are all destined for failure, and they are nothing more than the latest scam and a bubble that is sure to burst. At the other extreme, some Bitcoin enthusiasts say it is on track to replace gold and other assets as the preferred *store of value*, as they predict the price of Bitcoin continuing to rise for years to come. Some investors now believe cryptocurrency should be designated as a brand new separate asset class.

Special Purpose Acquisition Company (SPAC)

SPACs have no commercial operations. They are formed to raise capital via an initial public offering (IPO) for the purpose of acquiring an existing company. A traditional IPO is *a company looking for money*, whereas a SPAC IPO is *money looking for a company*. SPACs have existed since the early 1990s, but have been used more frequently in the last few years, becoming extremely popular in 2020 and 2021. SPACs are actually stocks, but because of their unique structure, they more appropriately belong in the *alternative investments* class.

Master Limited Partnership (MLP)

MLPs were a very popular way to invest in real estate, energy (oil and gas primarily), and in other assets or business operations in the 1980s. Regulations and tax laws made these attractive at that time. They still exist, but not with the popularity they once had.

SUMMARY

A *class* of assets is a group of assets or investments that share similar characteristics or features. Stocks, bonds, and cash are the most recognized classes, followed by real estate or tangibles. I listed seven distinct asset classes in the chapter—some investors divide assets into a few more or a few less classes than I did.

There are practical reasons individual investors can benefit from understanding the concept of different asset classes. Some classes are inherently riskier than other classes and much less predictable. Some classes are not very liquid, and therefore, it may take a long time to convert the asset to cash. Some classes have provided better rates of return over long time periods than others. For these reasons and others, investors may find it helpful to look at their personal investments in terms of how they are diversified by asset class.

In the simplest terms of investing, there are only two things you can do with your money: (1) *own* something, or (2) *loan* it. Stocks are ownership, and bonds are loans. Historically, the *own* (stocks) category has far outperformed the *loan* (bonds) group. The own group tends to be more volatile and less predictable. However, over the long haul, *owning* shares of companies has been far more profitable than *loaning* money to those same companies.

Mutual funds, ETFs, IRAs, Roths, 401(k)s, and other types of accounts are not specific asset *classes*. They are just types of *accounts* that assets are purchased within. For example, within an IRA or within a mutual fund, you can own stocks, bonds, cash, or even real estate. In other words, there can be a huge difference in terms of the risk and earnings for these various accounts, entirely depending on which assets you choose to own within them.

THE TIME I LOST 50% OF MY NET WORTH

During my last year in college at Southern Illinois University, I spent considerable time hanging out in a local commodity broker's office. I was following various markets, charting stocks and commodities, and learning technical jargon like resistance and support levels, trend lines, moving averages, head and shoulders patterns, etc. I was really into it and ready for the big time (or so I thought).

The trader who was mentoring me in spring 1983 traded a lot in hogs, pork bellies, and silver futures. After charting silver for several months, I was really itching to place a trade, my first trade. On a Friday, I entered that first trade for one silver contract.

Unfortunately, somebody bombed somebody else in the Middle East during the ensuing weekend, and the silver market went nuts. On Monday, silver was *limit down*, with no trades occurring (regulators set a daily limit as to how much the price is allowed to move before trading is halted for the day). I believe silver went limit down three or four days in a row before I could get out with a $4,056.30 loss, wiping out about 50% of my meager net worth at the time.

A lesson learned, indeed! Now for the most painful part of the story. To cover the loss, I sold $4,000 of the mutual fund in which virtually all of my savings was invested. Ignoring taxes, if I would have been able to leave that $4,000 in the mutual fund and reinvested all dividends and capital gains, as of January 31, 2022, it would have been worth more than $256,000.

Going from $4,000 to $256,000 in 39 years may sound like an extraordinary growth rate, but it comes out to approximately 11% compounded annually over that entire period. The particular fund I was invested in was started in 1934 and is still going strong today, investing primarily in large, well-established (blue chip) stocks. Nothing fancy, just ownership of good companies for the long haul.

CHAPTER 11

Stocks

I f investing were a baseball game, the stock ownership team would have won more World Series titles than the rest of the teams combined. Yes, the stock team lost some games, struck out a few times, made some errors on defense, and walked a few batters. However, the stock team has the most talented players in the game on their team, the best coaches, and the best minor league system with the stars of the future.

Over long time periods, the rate of return for stocks has far outpaced returns on bonds, bank accounts, insurance contracts, precious metals, real estate, commodities, and collectibles. Simply put, owning stocks has been the best way to consistently accumulate wealth over the long haul for *passive* investors. Passive investing means you are not involved with active management, as in owning and running a business.

For sure, there are plenty of examples of other asset groups far outperforming stocks for relatively short time periods. In fact, the overall stock market had a negative return in about 25% of the last 100 years, so in those years, you would have done better just holding cash.

After the coronavirus pandemic occurred, real estate prices increased substantially in many locations, and many commodity prices soared. There have been periods in which gold prices and other metals outperformed stocks. From time to time, certain types of collectibles and artwork have appreciated dramatically. In the last decade, cryptocurrencies such as Bitcoin have had meteoric price appreciation. However, stocks have consistently provided superior rates of return over generational time periods.

WHAT THIS CHAPTER IS *NOT*

No doubt some readers were expecting the chapter titled "Stocks" to be chock-full of advice and nifty tips on how to analyze and trade stocks. This chapter purposely has very little content on how to be a stock-picker for two reasons. First, the topic is beyond my core competency as I was never a stock analyst by vocation. Second, and more importantly, this book is about long-term wealth accumulation for the masses, and I believe investing in diversified funds is a much more appropriate option for most people than buying individual stocks, which will be explained in further detail in upcoming chapters.

INTRINSIC VALUE

A simple yet important thing to understand about investing, in general, and stocks specifically, is the concept of *intrinsic value*. Intrinsic means that which is naturally a part of something, innate, inherent, or native to. Many investors are oblivious to this concept and, as a result, take irrationally aggressive amounts of risk when investing, or, conversely, they are unwilling to accept any level of perceived risk, so they may avoid any chance of loss of principal.

For example, the intrinsic value of a bond is that the bondholder will receive interest payments as stipulated and receive the face amount at maturity. For bonds and other debt instruments, calculating the intrinsic value is fairly straightforward. For example, let's assume a bond has a $1,000 face value, matures in one year, pays a 2% interest rate, and the interest is due at maturity. Ignoring any risk of default, the owner of this bond will receive exactly $1,020 in one year (at maturity)—$1,000 for the face value and $20 interest for the year. Therefore, the *intrinsic value* would be something slightly less than the

$1,020 since the bondholder won't receive the money for a year. A method called *discounted cash flow* (DCF) analysis would be used to calculate the precise present value. Detailed discussion of DCF is beyond the scope of this writing, as entire books have been devoted to DCF analysis.

As compared to the relatively simple aforementioned bond value calculation, the determination of the intrinsic value of a home on an acre of land is somewhat more dynamic and more subject to opinion. Relevant factors would include the perceived value of the land, the replacement cost of a similar home, the recent selling price of comparable properties, the attractiveness of the neighborhood, and the proximity to desirable amenities, as well as other considerations.

INTRINSIC VALUE OF STOCKS

The intrinsic value of owning stocks is embedded in the fact that as a shareholder, you are an owner of the company, and therefore you are entitled to your proportionate share of the company's future earnings. Particularly from a long-term perspective, the intrinsic value of shares of stock is primarily based on the company's *ability to make money* in the future. The company's assets and liabilities are also important factors.

Let's say someone owned a pizza parlor that lost money every month and was only able to stay open because the owner continually put more money into the business. Eventually, they would go out of business, and the owner would lose whatever money they had invested. Owning publicly traded stocks is no different. Eventually, value comes back to the company's ability to make money.

In plain language, stocks have outperformed the aforementioned other types of assets because US businesses have prospered and made money for their shareholders over the long haul. As the American economy has grown and prospered, shareholders of quality companies have benefited accordingly. Consequently, if you believe our country and economy will continue to grow and thrive in the future, investing in stocks for the long haul is still the best choice for most investors, in my opinion.

HISTORICAL RATES OF RETURN

Various scholars have documented how stocks have a stellar historical track record of outperforming bonds, cash, gold, home prices, and inflation over the long haul. Without getting bogged down with too much data, going back more than 90 years to the late 1920s, historians show that inflation has averaged about 3% a year, the return on high-quality corporate bonds has been about 6% annually, and the return on stocks has averaged at least 9% per year (10% to 11% is probably a more accurate number). Conservatively, let's just say stocks have averaged 9%, including both capital appreciation and dividends paid.

Year by year, results for each have varied widely. There have been periods when inflation was more than 10% a year and other years when inflation was negative (declining prices). Stocks have had numerous years when the total return exceeded 30% for the year, and although there have generally been about three up years for every one down year for stocks, there have been at least five of those 90+ years when stock values declined by 20% or more for the calendar year.

Although the annual returns on bonds have not been as volatile as stocks (the highs or the lows), there have been numerous years in which bonds had double-digit returns, as well as more than a dozen years when bonds had a negative total return.

Earning 3% more per year; 9% for stocks vs. 6% for bonds may not sound significant, but that is 50% greater *earnings* per year for stocks over bonds. When compounded for many years, the difference is eye-opening. The following table shows how $100,000 would grow when compounded annually at 6%, 9%, and 11%. An 11% column is included because there are multiple mutual funds that invest in stocks that have produced average annual returns in excess of 11% for well over 50 years. It is staggering how much difference 3% and 5% greater earnings per year can make when compounded for decades. No consideration is made in the table for taxation of the earnings.

Growth of $100,000 Compounded Annually			
Years	6%	9%	11%
10	$179,085	$236,736	$283,942
20	$320,714	$560,441	$806,231
30	$574,349	$1,326,768	$2,289,230
40	$1,028,572	$3,140,942	$6,500,087
50	$1,842,015	$7,435,752	$18,456,483

Table 11.1

Perhaps the biggest risk relative to the stock market is not owning stocks at all. Historically, choosing to invest in supposedly *safe*, yet lower-performing interest-bearing accounts to avoid the *risk* of investing in stocks has been to the detriment of many long-term savers.

DIVIDENDS

One way companies deploy cash is to pay dividends to their shareholders. So, in addition to the potential for capital appreciation from a share price increase, shareowners may also receive a quarterly check for dividends.

Larger, more well-established companies with relatively predictable, ongoing revenue, commonly known as cash cows, are more likely to pay dividends than companies that are still rapidly growing and therefore need to retain earnings for their future growth or pay down the debt that fueled previous growth. Some very profitable companies choose not to pay dividends (for example, Amazon and Google).

Of the 30 stocks in the Dow Jones Industrial Average, 27 currently pay a dividend as of this writing in March 2022. The highest two yielding Dow stocks are IBM with a dividend yield of 5.28% and Verizon with a yield of 4.88%. The average yield for all 30 Dow stocks is currently 2.36%. (Note: the dividend yield is calculated by dividing the dollar amount of the annual dividend by the current share price.)

Many well-established companies have a history of increasing dividend payouts to shareholders year after year as their earnings have trended higher. For example, Coca-Cola has steadily increased their dividend annually for decades. As the price of a bottle of Coke went from a nickel to 50 cents to a dollar over the decades, their earnings increased, and so did their dividends paid to shareholders. This is a great example of why stocks are considered a hedge against inflation: as the cost of living, in general, increased over the years, so did the dividend checks for Coke shareholders.

Be aware that companies can also reduce or eliminate their dividends. For example, Boeing, the large aerospace company, had steadily paid dividends for decades until their business was pummeled by the coronavirus pandemic in 2020, which forced the company to completely eliminate dividends for the time being.

My 83-year-old mother has grown quite fond of receiving her quarterly dividend payments from her mutual fund accounts, which have steadily increased over the years, as has the value of her mutual funds. She affectionately calls those dividends her *fun money*.

Stock owners can profit in two ways
(1) Receive cash dividends
(2) Increase in share price

OWNING STOCKS THE EASY WAY

Question: Now that I have clearly stated my opinion that owning stocks is the best choice for most long-term serious investors, how do you go about deciding which individual stocks to buy?

Answer: You don't!

Bluntly stated, instead of buying individual stocks, most investors (not all, but most) would be far better off buying some type of *fund* that is broadly diversified into dozens or hundreds of different stocks, in my opinion. When I use the term *fund*, this could be an actively managed mutual fund, an unmanaged index fund, a variable annuity, an exchange-traded fund (ETF), or some type of managed account (which virtually all investment firms now offer), and all of those funds are available for non-tax-advantaged accounts as well as for tax-advantaged retirement accounts such as IRAs, Roths, and 401(k)s. The next chapter goes into depth about investing in stocks via diversified funds.

WHY NOT BUY INDIVIDUAL STOCKS?

Lack of diversification, time requirements, emotions, and lack of expertise (knowledge) are four significant reasons most investors would likely be better off buying some type of stock fund rather than individual stocks.

Diversification

Owning many stocks in different industries mitigates risk and reduces volatility. Few people have the time and expertise to analyze all the different variables to pass judgment on hundreds of companies to put together a well-diversified portfolio. So by default, many individual investors tend to focus on only a few companies with which they are most familiar and therefore overly concentrate their investments in a relatively small number of stocks.

Time Commitment

If you really enjoy reading annual reports, 10-Ks, and economic data or doing industry analysis, etc., etc., on an ongoing basis, then have at it! That is precisely what professional stock analysts do, and much more. Conversely, you could invest in a fund and then spend that extra time you didn't spend analyzing the financial markets doing more enjoyable things—like spending more time with your friends and family or enjoying your favorite hobby.

Emotions

A common investor affliction is that once someone owns a stock, the emotions of fear, greed, joy, disgust, and ego take precedence over intelligence and common sense when making buy/sell/hold decisions, and the objective brain is given a temporary leave-of-absence. For instance, an investor sells when they should have bought more because they are disgusted with owning a stock after it falls by 50%, or they refuse to sell because it hurts their pride to be wrong. Another example is when an investor falls in love with a stock that has increased dramatically, and they buy more shares instead of selling, even though its valuation deems the stock excessively overpriced.

Expertise

Individual investors often get fooled into thinking they are good at picking stocks, when in reality, they were just riding the wave of a raging bull market when it's virtually impossible not to make money. It's not that people can't have success buying individual stocks; in fact, they often do have success because stocks rise over time more often than not. On average, people will do better in some type of diversified fund, which will also reduce volatility (risk) and require considerably less time.

At a minimum, if someone doesn't understand the following basic investment terms, I would suggest they probably don't have the expertise to be a stock picker for serious amounts of money.

P/E ratio, book value, dividend yield, dividend payout ratio, sector, historical growth rate, cash flow, bid, ask, beta, moving average, short selling, market cap, common vs. preferred stock, fundamental vs. technical, listed and unlisted, TTM vs. forecasted, capital structure, market share, large cap vs. small cap, market order vs. limit order, 10-Q and 10-K, income statement, balance sheet, and price-to-sales ratio.

If someone is not a skilled carpenter or contractor, they are probably flirting with disaster if they attempt to build their own house. If someone lacks expertise and they choose to pick individual stocks with the bulk of their long-term savings, they may be inviting similar peril. Can the weekend carpenter build a birdhouse or a doghouse? Sure, and likewise, there is nothing wrong with investors occasionally allocating a small amount of their money to an individual stock they like, if that's what they enjoy and feel comfortable with.

PRICE-TO-EARNINGS RATIO

Price-to-earnings ratio (P/E) is the one analytical metric I would like to comment on. A stock's P/E ratio is calculated by dividing the stock price per share by the earnings per share. If a stock is trading at $20 per share and they earned $1 per share in the last year, their P/E ratio would be 20 ($20 divided by $1).

Historically, the overall stock market P/E ratio has averaged a little less than 20, give or take. Years ago, a famous investor said 20 minus the inflation rate is a reasonable P/E ratio for the overall market (in other words, if inflation is 3%, then a reasonable average P/E ratio for the entire stock market would be 17).

Understanding the concept of the P/E ratio may at least warn investors of the potential downside risk and magnitude of price volatility. For example, as a general rule, the more potential growth investors think a company has in the future, the more they are generally willing to pay for that stock today. A company that investors believe has only average earnings growth potential in the years ahead might trade at a P/E ratio of 20, whereas a highly innovative company that is a clear industry leader with phenomenal earnings growth potential may trade at a 50, 100, 200, or 500 P/E ratio.

However, if that high-flying industry leader stumbles and can't meet expectations, their stock may fall dramatically and quickly. How do you turn a 200 P/E ratio into a 20 P/E ratio? Drop the stock price by 90%, ouch! It gets even riskier when buying stock in companies that have never made money. There is no P/E ratio to calculate because there is no E. And if you really want to run with scissors, consider visionary startup companies that don't even have sales yet, let alone earnings.

Many industry-leading companies today had no earnings when they first went public, so I'm not saying high P/E ratio stocks (or no E stocks) are categorically bad investments, but they do tend to be much more volatile, and they tend to have more of a downside when things don't go well. Facebook worked out great for early investors. Myspace, not so much.

The P/E ratio is the most fundamental tool
to evaluate a stock's relative price.

TAX ADVANTAGES

When a stock is owned for more than one year and sold for a gain, it is a *long-term* capital gain for federal income tax purposes, and the gain is generally taxed at a lower rate than *short-term* capital gains, which are taxed as ordinary income. For 2022, there are three federal long-term capital gains rates (0%, 15%, and 20%, depending on your total taxable income), whereas ordinary income tax rates range from 0% to 37%. People with high levels of taxable income benefit the most from the lower long-term gain rates.

Also, dividends paid from most stocks are considered *qualified* dividends by the IRS and are taxed at the same rate as long-term capital gains. *Nonqualified* dividends are taxed the same as ordinary income. Capital gains and dividends earned by mutual funds pass through to the individual investor and receive the same rates as described above.

SUMMARY

Ultimately, the valuation (share price) of a stock is predicated on the company's ability to make money. The price-to-earnings ratio (P/E ratio) is the most fundamental way stocks are valued. Stock prices can fluctuate widely in the short term independent of earnings—but over the long haul, earnings dictate stock prices. For that reason, stocks have outperformed other investment alternatives over long time periods.

Assuming the US and worldwide economies continue to grow in the future, stocks have a high probability of continuing to perform well. However, selecting individual stocks can be a challenging and time-consuming task; therefore, most investors would be better off investing in stocks via one of the numerous diversified fund options that are available rather than buying individual stocks. Diversified fund investing is discussed in the next chapter.

Shareholders can benefit from the value of the stock appreciating as well as from cash dividends the company may pay to its shareholders.

THE DAVID YOUNG STORY

After graduating from college, David Young returned to his rural Missouri hometown to work in the family cattle business. The logical and easy choice would have been for him to be a lifelong cattleman. But around age 30, he decided to become a financial advisor with the brokerage firm Edward Jones, the same company for which I worked.

The career change resulted in David moving to North Carolina in 1984, where he built his client base by initially cold calling door-to-door, which was the norm for Jones brokers in that era. Over the next 25 years, he was consistently one of the firm's top-producing advisors as he steadily grew his business.

David and I developed a close friendship as we spent time together at various company meetings and conferences. Although he was making a good living, he was always striving to learn more and improve. He was always inquisitive and wanted to hear what other advisors were doing that might help him improve his business and better serve his clients.

In addition to running his office, he also served in various capacities to help the firm grow and to mentor new advisors in developing their businesses. He studied at night and on weekends to obtain various professional certifications, including an MBA from Duke University.

David's commitment to excellence and contributions to the company didn't go unnoticed. In 2008, he was invited to become a general partner and relocate to Jones' headquarters in St. Louis as a member of the management team. Over the next 10 years, before retiring in 2017, he was responsible for various roles in the leadership of the company's 12,000+ office locations.

Although becoming a general partner had a significant positive financial impact for David personally, that was never his primary focus. He is an excellent example of someone who simply strived to be the best he could be in whatever role he was in, and the rewards and opportunities followed.

DAVID'S LESSON: Never stop learning. High-performing team-oriented individuals who continue to seek personal growth and development throughout their careers are excellent candidates for upward mobility.

CHAPTER 12

Mutual Funds and ETFs

You might be thinking, "Kurt, all I want to know is, how should I invest my long-term money?" With a few caveats, my opinion for most investors is *diversified funds invested in high-quality stocks*. I believe in that answer so strongly that I'm going to repeat it three times for emphasis:

Diversified funds invested in high-quality stocks!
Diversified funds invested in high-quality stocks!
Diversified funds invested in high-quality stocks!

The two most common ways investors own stocks are direct ownership of individual stocks (as discussed in the last chapter) or investing in a pooled fund, which is then invested in stocks on their behalf, which is the focus of this chapter.

WHAT IS A MUTUAL FUND?

The combination of the two words *mutual* and *fund* is a perfect descriptor of what a mutual fund is. Literally, investors mutually pool their money together into one large fund that is then invested in a diversified portfolio by the fund's management company. Every investor in the fund earns the exact same rate of return for their portion of the fund.

I frequently use the term mutual fund or fund in this chapter to mean the entire universe of diversified funds, including mutual funds that are actively managed by professionals as well as unmanaged index funds, exchange-traded funds (ETFs), and various types of managed accounts offered by investment firms. Funds are available for regular individual accounts as well as for tax-advantaged retirement accounts such as IRAs, Roths, and 401(k)s.

BASIC TYPES OF MUTUAL FUNDS

There are more than 7,000 separate mutual funds as well as thousands of ETFs. Each fund has its own investment criteria and focus; therefore, it is vital to understand the objective of a particular fund before investing in it. Stock, bond, and money market are the three broad types of mutual funds in terms of asset type.

In the vernacular of investing, the word *equity* is often used to mean stock; *debt* is used for bond; and *cash* is used for money market funds. For example, an *equity-income fund* would be a fund that invests in stocks with a high-dividend yield or a history of increasing dividends.

Throughout this book, I present my opinion that stock funds are the best investment choice for long-term wealth accumulation for most investors. However, it is not as simple as just buying a random fund that invests in stocks, any more than an auto buyer would randomly buy a truck vs. a Ferrari. With so many stock funds available, it can be a daunting task even for an experienced investor to decide which fund(s) best fits their personal investment objectives.

Most of this chapter will focus on explaining the nuances of stock funds, which will hopefully assist readers in the fund selection process. At the end of the chapter, bond funds and money market funds are covered briefly.

APPEAL OF STOCK MUTUAL FUNDS VS. INDIVIDUAL STOCKS

Professional management and **diversification** are the two main compelling features of investing in a managed mutual fund vs. buying individual stocks. A mutual fund typically has millions or billions of dollars under management on behalf of thousands of different individuals who have invested in the fund.

The fund managers typically diversify the fund into dozens or hundreds of different stocks. The managers monitor the portfolio on an ongoing basis while buying and selling stocks (or other securities) to achieve the best results within the parameters of the fund's stated objectives.

The following are benefits investors hope to achieve by investing in mutual funds instead of buying individual stocks:

Simplicity and Less Time Required

It is easy to understand how selecting and purchasing a single mutual fund would be simpler and require dramatically less time than it would take to select a diversified portfolio of stocks, and then monitor and adjust the portfolio on an ongoing basis.

Less Risk/Volatility

Owning a fund that is diversified into many sectors and into dozens or hundreds of different stocks smoothes out overall volatility or fluctuation in value. Most individuals don't have the time or knowledge to make informed decisions to buy and monitor hundreds of stocks.

Lower Minimum Investment

Many funds only require $1,000 or less as the minimum investment to start an account, and then additions can typically be made at any time for virtually any amount, whereas it could require many thousands of dollars to buy a single share in enough individual stocks to be adequately diversified.

Better Return

Frankly, better earnings is probably the least compelling of the potential benefits of buying funds vs. individual stocks. The performance of the mutual fund industry as a whole is close to the overall performance of the broad market averages because of the very nature of the way most funds are so widely diversified. However, investing in funds keeps individuals from being catastrophically wrong and putting all their money in a small number of stocks that may all perform dismally.

Note: Years ago, lower cost was an additional benefit of mutual funds vs. buying individual stocks. That is no longer the case, since the major discount brokers no longer charge a commission to buy and sell stocks.

WHAT IS AN INDEX?

A stock market *index* is when a single number is calculated to represent the valuation of a particular set of stocks. For example, the Dow Jones Industrial Average (DJIA), which consists of 30 US stocks, is one of the oldest and most recognized indexes. The average of the prices of those 30 stocks is put through a calculation, resulting in a single number for the DJIA.

Indexes were developed as a way to communicate more concisely the performance of various stock markets or segments of those markets. Rather than having to examine the price of dozens or hundreds of different stocks, investors can look at the change of a single index—such as the DJIA and have a good idea of what the overall market did, whether that be the change over a day, a month, a year, or decades. For example, if the DJIA increased 50% over a given time period, that can then serve as an approximation of how stocks in general performed.

There are hundreds of different published indexes to track various portions of the world's stock markets. For example, there are indexes for the stocks of each individual country. There are indexes for only the largest US stocks, other indexes for only the smallest stocks, indexes that only track the stocks in one sector of the economy (for example, financials), indexes for just one industry (for example, airlines), and so on.

An index is also sometimes referred to as an *average* or as a *composite*. The following is a sampling of some of the other major stock market indexes in addition to the DJIA.

Standard & Poor's 500 (S&P 500): The S&P 500 includes 500 of the largest US stocks. It is considered a *broad* average because it includes 500 stocks versus only 30 for the DJIA. However, it is interesting how closely the results of the two averages usually are, even with such different sample sizes.

NASDAQ Composite: The NASDAQ Composite is also a very broad index that includes all of the companies that trade on the NASDAQ system (about 2,500). About 48% of the stocks on NASDAQ are technology companies, so this index is often viewed as a gauge of how tech stocks have performed.

The Russell Indexes: The FTSE Russell Company publishes numerous indexes, including:

$ Russell 3000 Index: includes the largest 3,000 US stocks.
$ Russell 1000 Index: a subset of the Russell 3000. It includes only the largest 1,000 US stocks.
$ Russell 2000 Index: includes the next largest 2,000 US stocks, excluding the 1,000 largest.

Nikkei 225: The Nikkei 225 tracks the performance of the top 225 companies listed on the Tokyo Stock Exchange in Japan.

FTSE 100: The FTSE 100 includes the largest 100 stocks listed on the London Stock Exchange.

STOCK MUTUAL FUNDS

Stock mutual funds are generally categorized based on the characteristics of the stocks they can own. Some of the most common criteria include the size of the company, geographic location of the company, sector or industry of the company, dividends paid history, and the company's growth prospects and stability.

Company Size

A stock's size is its *market capitalization* or market cap for short. Market cap equals the total number of shares outstanding for the company times their current per share stock price. For example, Apple's recent market cap of $2.83 trillion is the largest of all US stocks. Funds will often indicate the size of the companies they can or can't invest in—usually designated as large, mid, or small cap, but mega, micro, and nano are also used. The following are the commonly used market cap categories currently.

- $ Mega cap: $100 billion or more
- $ Large cap: $10 billion to less than $100 billion
- $ Mid cap: $2 billion to less than $10 billion
- $ Small cap: $250 million to less than $2 billion
- $ Micro cap: $50 million to less than $250 million
- $ Nano cap: Less than $50 million

Generally, the smaller the cap size, the more the perceived opportunity for future growth as well as greater volatility and risk (in other words, conservative investors would be more inclined to invest in large caps as opposed to micro or nano cap stock funds).

- $ *401(k) tip*: If the words *small, micro,* or *nano* are in the name of a fund being offered in your 401(k) plan, it means the fund invests in smaller companies that tend to be more volatile but may offer higher growth potential.

Geographic Location

Funds often designate which countries, regions, or continents the companies they invest in must be from. For example, a fund may be limited to only investing in companies based in the United States, or at least a certain percentage of the fund's assets must be in domestic stocks, or they may be able to invest with complete discretion anywhere in the world. Some funds invest exclusively in Europe or Asia, for example. Many financial advisors recommend clients have some exposure to or have a certain percentage of their holdings in international funds, as the United States' stock market isn't always the top performer.

$ ***401(k) tip***: If the words *global, international, world, emerging markets*, or a specific foreign region or country is in the name of a fund, it means the fund partly or completely focuses on stocks outside of the United States.

Sector or Industry

Unless otherwise stated by the fund, most stock mutual funds will have diverse holdings in most or all of the 11 sectors of the economy. However, in recent years, so-called *sector funds* have grown immensely in popularity, particularly sector ETFs (ETFs are explained later in this chapter). (Note: The economy is generally differentiated into 11 distinct sectors with multiple industries within each sector.) For example, *financials* is one of the 11 sectors; separate industries within the financial sector include banking, insurance, mortgage lending, and others.

In terms of providing safety and muting volatility, sector funds are somewhat halfway between owning a broadly diversified fund and putting all your money in only a few individual stocks. For example, the *Fidelity Select Utilities Portfolio* is a fund that invests exclusively in utility stocks. *The 3D Printing* ETF only invests in companies involved in the 3D printing industry. The *Calvert Global Water Fund* invests in stocks in the water industry. Chances are, if there is a niche you can think of, there is a fund or ETF that specializes in it.

$ ***401(k) tip***: If a particular sector or industry is in the name of a fund, or if the word *sector* or *industry* is in the name of a fund being offered in your 401(k) plan, the fund likely focuses on only a defined portion of the economy.

Dividends

In Chapter 11, "Stocks," I discussed how older and more established companies that generate excess cash flow will often pay a quarterly cash dividend to their shareholders, whereas companies that need their cash flow to service debt or for future growth often don't pay dividends. Likewise, mutual funds will often state whether or not they focus on companies that are paying dividends. This may be an important distinction for investors wanting to receive a regular income stream from their mutual fund investments. Such investors should be sure to understand what the dividend yield is for a fund before investing.

$ *401(k) tip*: If the words *dividend* or *income* are in the name of a stock fund, it means the fund focuses on stocks that pay dividends.

Capital Appreciation

Traditionally, stock funds were positioned as either a growth fund or as a growth and income fund, the distinction being that growth funds are focused solely on capital appreciation (increasing stock price) and not on dividend-paying stocks, whereas growth and income funds seek capital appreciation and healthy dividends. Growth funds generally invest in more rapidly growing companies with the potential for a higher overall rate of return but also more price volatility and risk, whereas growth and income funds invest in more mature and well-established companies, producing more generous cash flow but usually with fewer prospects for growth. With consideration of the long-term historical performance and relative volatility of each of these two types of funds, I am personally comfortable with long-term conservative investors owning both of them, as my 83-year-old mother has for years.

$ *401(k) tip*: Growth funds generally focus only on capital appreciation, whereas growth and income funds focus on appreciation and dividends. Often, one of those terms will be part of the fund's name. The term *blue chip* would indicate a growth and income fund.

Different categories of the market tend to go in and out of favor over time, depending on economic cycles and various trends. For example, large cap stocks may outperform small caps for a time, and then it may reverse and small caps will lead the way. Healthcare stocks may lead the way for a while and then give way to outsized performance by energy stocks or some other sector. Dividend-paying stocks are sometimes the market leaders. Any one country or continent doesn't always have the best performance. For these reasons, it may be advisable to own several different funds with different investment criteria to ensure less overall volatility, as different funds will often balance each other out. It's a way of being sort of right to make sure you are not completely wrong.

The main appeal of broadly diversified mutual funds is not outperforming the stock market, but rather an easy and efficient way to simply be in the market.

MUTUAL FUND POTPOURRI

The following section covers a number of miscellaneous details about mutual funds that many investors will find of interest.

Money Market Funds

The primary objective of money market mutual funds is no fluctuation of principal value and liquidity. Although not insured like bank deposits are, money market mutual funds generally serve the same purpose as money market accounts offered by banks. They are a good choice for short-term money and emergency fund accounts, but not a good way to accumulate wealth for long-term investors, as they are yielding less than 1% currently.

Bond Funds

There are four main types of domestic bond mutual funds based on the type of bonds they invest in, which are municipal (tax-free bonds), corporate, US government, and mortgage-backed bonds. Those four categories are further differentiated by the duration or term of the bonds in the fund, such as short-, intermediate-, or long-term bond funds.

Corporate and municipal funds are further divided by the quality (default risk) of the bonds in which they invest. For example, so-called *high-yield* or *junk-bond* funds invest in bonds with a higher interest rate but also entail a higher risk of default and loss of principal. There are also funds that specifically invest in bonds issued by foreign (non-US) corporations or governments.

Bond funds are a standard offering within 401(k) plans. With bond interest rates currently (March 2022) near all-time low levels, I am afraid many employees are unwittingly taking on more risk than they are aware of by investing in bond funds. In Chapter 16, "Bonds," I discuss interest rate risk in more detail, as well as other bond considerations.

$ **401(k) tip**: If the words *bond, balanced*, or *debt*, are in the name of a fund being offered in your 401(k) plan, the fund invests some or all of its assets in bonds.

With interest rates currently near all-time lows, bond fund investors should be aware that bonds decline in value when interest rates rise.

Balanced Funds

The term *balanced fund* indicates a fund that is balanced because it owns both stocks and bonds. In previous years, when interest rates were higher on bonds, balanced funds were considerably more popular than they are currently (March 2022).

$ ***401(k) tip***: If the word *balanced* is in the fund name, it means it invests in both stocks and bonds.

Managed Funds vs. Index Funds

Managed funds and index funds are the two broad categories for mutual funds and ETFs in terms of how the holdings are selected and adjusted. This is an important distinction, and I would encourage investors to understand whether a particular fund is actively managed or if it is an index fund before investing.

With a managed fund, the fund employs research analysts, portfolio managers, and other professionals to do research on companies, the overall market, the economy, and other factors to then decide how to allocate the fund's assets based on the fund's stated objectives and parameters. The fund's management team has wide discretion to determine which stocks to buy, how many shares to buy, when to sell, and often how much to leave in cash at any given time.

With an index fund, there are very few discretionary management decisions, but rather the fund's objective is to invest the fund's assets to replicate an index such as the Dow Jones Industrial Average or the S&P 500 index, or to replicate a particular sector, industry, country, region, etc. Index fund investing is referred to as a *passive* investment strategy, whereas managed funds are called *actively managed*. Investing in passive index funds has gained dramatically in popularity over the last decade.

As I described earlier in the chapter, there are many different indexes, and new indexes are invented frequently. It is paramount for an investor to clearly understand a fund's index parameters. The more narrowly a fund invests in a particular sector vs. the broader overall market, the more volatile (up and down) the fund will likely be. Since the majority of ETFs are index or sector funds, they are covered later in more detail in the ETF section of this chapter.

$ ***401(k) tip:*** If the word *index* is in the name, it means the fund seeks to replicate a particular index and it is not actively managed.

Fee-Based Accounts

Although they are not actually mutual funds per se; fee-based accounts are another type of fund possibility for investors to consider per my lumping of all diversified accounts under the broad generic title of funds. Over the last few decades, the retail investment industry has steadily transitioned away from commission-based accounts in favor of fee-based accounts. Traditionally, brokers charged a commission per transaction when executing trades for clients, but no fees were charged otherwise. For fee-based accounts, instead of charging commissions for each trade, customers pay an annualized fee based on the value of the account.

Within a fee-based account, some investment firms allow clients to own stocks, ETFs, mutual funds, bonds, and any other securities the firm would normally offer, while other fee-based accounts restrict investment choices to a variety of mutual funds or pooled funds managed by third parties. Fee-based accounts are discussed in more detail in Chapter 17, "Working With an Investment Professional...or Not."

$ *401(k) tip*: Fee-based accounts are generally not available in 401(k) plans.

The Prospectus

For the protection of investors, every mutual fund is required to have a document called a prospectus which discloses all the relevant information about the fund, including details on all fees and expenses, historical rates of return, the objective of the fund, the fund's investment strategies, and much more. A fund's prospectus should be easily obtained on the fund sponsor's website or by doing an Internet search.

Quote Symbol and Fund Information

Just like stocks, all mutual funds and ETFs have a unique quote/ticker symbol. All mutual fund sponsors/managers have a myriad of information on their websites about each of their funds. You can also get a quick fund overview on various sites. For example, on Yahoo Finance (finance.yahoo.com), type the fund's symbol or name in the Quote Lookup box. From there, you can select various pages, such as *holdings,* to see the largest 10 stock holdings for the fund. Morningstar.com provides independent and unbiased information on the entire spectrum of mutual funds.

Family of Funds

Virtually all mutual fund companies offer what is referred to as a family of funds. The typical family of funds includes a dozen or so different funds on the low end, to more than 100 funds for some of the large fund providers. For example, the basic types of funds most fund families offer will include a large cap, small cap, growth only, growth and income, global, corporate bond, municipal bond, money market, and various others. Beyond the basic fund categories, some fund families have numerous sector funds.

Some mutual fund families are owned by brokerage firms or banks, while others are independent companies with no other business operations. Some of the larger and more well-known mutual fund families include Vanguard, Fidelity, BlackRock, American Funds, T. Rowe Price, Invesco, Franklin Templeton, State Street, TIAA, PIMCO, JP Morgan, MFS, Dodge & Cox, and Schwab.

Load vs. No-Load

Traditionally, there are two types of mutual funds, load and no-load, in terms of whether there is a sales charge (commission) to invest in the fund. Load means there is a sales charge or fee paid to purchase the fund. Most or all of the load is paid to the brokerage firm offering the fund. No-load funds don't charge a fee to purchase the fund because there is generally no broker involved, so investors make their own selections. Years ago, no-load funds transacted their business with customers primarily by mail. Today, it is primarily done online with money being transferred electronically.

Load mutual funds generally offer a reduced fee for larger investments, referred to as breakpoints. For example, the following is a typical fee schedule with breakpoints for stock funds with a load.

$ Less than $25,000 invested, there is a 5.75% onetime sales charge.

$ $25,000 to $49,999 = 5.0%

$ $50,000 to $99,999 = 4.5%

$ $100,000 to $249,999 = 3.5%

$ $250,000 to $499,999 = 2.5%

$ $500,000 to $749,999 = 2.0%

$ $750,000 to $999,999 = 1.5%

$ $1 million and more = 0.0%

Fund families typically combine existing balances in all the funds an investor has with their fund family to achieve breakpoints. For example, if an investor had a combined balance of $90,000 in three of their funds and they were investing an additional $10,000, the investor would pay the reduced sales charge at the $100,000 break-point level. All accounts within a household can be used to qualify for breakpoints (for example, both spouses' IRAs and individual accounts). Fund owners can generally switch to different funds within the family of funds without incurring an additional charge.

Historically, so-called *full-service* brokerage firms offered load funds with the fee being their compensation for providing information, advice, and service for the client, whereas no-load funds were typically distributed directly by the mutual fund company without a broker involved to assist the investor (no personalized service, therefore no fee). Those distinctions have become blurred because there are now many fee structures and levels of service. It is not a matter of which is best or worst as a blanket statement, but rather based on the level of service and help a particular client may want or need. There is a need and a valuable place for both types of offerings across the retail investment spectrum.

Open-End vs. Closed-End

Both load and no-load mutual funds are referred to as *open-end* funds because they continually issue more shares of the fund as more money comes in from investors; hence, they are open to new money. There are also *closed-end* funds in which the fund is closed to new money flows; the only way to purchase the fund is to buy shares on the open market from an existing shareholder that is selling. The amount of money in closed-end funds is very small compared to the amount in open-end funds.

Shares, Dividends, and Capital Gains

Just like stocks, mutual funds are denominated in shares. For traditional open-end mutual funds, the share price is calculated at the end of each day, with all shares being bought or sold that day receiving the same price. During the year, the fund will receive dividends paid by stocks that the fund owns. Typically, the fund will pay those dividends to the fund's investors each quarter, and each investor has the option to receive their dividend in cash or to reinvest and buy additional shares of the fund.

Generally, once a year (commonly in December), funds will make a distribution to fund shareholders for *realized* capital gains during the year. Just like dividend distributions, shareholders have the option of taking their capital gain distributions in cash, or they may reinvest and acquire more shares of the fund. A realized gain means the fund sold stock at a profit, whereas an *unrealized* gain means a stock has increased in price but has not yet been sold. Regardless of whether distributions were reinvested, at the end of the year, mutual funds will issue all account holders a 1099 for tax purposes that provides details on dividends and capital gains paid.

Annual Expenses

In addition to whether a particular fund has a load or initial sales charge, all funds have various annual costs and expenses that are deducted before performance results are reported. In other words, the reported rate of return a fund achieves and reports to their shareholders is the net return after expenses have been deducted.

Actively managed funds generally have higher annual expenses than index funds because of the increased personnel and research costs to manage the fund. Annual expenses for a managed equity mutual fund are generally in the 0.50% to 0.75% range, but some funds are higher or lower. Some index funds have expense ratios below 0.10%, while larger funds often have lower expense ratios due to the economies of scale. A lower annual expense is one of the reasons some investors prefer index funds. Investors can review a fund's prospectus for details on all expenses.

Mutual Funds Within 401(k)s

One of the best things for the overall financial well-being of American workers is that mutual funds are the predominant investment choice offered in most 401(k) plans. For practical reasons related to administration, accounting, distribution, reporting, legal compliance, and other considerations, mutual funds are an ideal investment conduit for 401(k) plans. Some employers offer mutual funds from only one family of funds, while other employers may have funds from various fund families.

$ *401(k) tip*: Most 401(k) plans offer various stock, bond, and money market funds for employees to choose from. The rates of return and risks can vary substantially between funds. As stated numerous times throughout this book, stock funds have generally outperformed bond funds by a wide margin over the long term. Employees should take the time to understand the objectives and historical earnings for the funds they select.

Chasing Past Results ... Be Careful

Examining a mutual fund's past results can be meaningful as a comparative tool. The compound average annual rate of return for 1-, 3-, 5-, 10-, and 20-year time periods are common metrics quoted for mutual funds. However, stellar past performance may provide investors with unreasonable expectations of future results. For example, the dot.com stocks and NASDAQ funds of the late 1990s had phenomenal results ... until they didn't, and then things went south in a major way.

Sometimes, narrowly focused funds can have outsized results due to conditions that are unlikely to be repeated. One great year can dramatically skew the results for a three- or five-year average. Past results are best used as a tool to compare the performance of a fund with a benchmark index that is similar to the fund's objectives. For example, it is relevant how a large cap growth and income fund performed as compared to the S&P 500.

Websites

The following are a few websites pertaining to mutual funds, ETFs, retirement accounts, and other investing topics.

- $ investor.gov
- $ sec.gov/education
- $ finra.org/investor
- $ investopedia.com
- $ morningstar.com
- $ finance.yahoo.com

EXCHANGE-TRADED FUNDS (ETFs)

ETFs and traditional open-end mutual funds are similar in that both allow investors to purchase shares of a fund that owns a broadly diversified portfolio. Both fund types have passive non-managed index funds, and both have actively managed funds. In essence, the rates of return, ease of investing, and overall benefits of the two are generally very similar.

ETFs are relative newcomers to the investment world, as the first ETF, an S&P 500 index ETF, didn't come along until 1993, whereas traditional open-end mutual funds have been around since 1924. By 2002 there were about 100 ETFs, and for their first 15 years of existence until 2008, all ETFs were index funds (none were actively managed). In essence, ETFs were conceived as a low-cost way to replicate various indexes or market averages.

Although there are now a number of actively managed ETFs, the vast majority continue to be non-managed (passive) index funds in which the objective is simply to replicate a particular index rather than having fund managers making judgment decisions as to portfolio allocation.

ETFs have gained enormous popularity over the last decade, with more than 2,000 ETFs now in existence in the United States, with a total market cap exceeding $5 trillion. The following are three primary reasons ETFs are appealing to investors:

1. Low expenses.
2. The broad array of ETFs available focusing on specific portions of the market (sectors).
3. Real-time order execution whereby shares are bought and sold throughout the trading day, as opposed to traditional open-end mutual funds where all orders receive the same end-of-day price.

Low Expenses

A key selling point of managed mutual funds has always been professional management (in other words, investment experts managing your money). The implied expectation is that those experts will do a better job than you could and will outperform the market averages. In reality, most actively managed mutual funds don't consistently outperform the market, partially because they have to overcome their fees to do so. If a mutual fund has a 0.75% annual expense ratio and the overall market earns 10%, then the fund will have to earn 10.75% for its net return to equal the market's average rate of return.

Index ETFs and index mutual funds' basic goal is not to beat the market, but rather to reduce the fees to a bare minimum with the objective of simply replicating the market. Some of the largest index ETFs that seek to replicate averages, such as the Dow Jones Industrial Average or the S&P 500 have annual expense ratios as low as a miniscule 0.03%, whereas a typical actively managed equity fund has annual expenses in the range of 0.50% to 0.75%. Index funds can have such low expenses because the nature of an index fund basically allows computers to manage the portfolio; hence, there are no research expenses, professional analysts, or portfolio managers to pay. However, the annual expense ratio for actively managed mutual funds has steadily declined over the last decade, likely or at least partially as a response to the competitive pressure of lower expenses charged by ETFs.

In addition to the annual expense fee, there may be a brokerage fee to buy and sell ETFs. Since ETFs trade in the open market like stocks do, virtually all brokers charge the same commission to trade ETFs as they do to buy or sell stocks. However, most discount brokers went to commission-free stock and ETF trading in the last few years.

Index ETFs and index mutual funds are an efficient low-cost way investors can replicate the performance of various market averages and indexes such as the Dow and S&P 500.

Broad Array of Sector and Index Funds

ETFs have become the predominant way to invest in specific market sectors, as well as a way to replicate various averages or indexes across the entire stock market or specific portions of the market. There are hundreds of narrowly focused sector ETFs as well as hundreds of broader index ETFs.

Examples of broad-based index ETFs include those designed to replicate the S&P 500, Dow Jones Industrials, NASDAQ composite, Russell 1000, Russell 2000, Russell 3000, Wilshire 5000, or the entire US stock market, as well as foreign indexes such as Japan's Nikkei 225, the Hang Seng Index in Hong Kong, and hundreds more. There are also numerous ETFs that invest exclusively in various types of bonds.

Many new ETFs have been created in recent years that are commonly referred to as *sector funds* because they focus on a specific sector, industry, market niche, or sometimes just a common theme or concept (for example, environmentally friendly companies).

Sector ETFs are definitely a useful and attractive investment tool for professional money managers, in my opinion. For example, if a money manager wanted to allocate money to bank stocks, they could buy one or more of the many bank stock ETFs rather than having to buy dozens of different individual bank stocks. If they wanted exposure to stocks in Europe, they could buy a European index ETF. There are numerous ETFs for each of the 11 sectors of the economy as well as most of the specific industries within the sectors. For example, if you are high on marijuana stocks (bad dad joke), you can buy one of the many cannabis ETFs rather than trying to figure out which specific stock to buy.

I would caution individual investors against being too heavy in sector funds, as being in the wrong sector can be the equivalent of being too consolidated in just a few poor-performing individual stocks. For example, two ETFs that focus exclusively on Russia each declined more than 80% in value in less than three weeks when Russia invaded Ukraine in 2022. Primarily investing in funds that diversify across the entire economy is a prudent strategy for the majority of most long-term investors' portfolios, in my opinion.

Real-Time Order Execution

ETF shares trade in the market just like stocks in that the price can fluctuate during the entire trading day, and the price a buyer or seller receives is locked in at whatever point their order is executed in real-time. Conversely, all buy and sell orders for a given day for open-end mutual funds receive the same price, which is based on the closing value of the fund's assets for that day. Particularly during times of high market volatility, being able to execute real-time ETF trades has appeal. Real-time order execution is much more of an issue for professional investors and active traders than it is for long-term buy-and-hold investors.

In summary, ETFs are a viable investment option for individual investors, just like mutual funds. However, be sure to understand the investment objective and how the fund is invested before buying any ETF, as the strategies and risk profiles are quite diverse. A good document explaining ETFs in more detail can be viewed at *understandetfs.org*. Also, a guide to mutual funds produced by the Securities and Exchange Commission (SEC) is available at *sec.gov/investor/pubs/sec-guide-to-mutual-funds.pdf*.

$ *401(k) tip*: Most 401(k) plans do not offer ETFs.

SUMMARY

By investing in mutual funds, ETFs, or other diversified funds (collectively funds), investors can achieve rates of return that closely reflect the performance of the overall market or specific sectors of the market. Funds can enable investors to be more widely diversified than selecting individual stocks, therefore reducing volatility, and they also require dramatically less time since the fund handles all the investing and administration.

All things considered, owning diversified funds invested in high-quality stocks is the best way for most investors to accumulate wealth over the long term, in my opinion. The main issue is not whether you do so with a mutual fund or an ETF, not whether you invest in a load fund or a no-load fund, nor whether you invest in index funds or managed funds. The main issue is simply being invested in a broadly diversified portfolio of high-quality stocks. Doing so in a tax-advantaged account such as a 401(k), an IRA, or a Roth is even better.

CHAPTER 13

Don't Be "That Guy"

F ear, greed, and irrational thinking rather than wisdom and sound judgment often dictate investor actions. The following is a lighthearted view of some of the common characteristics that often yield unsatisfactory results. Admittedly, I have demonstrated a number of these behaviors myself from time to time. Calm, rational thinking is a constant work in progress for most investors.

I encourage you to read through this list with an open mind, and if you discover that you share some similarities with one of those *Guys*, maybe it will help you develop a different course of action for future investments. (Although I use the flippant term *Guy*, these behaviors can occur in both males and females.)

All-Eggs-In-One-Basket Guy: Familiarity results in an elevated sense of comfort and security. Nobody would logically advise you to invest most of your savings in the same company that employs you, but it frequently happens because people know how great the company is for which they happen to work.

In the 1980s, a new client of mine had just been wiped out financially by the collapse of his former employer, International Harvester (IH). Not only did he get laid off from his job, but he had also opted to have all of his retirement contributions invested in IH stock. He had also purchased IH stock with his other savings. In one calamity, he lost his job and more than 90% of his portfolio.

Stocks-Down-So-I-Can't-Sell Guy: This is one of the most common maladies of the brain for investors. The only thing that matters to this guy is the price he paid relative to the current price. Nobody wants to take a loss, but sometimes it is wiser to cut losses and move on.

Stocks-Up-So-I-Can't-Sell Guy: Some investors are so averse to paying taxes that they can't stomach the thought of selling at a profit. I once had a client who needed to generate some cash. As we reviewed his holdings, he either responded, "I don't want to sell that one, I'll take a loss," or "I don't want to sell that one, I'll have to pay taxes." The only way he would sell anything was if it were flat.

Lock-In-the-Profit Guy: This guy has an overwhelming urge to always sell once a certain profit is achieved. Up 20%, so that's an automatic sell signal. Many Lock-In-the-Profit Guys are also Stocks-Down-So-I-Can't-Sell Guys. What they end up doing is missing out on the good performers by selling them prematurely and holding the poor performers for too long. This is also called pulling the flowers and watering the weeds.

Average-Down Guy: When a stock declines in price, this guy never considers selling as a viable option; rather, his singular focus is to decrease his break-even point by obtaining more and more shares as the price cascades lower and lower. In a perverse way, the lower the price goes, the happier he becomes. He is a certifiable expert at being able to see things from his own perspective. He loves the taste of three-day-old donuts because they cost half as much as fresh. He almost filed for divorce 27 years ago until he realized it was cheaper to stay married.

Hot-Tip Guy: He validates his investment decisions with phrases like "They're developing the cure for ... ," "The FDA is going to approve them for ... ," "They're getting a patent for ... ," "They have the only ... ," "They have the exclusive rights to ... ," and "My buddy's uncle knows ... ." He likes anything with an inside scoop. He fancies himself a front-runner with many connections.

Lottery Guy: He uses statements like "It's all a crapshoot, anyway," "Might as well take a risk and see what happens," and "Nothing ventured, nothing gained." Known to hang out on the weekends with Hot-Tip Guy. He views investing as equal parts money, entertainment, and social interaction. Often justifies his stock picks with the phrase, "Who knows, they might be the next Apple or Amazon."

Make-Up-for-Lost-Time Guy: First cousin of Lottery Guy. He knows he's behind schedule with saving and investing, and therefore, he wants aggressive investments so his stellar stock selections can bail him out of a lifetime full of poor personal decisions.

(True story: a married friend around 40 years of age with two small kids asked for my opinion. He acknowledged he had done a poor job saving money and wanted to know what I thought about him investing in a company that had recently filed for bankruptcy. "I think they might come out of bankruptcy and make a lot of money," he stated. Yikes!)

Vision-of-Grandeur Guy: He went to high school with the Lottery Guy and Make-Up-for-Lost-Time Guy. He frequently daydreams about making $100 million by adroitly buying and selling Tesla and AMC stocks and fantasizes about one day being known as "the smartest guy in the room." Always looking to discover a stock for less than $2 a share that is destined to dominate an industry.

Sector Guy: Also known as the Next-Great-Thing Guy. He is absolutely convinced that some new technology is going to equate to a personal financial bonanza. He has the ability to talk for hours about topics such as 5G, electric vehicles, 3D printing, and renewable energy. Claims his grandfather made a fortune investing in plastics in the 1960s and is infinitely more concerned with investing in the right industry than picking the right company. Sector Guy's second cousin once removed is All-Eggs-in-One-Basket Guy.

Megatrend Guy: He roomed with Sector Guy in college. Makes all investment decisions based on what the world will be like in 50 years. His conversations always lead back to using phrases like disruptive technology, sustainability, next generation, 6G, global economic power, and eco-friendly. He talks about harvesting from the bottom of the ocean, planned communities on Mars, and the value of mineral deposits hundreds of miles below the Earth's surface.

Panic Guy: Aka Election Guy, aka Event Guy. He is often consumed with the impending financial peril associated with some future cataclysmic event, which is why his nickname in grade school was Chicken Little. Much to his spouse's chagrin, panic guy routinely sells everything prior to each presidential election out of fear the wrong party will win. He shifted his entire portfolio to gold bullion in 1999 to avoid financial ruin from Y2K. His favorite books are *Financial Apocalypse* and *Famine and Survival in America.*

News-of-the-Day Guy: The slightly less paranoid fraternal twin of Panic Guy. Stimulus package passes—Buy!! Interest rates are ticking up—Sell!! Positive jobs numbers—Buy!! COVID virus mutation—Sell!! He has been known to flip-flop between a leveraged-long position to an all-short position multiple times in the same month.

Market-Timer Guy: Also called All-In-or-All-Out Guy. Half brother of News-of-the-Day Guy. Believes he can outperform professional money managers by nimbly getting in and out of the market on a regular and ongoing basis using his vast insights. Ultimately, always concludes it's either time to sell everything or be 100% invested. He can impressively recite all the major and minor economic indicators. Constantly talks about the perils of an inverted yield curve. Spends four hours a night on *The Motley Fool* and *Seeking Alpha* websites gathering wisdom. Insists that he got it right, and it was the market that got it wrong.

Technical Guy: The nerdier uncle of the Market-Timer Guy. He trades stocks based solely on charts. Uses terms such as channel trading, death cross, triple top, golden cross, relative strength, reversal pattern, Bollinger bands, and moving averages. When analyzing a stock, he has no concern for what industry it's in or if the company is profitable. Has a library full of books on Elliott Wave Principle and the writings of Fibonacci.

SPAC Guy: If it has warrants and four letters in the symbol, he's interested. Thinks a company receiving a lot of Twitter comments equals good fundamentals. His concept of long-term is measured in hours after a merger announcement. Goes by the handle Deep-SPACing Kitty.

Stock-Split Guy: Is interested in buying any stock that announces a split. He still believes that when his mom cut his birthday cake in half that he had twice as much cake, since he then had two cakes instead of one.

Share-Price Guy: He finds a two-dollar stock considerably more attractive than a $100 stock because he will have 50 times more shares. He claims many stocks are too expensive, yet he has no idea what a P/E ratio is. Hunts and fishes with Stock-Split Guy.

Dividend-Yield Guy: Is only interested in buying the highest dividend-yielding stock in a given industry. He sees no correlation between a company paying out three times their earnings in dividends and the likelihood of a future dividend cut.

I'm-Too-Old Guy: His investing philosophy is based on the phrase, "I'm gonna retire soon, so I can't take any risk." Suspicious of anything that appears profitable. Doesn't trust the government or any person who provides services and not tangible products. His aunt is known as Nervous Nelly.

Robinhood Guy: Also known as Webull Guy. Thinks thoroughly researching a stock means reading all the related Twitter and Reddit comments. Confident that he knows how to pick winners because he made $312 total on his first 17 GameStop trades (even though he lost $784 on the 18th trade). Considers investing either easy or stupid, depending on which way the market is trending. Thinks Dave Portnoy will one day be president. Since he didn't graduate, it pisses him off that people actually think he should still have to pay back his student loans. His biggest fear is that his parents may start charging him rent.

I'll-Invest-Next-Year Guy: He gets a new car every other year, owns a beach house, has season tickets for multiple sports teams, and takes his family on frequent vacations, but he never gets around to saving or investing.

Rearview-Mirror Guy: Makes investment decisions based on what just happened. Could be called a momentum investor, but he has no clue whether the momentum has changed or not. He just knows somebody that made money on this in the past, so he wants some of it. COVID era trading has been particularly treacherous for him; he sold his airline and energy stocks at the bottom in 2020 and loaded up with GameStop at the peak. Back in the 1980s, he made all of his investment moves based on *Money Magazine's* previous year's mutual fund rankings.

CHAPTER 14

Tax-Advantaged Retirement Accounts
IRAs, Roths, 401(k) Plans, 403(b) Plans

Chapter Abbreviations

IRA:	Individual Retirement Account
IRS:	Internal Revenue Service
RMD:	Required Minimum Distribution

L et me be clear upfront—tax-advantaged retirement accounts are generally the most lucrative option for the vast majority of serious long-term investors to accumulate wealth and improve their financial well-being.

Tax-advantaged retirement accounts are made available to us courtesy of the tax laws of the federal government. However, unlike many government initiatives, they are not freebie welfare programs. They are incentivized opportunities to turbo-charge the wealth accumulation process for those who are diligent enough to save and invest on the road to financial freedom.

Providing such tax advantages has been lawmakers' primary tool to encourage people to save on their own for retirement and thus avoid dependence on government assistance in their golden years. This has resulted in tens of millions of Americans contributing trillions of dollars to various tax-advantaged retirement accounts.

The federal tax code provides tax advantages based on putting money into certain types of accounts or plans. Examples of tax-advantaged accounts include individual retirement accounts (IRAs), Roth IRAs, 401(k) plans, 403(b) plans, 457(b) plans, profit-sharing plans, health savings accounts (HSAs), and flexible spending accounts (FSAs), as well as various others. Each of these accounts has its own unique tax advantages as well as its own rules, conditions, and limitations mandated by law. Tax-advantaged retirement accounts are generally easy to establish and readily available to anyone with earned income (wages). This chapter focuses on the details and significant financial benefits of the most popular tax-advantaged retirement accounts.

Note: At the end of Chapter 15 "Other Tax-Advantaged Accounts," there is a Tax Terminology section that provides a definition of various tax terminology such as after-tax, pre-tax, tax deferred, etc.

Tax-advantaged accounts turbo-charge the wealth accumulation process. Simply put, they are the best opportunity for most long-term investors to consistently save and grow their net worth.

WHY IS TAX-ADVANTAGED SO BENEFICIAL?

Before explaining the differences between the most popular tax-advantaged retirement accounts, let's look at a comparison of how money would grow when invested *after-tax* in a non-tax-advantaged account vs. being invested *pre-tax* in a tax-advantaged account.

After-Tax Investing:

Let's assume the following about a hypothetical employee investor:

$ Employee chooses to *not* invest in a tax-advantaged account.

$ Employee has a marginal income tax rate of 25% for combined federal and state income taxes.

$ At the end of the year, after paying all taxes and cost-of-living expenses, employee has $4,500 left over to invest, which requires them to earn $6,000 in wages to net $4,500 after paying 25% in taxes.

$ Employee invests the $4,500 in a mutual fund invested in stocks and reinvests all earnings.

$ The mutual fund produces average annual earnings of 9%.

$ Employee pays 18% in taxes out of the mutual fund on the earnings each year. This assumes a 15% federal rate for capital gains and dividends and a 3% state tax rate.

$ The employee repeats all the assumptions above annually. That is, they invest an additional $4,500 into the mutual fund year after year, and the earnings rate and tax rates are also the same every year.

$ The table below shows how the account would grow over time based on the assumptions above.

After-Tax Investing With 9% Average Annual Earnings Rate			
Years	Annual Investment Amount	Cumulative Amount Invested	Total Account Value
10	$4,500	$45,000	$65,637
20	$4,500	$90,000	$199,414
30	$4,500	$135,000	$472,072
40	$4,500	$180,000	$1,027,785

Table 14.1

Pre-Tax Investing:

Now, let's assume the same hypothetical employee invests in the 401(k) offered by their employer.

$ Instead of investing $4,500 after-tax, the employee invests an annual total of $6,000 on a pre-tax basis in the 401(k).

$ Since the $6,000 is invested in the 401(k), it is not included in taxable income, therefore saving the employee $1,500 in income taxes based on their 25% tax bracket; hence, they are able to increase their annual investment from $4,500 to $6,000 due to their reduction in income taxes. (Note: Money contributed to a 401(k) and other retirement accounts are subject to Social Security tax.)

$ Within the 401(k), the employee elects to have the money invested in a stock mutual fund that produces an average annual return of 9%; hence, we are assuming the same rate of earnings in both examples.

$ Also, the employer matches employee contributions dollar for dollar up to a maximum of $6,000 per year per employee.

$ The table below shows how the 401(k) account would grow based on these assumptions.

Pre-Tax Investing with 9% Average Annual Earnings Rate				
Years	Annual Investment Amount	Cumulative Amount Invested	Total Account Value *Without* the Employer Match	Total Account Value *With* the Employer Match
10	$6,000	$60,000	$95,260	$190,520
20	$6,000	$120,000	$320,774	$641,548
30	$6,000	$180,000	$854,648	$1,709,296
40	$6,000	$240,000	$2,118,523	$4,237,046

Table 14.2

Analysis of the Examples Above

$ Looking at the total account value column, it is easy to see the power of long-term compounded earnings on a pre-tax basis.

$ The 401(k) offers three distinct benefits that resulted in the account being more than $3 million larger after 40 years than the after-tax account. First, the employee was able to invest $6,000 each year instead of $4,500 because they saved $1,500 in taxes. Second, they didn't have to pay taxes each year on their earnings. Third, the employee is fortunate to have an employer that matches up to $6,000 per year, thereby doubling the employee's account balance. The combination of those three benefits resulted in this hypothetical 401(k) account balance being $4,237,046 after 40 years, as compared to $1,027,785 in the after-tax hypothetical investment scenario.

$ Be aware that all taxes have been paid on the after-tax account, whereas no taxes have been paid on the 401(k) account, but the 401(k) is still dramatically more beneficial in terms of producing a lifetime income stream. Since the 401(k) grew to more than four times the value over 40 years, it will produce more than four times the income throughout retirement. For example, let's assume the employee elects to withdraw 5% of the account balance annually from each account after 40 years:

- After-tax account balance of $1,027,785 x 5% = $51,389 annual income.
- 401(k) account balance of $4,237,046 x 5% = $211,852 annual income.

$ The examples also graphically show how investing a fairly modest annual amount of $6,000 can grow into a substantial sum. In other words, significant wealth accumulation is an attainable goal for those who diligently save and invest consistently.

$ You may be thinking $1 million or $2 million won't be worth as much in the decades ahead due to inflation. True, but the hypothetical employee's wages will increase from inflation as well, and it is fair to assume the amount they will invest annually will also steadily increase with inflation.

THE MOST POPULAR TAX-ADVANTAGED RETIREMENT ACCOUNTS

The three most widely used tax-advantaged accounts currently are **traditional IRAs,** which were first available in 1975, employer-sponsored **401(k)** plans, which began in 1980, and **Roth IRAs,** which arrived in 1998. Wage earners have contributed trillions of dollars to these three popular plans since their inception.

IRAs, 401(k) plans, and profit-sharing plans were the predominant tax-advantaged accounts prior to the Roth. All of these pre-Roth plans had the same four basic tax features:

1. **Pre-Tax Contributions:** Contributions (money added) are pre-tax or tax deductible.
2. **Tax-Deferred Earnings:** No income taxes are paid until a distribution (withdrawal) is made.
3. **Taxable Distributions:** All distributions are taxable in the year of the distribution.
4. **Mandatory Distributions:** Beginning at age 72 (formerly age 70½), minimum annual distributions must be made based on published IRS life expectancy tables.

Note: Other plans have these same features, such as 403(b) plans, 457(b) plans, SEPS, SARSEPS, Keogh plans, and SIMPLE IRA plans.

There are only two significant distinguishing features among all these various plans: (1) Annual contribution limits vary substantially from one plan to another, and (2) availability of the plan based on someone's employment (not all plans are available to everyone). I'll say more on those two issues later.

The advent of the Roth IRA in 1998 was the first really significant innovation for tax-advantaged retirement accounts since the inception of the traditional IRA in 1975. The Roth for the most part, has exactly the opposite tax treatment from all the other previous plans as follows:

1. **After-Tax Contributions:** There is no tax deduction for contributions.
2. **Tax-Free Earnings Accumulation:** Earnings are not taxed as they accumulate.
3. **Tax-Free Distributions:** Distributions are not taxed.
4. **No Mandatory Distributions:** There is no requirement to take distributions at any age.

The table below shows a side-by-side comparison of the Roth and the traditional IRA.

	Roth	Traditional IRA
Contributions	Not tax deductible	Tax deductible
Taxation While Earnings Accumulate	Not taxed	Not taxed
Taxation of Distributions	Not taxed	Fully taxable
Mandatory Distributions	None	Annually beginning age 72
Contribution Age Limit	No age limit	No age limit

Table 14.3

A Little History

When IRAs began in 1975, they were just called *IRAs*. Then, in 1998, Congress invented Roth IRAs. To differentiate between the two, everyone started calling the non-Roth IRAs *traditional IRAs*. Eligible individuals can contribute to traditional IRAs or Roth IRAs, or both. Likewise, many employers now offer both traditional accounts and Roth accounts within their 401(k) or 403(b) plans, whereby employees can choose to invest in either the traditional or Roth options, or both.

The common features of all traditional accounts are pre-tax contributions and taxable distributions, whereas the common features of all Roths are after-tax contributions and tax-free distributions.

TRADITIONAL IRA VS. ROTH IRA: WHICH IS BETTER?

Which is better, contributing to a Roth IRA or a traditional IRA? It depends. A strong case could be made for either account type based on various factors, such as your current income tax rate vs. what you believe your tax rate will be in the future, your need for income from the account in retirement, and other possible factors (more on this below).

Note: When I use the term *traditional IRA*, I am universally referring to any of the numerous accounts that have the same tax treatment as the traditional IRA, such as a 401(k) or a 403(b) plan.

First, let's clear up one important fact that is often misunderstood. Mathematically, if someone's tax bracket remains constant, the Roth IRA and the traditional IRA yield *identical* returns to the penny! There is a common misconception that the math works out in favor of the Roth.

The following is a simplistic math example: Let's assume a constant 25% tax bracket, a single contribution of $6,000, and a constant 9% annual compounding rate of return for 20 years.

- $ For the traditional IRA, $6,000 grows to $33,626. All the money is withdrawn after 20 years, and 25% is paid in tax, netting $25,220 after taxes.
- $ For the Roth IRA, after paying 25% tax ($1,500) on the $6,000, the remaining $4,500 is invested, and it grows to an identical amount of $25,220.

Since the two account types produce identical results if the rate of taxation is constant, then the dilemma of deciding which is better should be resolved with respect to other considerations. One primary factor is each individual's opinion as to whether their personal rate of taxation will be higher or lower when funds are withdrawn, vs. when the funds were contributed.

The following are examples of how a potential change in someone's tax bracket could favor each of the two.

Example Favoring a Traditional IRA

You are currently working and paying income taxes; therefore, contributing to a traditional IRA now would reduce your income taxes while you work. However, you plan to retire in a few years, and after retiring, you will likely have very little taxable income. In fact, you anticipate being in a zero-tax bracket after retiring; therefore, you may be able to take distributions from the IRA after retirement without incurring any income taxes.

Example Favoring a Roth IRA

You are a young wage earner in a low tax bracket (or paying no income taxes), and your income will likely increase in the years ahead, causing you to be in a higher tax bracket later.

IRA distribution rules are a factor that favors Roth accounts. Beginning at age 72 (formerly age 70½), traditional IRAs have a *required minimum distribution* (RMD) each year per IRS rules, but there is never a required distribution for a Roth. This distinction could make a Roth account substantially more appealing for someone who has a large account balance, doesn't need the income for living expenses, and who continues to be in a high tax bracket after age 72. This is particularly true if such a person lives for many years beyond age 72. In other words, beginning at age 72, the traditional IRA could require the account owner to take substantial amounts out of the account, causing the owner to pay income taxes on those distributions and then have to do so year after year, whereas money in a Roth is allowed to continue to accumulate tax free for as long as someone lives, and then the Roth proceeds pass to their heirs without incurring income taxes.

A psychological factor that appeals to many investors about Roth accounts is the peace of mind, knowing no income taxes are due in the future for themselves or for their heirs that may inherit their Roth. In other words, many people are more at ease having a smaller amount in a Roth on which no future tax is due, than having a larger sum in a traditional account that will be taxed upon distribution.

Due to the various uncertainties of the future relative to tax brackets and personal considerations, I think it's logical for many people to split their contributions between a Roth account and a traditional IRA. This would allow for some immediate tax reduction from traditional IRA contributions while also having some money in a Roth that is not subject to mandatory distributions but could be accessed as needed without any tax liability.

SHOULD YOU CONTRIBUTE TO A ROTH *AND* A TRADITIONAL IRA?

Having both types of accounts may provide a nice blend of flexibility and tax benefits. IRAs provide immediate tax relief since contributions are tax deductible. Whereas, tax-free distributions can be made from Roths, and there are no mandatory distributions for Roths.

RULES, RULES, RULES, AND MORE RULES

Unfortunately, there is a somewhat daunting myriad of additional IRS rules and restrictions related to all the different tax-advantaged retirement accounts. A detailed explanation of all rules is beyond the scope and primary focus of this book. However, it is useful for investors to receive an introduction to some of the benefits and key rules of various tax-advantaged accounts. The balance of this chapter is devoted to an overview of many, but not all, of the key rules of various tax-advantaged retirement accounts. Readers should seek competent advice to determine the best investment strategy for themselves.

401(k) PLANS

Whereas IRAs are established by each individual wage earner at the financial institution of their choosing, the only way to participate in a 401(k) is if your employer offers a 401(k) plan. As far as the tax benefits of the two are concerned, they are identical, meaning account contributions are pre-tax and distributions are fully taxable.

Similar to the way individuals have the choice between a traditional IRA and a Roth IRA, 401(k) plans may also offer a traditional 401(k) or a Roth 401(k). Some employers choose not to offer a Roth 401(k) in their company's plan.

Due to some of the unique aspects of 401(k) plans, they are often the most convenient and profitable way for many individuals to accumulate wealth consistently.

THE GREATEST OF ALL TIME!

Some say Muhammad Ali was the greatest boxer of all time. I say the 401(k) is the greatest investment opportunity of all time for most investors, for four reasons.

#1 The lucrative tax advantages for 401(k) plans.

#2 The opportunity to receive employer-matching contributions.

#3 The opportunity to invest in diversified portfolios of stocks within the 401(k).

#4 The convenience of automatic payroll deduction to make the contributions.

If a matching contribution is offered by an employer, contributing enough to take advantage of the maximum match is a wise decision if possible. This is the single best wealth accumulation opportunity most investors will ever have.

401(k) Contribution Limits

For 2022, employees can contribute a maximum of $20,500 to a 401(k), or $27,000 if the employee is age 50 or older during the year. This is a major appeal of 401(k) plans over IRAs and Roth IRAs, in which the annual limit is only $6,000 ($7,000 if age 50 or older). It becomes even more attractive if there is an employer match, as discussed below. Employees can contribute up to 100% of their wages as long as they don't exceed the maximum dollar limits each year.

Investment Options

Historically, employees have generally been able to select from an array of various stock, bond, and money market mutual funds for investing their 401(k) contributions. In recent years, some employers have added *self-directed* brokerage accounts as an option. In self-directed accounts, employees can usually buy individual stocks, bonds, and exchange-traded funds (ETFs). In 2022, a few 401(k) plans began allowing investments in a few cryptocurrencies, such as Bitcoin.

Employer Match

Many employers match their employee's contributions up to a certain percentage of the employee's wages. Around 5% is a typical match. For example, if an employee is making $80,000 per year and the employer offers a dollar-for-dollar 5% match, then if the employee contributes $4,000 for the year to their 401(k), the employer will match that amount and contribute an additional $4,000 to the employee's account. The employee can still contribute more than 5%, but the employer doesn't match it.

- $ Not all employers match contributions, and the match can vary substantially as set by the employer. For example, the match could be dollar for dollar, or they could put in $0.50 for every $1 the employee contributes, or the match could be capped at 2% of wages or 10% of wages, etc.
- $ The combination of employee and employer contribution limit for 2022 is $61,000, up to 100% of compensation. For those aged 50 and over, the maximum is $67,500.
- $ Taking full advantage of the employer match is a HUGE benefit that I would encourage every employee to take full advantage of if possible. Consistently contributing the full amount the employer will match is the best long-term wealth accumulation strategy that investors can make, in my opinion.

Vesting Schedules

Don't confuse the terms *vesting* and *investing*. They are two completely different things. Vest simply means to become the owner of. Vesting schedules relative to retirement accounts means the time period (in years) until the employee becomes the irreversible owner of the contributions made to the employee's retirement account by the employer.

Once an employee is vested, the money contributed by the employer cannot be taken back by the employer for any reason. Employees are always 100% vested in the contributions they made themselves. Vesting schedules only relate to the employer contributions. Most retirement plans use one of three methods for vesting: *immediate, cliff,* or *graded.*

- $ **Immediate Vesting:** This is when the employee is always 100% vested. There is no waiting period. This is the most employee-friendly form of vesting. Many plans have immediate vesting.
- $ **Cliff Vesting:** As the term cliff implies, this type of schedule is when the employee is 0% vested for some time period, and then becomes 100% vested after a certain length of employment. By law, employees must be 100% vested after no later than three years if cliff vesting is being used.
- $ **Graded Vesting:** This is when the vested percentage increases a certain amount each year. A common graded vesting schedule is 0% after one year, 20% after two years, 40% after three years, 60% after four years, 80% after five years, and 100% after six years.

Payroll Deduction

For some people, the fact that 401(k) contributions are deducted from the employee's wages automatically each pay period may actually be the most powerful wealth accumulation aspect of 401(k)s vs. IRAs or other investment options.

Roth's Within 401(k)s

Employers can choose to allow their 401(k) plans to offer a traditional 401(k) option and a Roth 401(k) option. As covered earlier in this chapter, the tax aspects of the traditional retirement account vs. the Roth are substantially different. Offering both allows each 401(k) participant to decide which option is best for them.

Note: If an employee selects a Roth 401(k) and the employer has a match, the employer's matching funds must be contributed to a separate *traditional* account for the employee.

No Income Restrictions

401(k) contributions can be made regardless of the employee's income level. For high wage earners, this could be a key feature since IRAs and Roth IRAs have limitations based on income.

Required Minimum Distributions (RMDs)

Just like for IRAs, beginning at age 72, annual distributions are required for 401(k) accounts. However, if someone has not retired, there is no age at which RMDs must commence from a 401(k). This rule doesn't impact many employees, but for those that may choose to work into their 70s and older, it could be meaningful.

$ The *no RMD* rule, if not retired, does not apply to anyone owning more than 5% of the company. Consult with an expert for the IRS' definition of *retired* as it relates to this rule.

$ The IRS penalty for failing to meet an RMD is a whopping 50% of the amount that was supposed to be distributed but was not.

Early Distributions

Distributions (withdrawals) from traditional 401(k)s and IRAs before age 59½ generally result in a 10% penalty paid to the IRS, in addition to reporting the distribution as taxable income.

$ **10% Penalty Exceptions:** The 10% penalty is waived when funds are used for various exceptions as defined by the IRS, such as distributions to the beneficiary after the account owner's death, certain unreimbursed medical expenses, total and permanent disability, court-ordered qualified domestic relations orders (QDROs), substantially equal periodic payments as defined by IRS section 72(t), an IRS levy, and the rule of 55 (see below). The 10% penalty is not waived for 401(k) distributions to pay qualified education expenses (QEE) as it is for IRAs.

$ **The Rule of 55:** This is a special rule for 401(k)s, but not for IRAs. If a 401(k) participant separates employment at age 55 or older, they may take distributions without incurring the 10% penalty.

Borrowing From a 401(k)

If the employer chooses to allow loans, 401(k) participants can borrow from their account balances rather than taking a taxable distribution. Loans are not allowed for IRA accounts and, frankly, having the ability to borrow could encourage employees to unwisely take out loans they later regret. By law, 401(k) loans are limited to the lesser of $50,000 or 50% of the account value. Generally, loans must be paid back within five years to avoid taxes and a 10% penalty.

Limited Advice

One negative aspect of 401(k) plans is investment advice is often limited. An abundance of brochures and documents explaining the investment options is the norm, but individualized help is sometimes limited to calling a help desk. Seeking help from a financial advisor is often a good idea.

401(k) HIGHLIGHTS

$ 401(k)s are employer-sponsored plans. Not all employers offer them.

$ Employees contribute to their 401(k) via systematic payroll deduction.

$ Contributions are on a pre-tax basis unless the employee elects a Roth 401(k).

$ Earnings accumulate tax-deferred until a distribution is made.

$ Distributions are fully taxable except for Roth 401(k)s.

$ 401(k) annual contribution limits in 2022 are $20,500
($27,000 if age 50 or over).

$ Many employers match employee contributions up to a certain level.

$ There may be a vesting schedule for contributions made by the employer.

$ There is no income level that restricts 401(k) contributions.

$ Although not required to do so, some plans allow employee loans.

$ There are generally no required distributions if an employee has not retired.

$ After an employee retires, required minimum distributions must begin at age 72.

$ A 10% penalty is imposed for distributions prior to age 59½
(some exceptions).

$ Some 401(k)s have a Roth option as well as the traditional pre-tax 401(k).

$ Most 401(k)s offer a wide selection of mutual funds in which to invest.

$ Some 401(k)s offer self-directed brokerage accounts as an investment option.

$ Upon termination of employment, employees may roll their 401(k) into an IRA.

$ Each employee's account will grow based on the performance of the specific
investment options they select.

TRADITIONAL IRAs

The fundamental difference between an Individual Retirement Account (IRA) and a 401(k) is that the 401(k) is sponsored by an employer, whereas IRAs are established by individuals at whatever financial institution they choose. Because each has some unique advantages, some people contribute to one or the other, and some people contribute to both.

If your employer doesn't offer a 401(k) or some other similar plan, such as a 403(b), then an IRA or a Roth may be your only option. If your employer offers a 401(k) with matching employer contributions, it would be wise to consider contributing enough to the 401(k) to receive the maximum employer match before contributing to an IRA.

Taxation

Contributions to IRAs and other traditional qualified plans are tax deductible or are made pre-tax. However, all distributions are generally fully taxable.

Contributions Require Earned Income

To contribute to a traditional IRA or a Roth IRA, you must generally have *earned* income (wages). Dividends and interest, for example, don't qualify as earned income.

Annual Contribution Limits

For 2022, the annual combined contribution limit for IRAs and Roths is $6,000, or $7,000 for those age 50 and older. You can contribute to both an IRA and a Roth as long as the combined total for the two doesn't exceed the limit. In 1975, the first year for IRAs, the annual limit was $1,500. The limit has been increased frequently over the years.

$ **Spousal Contributions:** A contribution can also be made for up to $6,000 to a spouse's IRA who does not have earned income, as long as the wage earner has wages equal to the combined contributions of both spouses.

No Age Limit for Contributions

For the first time, starting in 2020, there is no age limit to contribute to an IRA. Previously, contributions could not be made after reaching age 70½. Now, anyone regardless of their age, may contribute to an IRA as long as they have earned income.

Nondeductible Contributions

If you or your spouse is covered by a retirement plan at work, such as a 401(k) or a 403(b), an IRA contribution may not be tax deductible, depending on your income level. The stipulated income levels are phased in with partial deductibility between the high and low ends of the range. Also, there are different income ranges for single tax filers vs. joint tax filers, as well as different ranges depending on whether your spouse has a retirement plan at work as opposed to you having a plan at work.

You can still contribute to an IRA regardless of your income level or whether you or your spouse have a plan at work, but you may not receive a tax deduction for your IRA contribution as you otherwise would.

Generally, I find little appeal to nondeductible IRA contributions, unless you intend to do a Roth conversion (see *backdoor conversions* in the following Roth IRA section). There is no deduction for the contribution, and the distribution of earnings is fully taxable with no capital gains treatment. Additionally, you have to keep excellent records for years to document how much of the IRA has and has not been taxed previously. A nondeductible IRA is essentially the equivalent of a tax-deferred annuity, but with more recordkeeping hassle.

You Can Contribute to an IRA and a 401(k)

$ It is permissible to make the maximum contributions in a 401(k) and to an IRA/Roth. For example, in 2022, an employee could contribute $6,000 ($7,000 age 50 and older) to an IRA and/or a Roth and contribute the maximum of $20,500 ($27,000 age 50 and older) to their 401(k). This could be a good option for those nearing retirement who would like to bolster their retirement funds. However, as described in the previous section, if your income is too high, you may not get a tax deduction for your IRA contribution if you also have a 401(k).

Required Minimum Distributions (RMDs)

Annual RMDs begin the year in which the account owner reaches age 72. The required withdrawal each year is calculated by dividing the year-end value of the IRA from the previous year by the owner's life expectancy per the IRS tables. RMDs are not required from 401(k) plans at any age if the participant has not retired, whereas IRAs have no such provision.

- $ **50% Penalty for Missed RMDs:** Perhaps the most onerous and unreasonable penalty related to tax law is the whopping 50% penalty for a missed RMD. For example, let's assume your RMD for the year was $10,000, but you only took a distribution of $6,000, which means you should have distributed $4,000 more than you did; therefore, you owe a $2,000 penalty (50% of $4,000). The good news is the IRS realizes this huge penalty is extreme, and they will often waive the penalty if they deem you have an acceptable excuse for not taking the RMD.
- $ **Contributions and RMDs in the Same Year:** RMDs must be taken annually after age 72, but contributions may continue to be made at any age. Therefore, someone who has earned income after age 72 may continue to contribute up to $7,000 a year, but they will also be required to take an RMD every year.

Penalty Before Age 59½

Generally, if a distribution is taken before age 59½, there is a 10% federal penalty in addition to paying income taxes. However, the 10% penalty is waived for IRAs for various exceptions as defined by the IRS.

Most of the exceptions when the 10% penalty is waived are the same for all retirement plans, as described in the preceding 401(k) section, but there are a few notable differences between IRAs and 401(k) plans. The following are three situations when the **10% penalty is waived for 401(k) plans but not for IRAs:**

1. When separating from employment after age 55 (the rule of 55).
2. Distributions made related to a qualified domestic relations order (QDRO).
3. Distributions from an employee stock option plan (ESOP).

There are also three situations when the **10% penalty is waived for IRAs, but not for 401(k) plans**:

1. Qualified first-time homebuyer expenses up to $10,000.
2. Health insurance premiums paid while unemployed.
3. Qualified higher-education expenses (QEEs) for the account owner, their spouse, their children, or their grandchildren.

The 10% penalty being waived on IRA distributions relative to QEEs is a significant advantage for IRAs over 401(k) plans for families with young children planning for future potential college expenses. This rule may, in fact, make an IRA account the most attractive savings tool for many families trying to save for retirement as well as for potential college expenses for their children. I discuss this consideration in greater detail in the 529 Education Savings Plan section in Chapter 15.

No Loans

By law, loans are not permitted for IRAs (or Roths), whereas 401(k) plans, 403(b) plans, and other employer-sponsored plans are permitted to allow plan participants to borrow from their personal account balances.

More Investment Options

One distinct advantage for IRAs and Roths vs. most employer-sponsored plans is a much broader array of investment options. Most employer-sponsored plans limit investment options to a specific set of mutual funds. Individuals can establish IRAs with any mutual fund and with any investment broker, bank, credit union, or insurance agent they choose. Additionally, self-directed IRA accounts with investment brokers allow individuals to buy and sell stocks, bonds, and mutual funds within the IRA. Some IRAs allow investing in real estate, precious metals, cryptocurrencies, and other assets.

ROTH ACCOUNTS

Previously, I opined that a 401(k) with an employer-matching contribution is the greatest investment of all-time for most people. Many 401(k)s allow the choice of either a traditional account or a Roth 401(k) account; therefore, I would add that a *401(k) Roth* with an employer match may be the greatest of all time for *some* people.

Various rules and features of Roths have been discussed piecemeal through-out this chapter. Below, the key aspects of Roth accounts are more concisely listed.

Taxation

Contributions to Roths are not tax deductible; they are made with after-tax money. However, distributions are tax free when held for the required time period.

Contributions Require Earned Income

To contribute to a Roth (or an IRA), you must generally have earned income (wages). Dividends and interest, for example, don't qualify as earned income.

Annual Roth Contribution Limits

Contribution limits and the rules for spousal IRAs are the same for Roth IRAs and traditional IRAs, as described in the previous section on traditional IRAs. The 2022 limit is $6,000 if under age 50, and $7,000 if age 50 or older.

No Age Limit for Contributions

There is no age limit for making contributions.

Income Restrictions

Those with *modified adjusted gross income* (MAGI) over certain levels cannot contribute to a Roth. For 2022, joint tax filers with MAGI under

$204,000, and single tax filers with MAGI under $129,000 can make a full maximum Roth contribution. Contributions are phased out for higher MAGI levels. Joint filers with MAGI of $214,000 or more and single filers with MAGI of $144,000 or more cannot contribute any amount to a Roth in 2022.

No Mandatory Distributions

Unlike IRAs, there are no required distributions from Roth accounts. This is a significant advantage relative to wealth accumulation as compared to traditional IRAs if the account owner doesn't need the income. This feature has the potential to allow Roth owners to accumulate tax-free growth of their entire account for 20, 30, or more years longer than what is allowed for traditional IRAs, in which distributions must begin at age 72.

Distribution Rules

One attractive Roth feature is that the IRS deems contributions come out first before earnings. You can withdraw contributions at any age for any reason, with no taxes or penalties. For example, if you have contributed $12,000 to your Roth and the account is now worth $15,000, you can draw out the $12,000 you contributed, with no taxes or penalties at any time and at any age. If you withdraw more than the $12,000 you contributed, the excess is considered earnings, and you may have taxes and a 10% penalty if you don't meet one of the many exceptions (see below).

Relative to Roth earnings, if someone withdraws money from their Roth, the distributions are free of taxes and penalties if the owner is 59½ or older, and they established a Roth account at least five years before the distribution. If either of those conditions is not met, then the distribution of earnings may be taxable and subject to a 10% penalty.

Penalty Exceptions: No taxes or a 10% penalty are due on Roth distributions if any of the following exceptions apply:

- $ The distribution is contributions only (not earnings).
- $ The owner is age 59½ or older, and they established a Roth at least five years prior.

$ Any of the exceptions as detailed in the previous traditional IRA section are met, such as disability, death, first-time homebuyer, certain education and medical expenses, certain health insurance premiums while unemployed, qualified first-time homebuyers, and distributions pursuant to IRS section 72(t).

Roth Conversions

The IRS allows IRAs and other qualified retirement accounts to be converted to Roths. However, any previously untaxed portion of the amount being converted will be included in taxable income for the year of the conversion; therefore, the tax liability could be substantial if converting a significant amount. Conversions can be for any portion of or all of the IRA account. Fully understanding the tax implications in advance is advisable.

$ **Backdoor Conversion:** So-called backdoor conversions have become popular for high wage earners who are not allowed to contribute to a Roth because their income is too high. Since there is no income limit for nondeductible IRA contributions, such individuals make a nondeductible contribution to an IRA and then immediately convert it to a Roth. I find this to be a fine example of the legislative idiocy we sometimes get from our elected lawmakers.

$ **Beware of the Aggregate Rule:** When doing a Roth conversion, you are required to aggregate all of your IRAs for tax purposes. For example, assume you have $100,000 total in IRAs, of which $94,000 has never been taxed and $6,000 is the nondeductible contribution you just made. You cannot convert $6,000 to a Roth and claim you are specifically converting the $6,000 that has already been taxed. Since 94% of your total IRA balance has not been taxed, you would have to report 94% of the $6,000 as taxable income. This can become an accounting nightmare. Personally, I would only make nondeductible IRA contributions if I were intending to convert all of my IRA balances to a Roth, but others may disagree.

Recordkeeping

It is important to keep documented proof of all Roth contributions until the latter of age 59½, or five years after you established a Roth IRA. This is because your contributions may be withdrawn anytime without penalty or taxes, whereas earnings may be subject to penalty and taxes if withdrawn before age 59½ and before five years has passed since establishing a Roth.

I would suggest keeping a file of all account statements showing the dates and amounts of all contributions. For example, if someone is 50 years old and they have contributed $100,000 to their Roth over the years, and they want to take out all of their contributions but not withdraw any earnings, they need to know exactly how much they put in, and they need to be able to prove it if they are audited after they take a distribution.

Roths for Children

Roths for young children could be an attractive option for the following reasons and pursuant to certain conditions as follows:

- $ There is no minimum age limit to contribute to a Roth (or an IRA).
- $ The child must have earned income (wages). Interest, dividends, and gifts from Grandma don't count as earned income. If the child made legitimate money babysitting, delivering papers, or other jobs allowed by law, that money could be contributed to their Roth.
- $ Contributions can always be withdrawn without taxes or penalties if the child wants their original contributions back at some point. However, if the money remains in the Roth, it has the potential to grow for many years completely tax free.
- $ Income taxes, as well as FICA taxes, may be due on the wages depending on the child's total income circumstances.
- $ Generally, a Roth is substantially more attractive for children than an IRA, since most children don't pay income taxes and therefore would not benefit from an IRA deduction.

403(b) PLANS

A 403(b) plan, often referred to as a tax-sheltered annuity (TSA), is another type of employer-sponsored plan that has many similarities to a 401(k) plan. The primary difference is that by law, 403(b) plans may only be offered by school systems and certain other 501(c)(3) tax-exempt organizations, such as churches, hospitals, and other entities.

403(b) plan similarities to 401(k) plans include the following:

$ The same annual contribution limits.

$ They may offer Roth and traditional (pre-tax) options.

$ The employer may (but is not required to) contribute to the plan for employees.

$ The plan may (but is not required to) allow loans.

$ Distribution rules are generally the same, such as a 10% penalty for withdrawals prior to age 59½, with certain exceptions.

$ Mutual funds are commonly the preferred investment option offered. Prior to 1974, 403(b) plans were required to be invested in annuity contracts; hence, the TSA moniker still lingers.

$ Contributions are generally made via payroll deduction from the employee's wages.

MISCELLANEOUS

This final section of the chapter contains information on five miscellaneous topics that all relate to tax-advantaged accounts in some way.

Rollovers and Transfers

A *rollover* or *transfer* is when money is moved from one retirement account to another. For example, when someone separates from employment, they might roll over their 401(k) balance to their new employer's 401(k) or to an IRA. The fundamental purpose of doing a rollover or transfer is to maintain the tax benefits of the previous plan in which the funds were invested, as opposed to taking a taxable distribution.

A *direct rollover* or transfer is when the plan administrator makes the payment directly to the new plan administrator or IRA trustee rather than to the plan participant. In this case, no taxes are withheld or owed.

A *60-day rollover* is when the proceeds are paid directly to the account owner rather than to the new administrator. The owner then has 60 days from receipt of the payment to roll over (deposit) the money into an IRA or another retirement plan to avoid taxes. If the owner is under age 59½, they will generally owe a 10% penalty on any amount not rolled over in addition to any applicable income taxes. As previously discussed in this chapter, there are a number of exceptions when there is not a 10% penalty.

Donating Tax-Deferred Retirement Accounts to Charity

Naming a 501(c)(3) tax-exempt charity as the beneficiary can turn a tax-deferred retirement account into a tax-free scenario. Normally, if the beneficiary of a tax-deferred account, such as a traditional IRA or 401(k) is any person other than your spouse, the beneficiary will have to include the distributions in their taxable income. Affluent and philanthropically inclined individuals can arrange their affairs to minimize taxes and maximize gifts by strategically planning their bequeaths.

A simple example: Aunt Mildred has $1 million in a traditional IRA and $1 million in a bank account. She wants to leave $1 million to you (her sole heir), and $1 million to the local hospital, which is a 501(c)(3).

The hospital could be designated as the beneficiary of either account and pay no taxes, since it is a 501(c)(3) tax-exempt entity. If she bequeaths the bank account to you, no income taxes will be due, since the bank account was not a tax-deferred account. However, if she leaves the IRA to you, the entire account value will be taxed when you receive distributions from the account. If the entire distribution were taxed at the 2022 maximum individual federal tax rate of 37%, a $1 million distribution would result in $370,000 in federal taxes (not to mention potential state income taxes). Conversely, by leaving the IRA to the hospital and the bank account to you, Aunt Mildred could allow all $2 million to transfer free of federal income taxes.

Note: When a non-spouse is an IRA beneficiary, there are several distribution options available. A non-spouse always has at least a five-year time period they can spread distributions over. Any applicable income taxes would be payable for each year in which the beneficiary received a distribution. Help and planning from a competent tax professional would be advisable if you are a non-spouse beneficiary.

Target-Date Accounts

To the point, I am frankly not a fan of target-date retirement accounts with near-term dates. They have a wonderful marketing hook that lends itself well to glossy brochures and marketing plans. The name has a warm fuzzy comforting feel to it that appeals to the desire to be prudent and appropriate: "Gee whiz, this is perfect for us, honey. It says they have a *2025 Target-Date Fund*—that's exactly when we plan to retire!" The name implies the ideal investment, since it "targets" the year you plan to retire.

From a portfolio allocation perspective, it simply means as you get closer to retirement, they shift more out of stocks and more into bonds. Why? Because you are old, and old people are supposed to take less risk, right? And bonds are less risky than stocks, right? Hmm, I'm not sure about all that.

The problem I have with target-date funds currently is that interest rates (bond yields) are near all-time lows. In fact, bond yields have been extremely low for the last decade, from a historical perspective. When interest rates rise, fixed-rate bond values decline, so the notion that bonds are safer than stocks is a sketchy assertion, given the current low-interest rate environment.

In decades past, the interest rate on bonds far outpaced the dividend yield on the vast majority of stocks. That's not the case currently. Not to mention that stock dividends tend to rise over time as well. So, from an income perspective, shifting to bonds because you are retiring and want income doesn't make sense now, as it once did.

My 83-year-old widowed mother is thankful nobody sold Dad on the idea of a target-date fund years ago. She is still primarily invested in stocks and has thoroughly enjoyed the way her dividend checks have steadily increased over the years. My siblings and I also like the way her portfolio value has multiplied several times over along the way.

Other Tax-Advantaged Investments

Relative to investing, the federal tax code primarily gives tax preferences based on three broad parameters. One parameter is based on the type of account in which money is invested; that's what was covered in this chapter pertaining to IRAs, 401(k) plans, etc.

A second way tax advantages are given is based on the type of investment (asset type). Examples would include interest on municipal bonds being tax free, a reduced tax rate for qualified dividends from stocks, and depreciation allowances for certain types of real estate.

The third way tax preferences are allowed is based on the holding period of the asset. If an asset is held (owned) for one year or more, it is considered *long term*, and any capital gain is potentially taxed at a lower rate. However, capital gains rates do not apply for assets held in retirement accounts.

The Demise of Pensions

A pension typically provides a guaranteed monthly income for the remainder of the recipient's life, but with no ownership or access to the principal. Pensions are typically funded and paid by the employer. The retirement accounts we covered in this chapter are basically the opposite of pensions in that the employee has ownership of and access to the principal, but there is no guaranteed income, and the employee more often funds the account rather than the employer.

Decades ago, pensions were omnipresent in big corporate America. Then people started living longer, and a number of large companies went bankrupt due in part to their pension and health-care obligations to their retired employees (General Motors, for example).

Now, pensions are primarily associated with government employees, such as the military, state and federal workers, teachers, etc. The burden of retirement funding has largely been shifted to the employee via 401(k) plans, IRAs, Roths, etc.

Social Security was never intended to provide 100% of someone's retirement income. With the demise of pension plans, it is advisable that workers carefully consider how they are saving and accumulating wealth in preparation for their retirement.

SUMMARY

Tax-advantaged retirement accounts are the most effective way for the majority of long-term investors to accumulate wealth. Congress passed laws that provide generous tax incentives to encourage working Americans to contribute to one or more of the several tax-advantaged accounts. IRAs, Roths, and 401(k) plans are the three most widely used options. The best of those three would generally be the 401(k) if the employer offers a matching contribution.

Traditional IRAs and 401(k)s allow for a tax deduction for contributions and tax-deferred earnings accumulation. Roth contributions don't provide for a tax deduction but the earnings and distributions are generally tax free. When compounded for years, the additional amount that can accumulate due to these tax advantages can be quite significant.

In addition to the tax advantages, other reasons these accounts work so well to accumulate wealth include being easy to establish and contribute to—either automatic payroll deduction or automatic monthly fund transfers are popular choices. Once people set up automatic contributions, they tend to stick with it. Stock mutual funds are popular investment choices within retirement accounts and they have generally provided excellent long-term performance for participants. Most people don't take withdrawals from these accounts until after age 59½ to avoid taxes and penalties, which is actually another added benefit to keep these accounts growing.

The combination of tax advantages, ease of contributing, attractive long-term earnings rates, and the tax disincentive to make early withdrawals has made tax-advantaged retirement accounts an enormous success. Workers and retirees now have trillions of dollars invested in these lucrative accounts.

THE ALLEN THOMAS STORY

A side benefit of being a diligent hard worker is how it often begets opportunities you weren't even looking for. Employers recognize and often value individuals who demonstrate exceptional passion and effort as much as someone with more impressive credentials and years of experience.

Allen Thomas was a gifted and hardworking athlete, a two-time collegiate baseball All-American who was also a dedicated student. He graduated on schedule in four years with a sports medicine degree from Wingate University. The following month, he was drafted by and signed with the Chicago White Sox.

After playing two seasons in the minor leagues, the White Sox released Allen, effectively ending his playing career and his lifelong dream of playing in the big leagues. However, the White Sox were so impressed with his work ethic and professionalism as a player, as well as his college degree, that they offered him a position as a strength and conditioning coach in their minor league system.

Allen's hard work and dedication as a coach was recognized by the White Sox as they steadily promoted him through the minor leagues over the next six seasons. Ultimately, Allen achieved his dream of making it to the big leagues, but as a coach rather than a player. At the age of 29, he was offered the position of director of strength and conditioning for the White Sox major league team, making him the youngest strength coach in all of Major League Baseball.

Simply put, the effort and professionalism Allen displayed in his short tenure as a player were pivotal traits that earned him the opportunity to rise to the top of his profession. In 2021, Allen completed his 18th season in Major League Baseball. He is a great example of the adage, "when one door closes, another door opens." I was fortunate to meet Allen in the summer of 1984 when he was a 10-year-old on the recreation team I helped coach. We have maintained a close friendship ever since, and I'm happy to say that in spite of my coaching, he still made it to the big leagues!

ALLEN'S LESSON: Always do your best and work hard. Your diligence and professionalism in an entry-level position may be the pivotal point to launching a highly successful career.

CHAPTER 15

Other Tax-Advantaged Accounts

HSAs, FSAs, 529 Plans, UTMAs, Annuities, and Tax Terminology

Chapter Abbreviations

FSA:	Flexible Spending Account
DCFSA:	Dependent Care FSA
LPFSA:	Limited Purpose FSA
HDHP:	High-Deductible Health Plan
HSA:	Health Savings Account
QEE:	Qualified Education Expense
QME:	Qualified Medical Expense
UTMA:	Uniform Transfers to Minors Act

The previous chapter was devoted entirely to tax-advantaged *retirement* accounts, which are accounts that provide tax incentives to leave the money in the accounts until retirement age (generally age 59½).

There are also specific accounts that provide tax advantages to pay for medical or educational costs. Those accounts are the primary focus of this chapter. Also, at the end of the chapter, the definitions of the numerous and often confusing tax-related terms are provided.

HEALTH SAVINGS ACCOUNTS (HSAs)

For those who qualify, a health savings account (HSA), is a must-do no-brainer in my opinion. Like a traditional IRA, HSA contributions are tax deductible **and** like a Roth, qualified HSA distributions (withdrawals) are tax free—the best of both worlds. What a beautiful thing!

> **For eligible individuals, HSAs are the absolute best of both worlds. Contributions are tax deductible and qualified distributions are also tax free. Sign me up!**

IRS Publication 969 covers all the rules and information pertaining to HSAs. The following is a summary of some (not all) of the key points of HSAs.

Who Qualifies for an HSA?

Regardless of your employment status, as long as you are covered under a qualifying *high-deductible health plan* (HDHP), you are eligible to contribute to an HSA. An HDHP is defined by the IRS as a health insurance plan having an annual deductible for 2022 for self-coverage (one person) of at least $1,400 and at least $2,800 for family coverage, and having total annual out-of-pocket expenses (including deductibles, copayments, and coinsurance) of no more than $7,050 for self-coverage or $14,100 for family coverage. Family coverage is when the owner and at least one other person are covered. If your health insurance plan is below these minimums or above these maximums, you are not eligible to contribute to an HSA.

Additionally, you can't be enrolled in any other health insurance plans, including Medicare and *general-purpose* flexible spending accounts (FSAs). Since many people begin Medicare at 65, that is a common age when many participants can no longer contribute to their HSA. However, having a limited purpose FSA (LPFSA) that covers eligible dental or vision expenses does not affect HSA eligibility, nor does having a dependent care FSA (DCFSA). Accidental and disability insurance plans do not affect HSA eligibility either.

Annual Contribution Limits

For 2022, self-only (individuals) HDHP participants may contribute a maximum of $3,650 to their HSA, and a family plan has a maximum contribution of $7,300. Those age 55 and older may contribute an additional $1,000 per year. HSA limits are completely unrelated to other retirement account contributions. In other words, contributing to a 401(k) or to an IRA doesn't impact your HSA limit, and vice versa.

HSA Tax Benefits

Contributions to an HSA are tax deductible even if you don't itemize; there is no tax on the earnings that accumulate in the account, and distributions used for qualified medical expenses (QMEs) as defined by the IRS are tax free. To my knowledge, HSAs, FSAs, and related accounts are the only tax-advantaged accounts that offer both tax-deductible contributions and tax-free distributions. For these reasons, I would strongly encourage consideration of an HSA for anyone who is eligible.

What Can HSAs Be Used for?

HSA funds can be used to pay for health plan copayments, coinsurance, and deductibles, as well as for many items that are QMEs. IRS Publication 969 states that QMEs are "those expenses that generally would qualify for the medical and dental expenses deduction," which are explained in IRS Publication 502.

A few of the QMEs are medical care, vision and dental care expenses, chiropractic care, physical therapy, glasses and hearing aids, prescriptions, and payment for long-term care services, as well as dozens of medical-related over-the-counter items such as Band-Aids and medicines. However, HSA funds may not be used to pay premiums for a health plan.

Whose Expenses Can an HSA Pay?

HSAs can be used to pay qualified medical expenses for the account owner and their spouse, all dependents the owner claims on their tax return, and certain other people the owner could have claimed but didn't (consult with your tax advisor).

Accessing the HSA

HSA owners may access their HSA funds by using a debit card or checks issued by their HSA provider, or the owner may pay the expense and then get reimbursed from the HSA.

Investing Within the HSA

Traditionally, most HSA balances were deposited in interest-bearing accounts. Now, most HSAs also offer participants a selection of mutual funds invested in stocks and bonds, so participants may benefit from investment gains on their account balances. There is no taxation on earnings within the HSA account.

Do You Have to Use All the Money Each Year?

Any money not used each year remains in the account and can continue to grow tax free until needed for a QME. Even when the owner is no longer eligible to make new annual contributions, they can leave money in the account indefinitely until they have a QME for which to use it. There is no age when mandatory distributions must commence like there is for IRAs. For example, someone may let their HSA balance grow tax free for decades and ultimately use the funds for nursing home expenses years after they last contributed to the HSA.

Taxable Distributions

Distributions (withdrawals) can be made for any reason at any time, but if a distribution is made for purposes other than a QME, it is taxable. Also, any nonqualified distribution made before reaching age 65 is subject to an additional 20% penalty. If possible, it is certainly advantageous to leave money in the HSA until a withdrawal can be made for a QME to avoid taxation.

What Happens if the HSA Owner Dies?

Only one person can be the owner of an HSA. They can't be jointly owned with a spouse or anyone else. A beneficiary can and should be designated for an HSA. If the spouse is the beneficiary, then the HSA may simply be transferred into their name when the owner dies, and they will continue on as the new owner with all the same benefits and usages of the account.

If someone other than the spouse is the beneficiary, then upon the owner's death, the account stops being an HSA, and the fair market value of the HSA is taxable to the beneficiary for the year in which the owner died.

Who Provides HSAs?

Individuals may choose from dozens of providers to establish an HSA, such as banks, insurance companies, or other trustees approved by the IRS. Often the health insurance provider will have an affiliation with an HSA provider. Employees can select a different HSA plan other than what their employer may offer, but their employer may not allow them to fund another plan via payroll deduction.

Contributing to an HSA has been a wonderful tax-advantaged strategy for my family. Over the last 13 years, we have made tax-deductible contributions totaling $96,200 to our HSA and then made tax-free withdrawals to pay for deductibles, copayments, and coinsurance for two hip replacements, a shoulder surgery, a knee surgery, countless doctor visits, dozens of prescription medications, and numerous other QMEs.

HSA HIGHLIGHTS

$ You must have a high-deductible health plan (HDHP) to contribute to an HSA.

$ To contribute to an HSA, you can't have any other health plans, including Medicare.

$ Contributions are tax deductible, even if you don't itemize.

$ Earnings in the HSA are not taxed.

$ Distributions are tax free if used to pay qualified medical expenses (QMEs).

$ Distributions may be used to pay health plan deductibles and copayments, and coinsurance as well as many other QMEs.

$ HSA owners can use debit cards, checks, or reimbursement to pay for QMEs.

$ Nonqualified distributions are subject to taxation.

$ Nonqualified distributions are subject to a 20% penalty if under age 65.

$ There are no mandatory distributions or age by which distributions must be made.

$ Balances in an HSA may be invested in a variety of ways, including mutual funds and fixed interest rate accounts.

FLEXIBLE SPENDING ACCOUNTS (FSAs)

Flexible spending accounts (FSAs) are plans offered by employers, and employees choose whether or not to participate. FSAs are commonly used to pay QMEs that are not covered under general health insurance plans. There are two general types of FSAs—Health Care FSAs and Dependent Care FSAs (DCFSA). There are also *limited purpose* FSAs (LPFSA) designed to pay for dental or vision care.

There are many similarities between an HSA and an FSA, but there are also some significant differences.

Key Similarities of FSAs and HSAs

- $ **Pre-Tax Contributions:** FSAs and HSAs have the same net tax savings for the participant in that contributions are made on a pre-tax or tax-deductible basis.
- $ **Tax-Free Withdrawals:** Withdrawals are tax free if used for QMEs for the FSA and the HSA.
- $ **QMEs:** Qualified expenses for both FSAs and HSAs include health insurance plan copayments, coinsurance, and deductibles; prescribed and over-the-counter drugs; and many other medical-related expenses as defined in IRS Publication 969. However, payment of health insurance premiums is not a QME for either.
- $ **Employer Contributions:** Although not required to do so, employers can make contributions to both FSAs and HSAs.

Key Differences Between FSAs and HSAs

- $ **Employer-Established:** Whereas individuals establish, control, and have ownership of their own HSA, FSAs may only be established by an employer and then offered to employees.
- $ **Annual Contribution Limits:** The 2022 individual contribution limit for an FSA is $2,850. If married, each spouse may contribute the maximum to an FSA for a total of $5,700 for the couple. The 2022 HSA individual limit is $3,650 and $7,300 for family coverage. Those age 55 and older may contribute an additional $1,000 to an HSA.

$ **Use-It-or-Lose-It:** For an HSA, funds not used to pay medical expenses simply remain in the account. Money can be left in an HSA indefinitely for years and used when needed. The money in the account belongs to the individual, and an employer is never entitled to take any money back. This is not the case with an FSA. Any funds not used each year in an FSA are forfeited by the employee and are claimed by the employer. Although not required to do so, employers can allow employees to roll up to $570 (annual maximum for 2022) of unused money into the next year or allow employees an extra 2½ months to use all funds from the previous year. This use-it-or-lose-it rule makes it important for employees to carefully estimate how much they think their QMEs will be for the upcoming year, so they don't over-contribute to their FSA.

$ **Investing:** FSA cash balances may not be invested, whereas most HSA providers now offer an array of mutual funds to invest cash balances in. Earnings grow tax free and can be used to pay for QMEs, just like your contributions.

$ **Eligibility:** Self-employed and unemployed individuals may not contribute to an FSA, but they can with an HSA as long as they are covered under a qualifying high-deductible health plan (HDHP). You can't be enrolled in Medicare or any other general-purpose health insurance plans and contribute to an HSA, whereas you can with an FSA. If you are enrolled in a general-purpose FSA, you can't contribute to an HSA. But you can contribute to an HSA and also have a DCFSA, or an LPFSA for dental or vision.

OTHER TAX-ADVANTAGED MEDICAL ACCOUNTS

In addition to FSAs and HSAs, there are a few other tax-advantaged medical accounts, including health reimbursement arrangements (HRAs), dependent care flexible spending accounts (DCFSAs), Medicare advantage medical savings accounts (MSAs), and the Archer MSA.

An HRA is sponsored by and funded by the employer as an employee benefit to pay for QME. The employer has considerable latitude in terms of what the HRA covers and how much is covered for each employee. A DCFSA allows for qualified child and dependent care expenses to be paid from the account pre-tax. The Medicare Advantage MSA is a type of Medicare Advantage plan that combines an HDHP with an MSA. The Archer MSA was discontinued in 2007, but existing accounts were allowed to continue, and many still exist today. An Archer MSA is an MSA for the self-employed and businesses with 50 or fewer employees.

529 EDUCATION SAVINGS PLANS

529 Overview

The financial incentive to establish a 529 account is that distributions of earnings for *qualified education expenses* (QEEs), as defined by the IRS, are tax free. There is no federal income tax deduction for the contribution, although many states do offer some type of credit or deduction on state income taxes for contributions.

In effect, a 529 is sort of like an education-oriented Roth in that both have the same basic tax treatment—no deduction for contributions, earnings grow within the account without taxation, and withdrawals are tax free when certain conditions are met.

529 plans must be sponsored by state governments; however, numerous investment brokers and mutual funds distribute those state-sponsored plans. All 50 states and Washington DC sponsor 529 plans, and there are typically several different providers to choose from in each state.

For some parents and grandparents, 529s make a lot of sense as a way to pay for QEEs via a tax-advantaged account. However, there are numerous considerations that make 529s less appealing for many families. Unlike HSAs and tax-advantaged retirement accounts, I don't think everyone needs a 529 just because they are available to them. As I will explain later in this section, for most families, I think there are better ways to save for potential college expenses than 529 plans.

Like most tax-advantaged accounts, there are numerous federal laws and rules, as well as exceptions to the rules. Laws also vary substantially from state to state for 529 plans, and it is beyond the scope of this book to attempt to address the various state laws. The following are *some* of the key *federal* rules and other considerations for 529 education savings plans.

Note: The following overview relates to *529 education savings plans*, not to *529 prepaid tuition plans*.

What Can the Money Be Used For?

For a distribution to be tax free, it must be used for a QEE. When 529 plans started in 1996, they were only for post-high school (college) QEEs. As of 2018, kindergarten through high school *tuition* is now included as a QEE as well. K-12 QEEs are capped at $10,000 per year (tuition only), per beneficiary (student), whereas there is no cap on the amount of college QEEs. 529s can be used to pay QEEs for public, private, or religious-based schools.

To be a QEE for a college student, the institution must be on the US Department of Education's Database of Accredited Postsecondary Institutions and Programs (DAPIP) list. The DAPIP list includes thousands of institutions ranging from trade schools, two-year and four-year schools, and public and private schools. Both undergraduate and postgraduate studies qualify, including medical, law, business, and other graduate schools. Virtually all accredited institutions are on the DAPIP list.

Whereas QEEs for K-12 are for tuition only (no other expenses qualify), QEEs for post-high school institutions include tuition and fees, room and board (on or off campus), textbooks, computers and accessories, supplies and equipment, and required items for special needs students. Also, the SECURE Act enacted in 2019 allows for a lifetime limit of $10,000 to repay the beneficiary's student loans.

Who Can Have a 529?

Although anyone can establish a 529, typically, these accounts are set up by parents or grandparents for the benefit of their children or grandchildren.

Ownership and Beneficiary

A 529 account designates a person as the owner, who may or may not be the person providing the funds. Only one beneficiary can be named per 529 account. The beneficiary is the person/student for whose QEEs the 529 can be used. The owner controls the account and decides if and when to distribute money for the beneficiary's benefit. Although there can only be one beneficiary per account, the owner may change the beneficiary at any time. Also, the owner may transfer money from one child's account to another. Some plans allow for joint ownership (for example, spouses), while other plans require that only one person be the owner.

The following is an example: Grandma funds a 529 with herself as the owner and the eldest granddaughter, Jane, as the beneficiary. After Jane finishes college, there is still money left in the 529 account. Grandma then names one of the other grandkids as the account beneficiary, and she also moves half of the remaining balance by doing a plan-to-plan roll over to a second 529, in which the third grandchild is named as the beneficiary.

Successor Owner: In addition to designating an owner and beneficiary, many 529 plans allow for the naming of a successor owner. So, using the above example, if Grandma (owner) dies, the plan stays in effect, and the successor owner becomes the new owner. Having a successor owner is an attractive feature.

Contribution Limits and Aggregate Account Balance Limits

Rather than having a contribution limit, the way most retirement accounts do, 529 plans have an aggregate account balance limit. Since 529 plans are state-sponsored, each state sets its own limit. If the aggregate balances in all 529 accounts, administered by that state for a single beneficiary, reach the maximum, then no future contributions can be made to any account administered by that state for that beneficiary unless the aggregate account balances fall below the limit.

The limit is based on the state's estimate of the cost to attend an expensive four-year college and graduate school in that state. On the high end, California and New York have aggregate account balance limits over $500,000. On the low end, some states are closer to $300,000.

Gift Tax Implications

Although there are no annual or lifetime contribution limits for 529s, large contributors need to consider gift tax implications. Even though the money in a 529 plan has not yet actually been given to the child, federal tax law treats contributions to a 529 as a gift. As of 2022, any individual may gift up to $16,000 to any other individual with no gift taxes each calendar year. There are numerous exceptions and aspects of the gift tax rules, which are beyond the scope of this book. Simply put, consult with a competent tax advisor before your combined gifts and 529 contributions to any one individual exceed $16,000 in a year. That is $16,000 per person, so two grandparents with five grandkids could gift a total of $160,000 per year and stay under the threshold. Two grandparents x five grandkids = 10 gifts of $16,000 each.

Investment Options

Much like employer-sponsored retirement accounts, most 529 plans offer participants a smorgasbord of stock, bond, and cash mutual funds in which to invest. Each individual 529 account will increase or decrease in value based on the performance of the specific investment options selected by the account owner.

Taxation of Nonqualified Withdrawals

What if none of your kids go to college, or you just want/need the money for other reasons? The owner (parent or grandparent) of the 529 account owns the account and can withdraw the money at any time for any reason. However, if the withdrawal is not used for a QEE, then the earnings portion of the withdrawal is subject to ordinary income tax and a 10% penalty. Since there was no tax deduction for contributions (basis), there is never tax or a penalty on basis distributed.

Unfortunately, 529s are not like Roths, from which you can withdraw the basis first without tax or penalty. 529 withdrawals are deemed pro rata between basis and earnings. For example, if 70% of the 529 account was earnings and 30% basis, and a nonqualified withdrawal was made, then 70% of the amount would be subject to income tax and a 10% penalty. The plan's administrator keeps track of the basis and issues a 1099-Q for each year withdrawals are made, showing how much of the withdrawal is earnings and how much is basis.

The earnings portion of nonqualified withdrawals is always taxable, but there are several situations when the 10% penalty is waived, such as if the beneficiary (student) dies or becomes disabled, when the beneficiary receives a tax-free scholarship, when the beneficiary attends a US military academy, as well as several other circumstances. If you take a nonqualified withdrawal and you received a state tax break when you made the contribution, you may have to repay the state, depending on the state.

Financial Aid Consideration

If a family's income and assets are at a level that makes receiving federal student aid unlikely, then a 529 plan may be an excellent choice. But for students who may otherwise qualify for student aid, be aware that 529 balances and withdrawals must be included on the FAFSA (student aid) application. In other words, it may be better for grandma to assist in other ways besides contributing to a 529 plan relative to maximizing the opportunity to receive student financial aid.

---

529 accounts can negatively impact financial aid opportunities. Income received from 529s and assets within 529s must be listed on the FAFSA financial aid application.

Starting Early

The benefit of a 529 is to benefit from the tax-free earnings that accumulate in the 529 account. If you wait until the child is a senior in high school to fund a 529, the tax benefit will probably be minimal. But, $20,000 invested in an infant's 529 plan that grows at a compounded annual rate of 9.4% will be worth over $100,000 in 18 years, hence, avoiding taxation on $80,000 worth of earnings if the money is used for QEEs.

State Tax Considerations

State tax laws vary substantially relative to 529 plans. For example:

$ Many states (but not all) offer a state income tax credit or tax deduction for contributions.

$ Some states offering state income tax benefits require that the contribution be to an in-state 529 plan, while other states offer tax benefits for contributions to any 529 plan.

$ Some states cap the contribution amount that can be deducted from state taxes.

$ Some states tax QEEs if the withdrawal was from a 529 administered by another state.

$ Some states impose a state tax penalty for nonqualified distributions in addition to the federal 10% penalty.

$ Many states follow or conform to the federal 529 tax laws.

529 Prepaid Tuition Plans

There are two types of 529 plans: (1) education savings plans and (2) prepaid tuition plans. The two plan types have the same tax advantages but are substantially different in other ways. The preceding pages focused on education savings plans, not on prepaid tuition plans.

I purposely did not discuss prepaid tuition plans because they have a much narrower focus and less flexibility compared to education savings plans. Also, less than half the states offer prepaid tuition plans. Personally, I find very little appeal to prepaid tuition plans as opposed to education savings plans.

With a prepaid tuition plan, you are basically paying money today into a fund in lieu of tuition in the future. If the child doesn't attend one of the specific colleges the plan covers, then you may lose part or all of your investment. Prepaid tuition plans are a great idea from the college's perspective to help encourage a steady stream of students for years to come. From a future student's perspective, however, a prepaid tuition plan may apply unwanted pressure to attend a particular college only because the tuition is prepaid.

529s VS. RETIREMENT PLANS

One financial dilemma for many parents is determining the best strategy to save for their own retirement while at the same time preparing for their children's future college expenses.

For high-income parents who are contributing the maximum to their retirement accounts and have additional investable money, 529 contributions may be a good option. However, for most middle-class parents, contributing to a tax-advantaged retirement account is more advantageous and flexible than contributing to a 529 plan for both retirement savings and potential college expenses.

When planning for retirement as well as for potential college expenses for children, for many parents it is more advantageous to contribute to their own retirement account rather than a 529 account.

The following are examples of regulations and tax aspects that support my view that contributing to an IRA, a Roth, or a 401(k) may make more sense than contributing to a 529 plan.

- $ **IRA Key Feature:** For IRAs, the 10% penalty for withdrawals before age 59½ is waived for QEE for college. This penalty waiver does not apply to 401(k) or 403(b) plans.
- $ **Roth Key Feature:** Contributions to Roths may be withdrawn at any time with no taxes or 10% penalties. For example, if you contributed $60,000 over the years to a Roth that has grown to $150,000, and then you need some money for college expenses, you can withdraw the $60,000 you contributed tax- and penalty-free—and leave the $90,000 of earnings in the account.
- $ **401(k) Key Feature:** Many 401(k) plans allow borrowing from your account. This feature allows access to the money without incurring any

taxes or penalties. Then, instead of making new contributions to the 401(k), you could apply monthly payroll deductions to paying back the loan. By law, the maximum 401(k) loan amount is the lesser of $50,000 or 50% of your account balance. Also, generally, the loan must be paid back within five years, or taxes and a 10% penalty apply.

A strategy that could provide the most flexibility for the future would be diversifying contributions and having some money in a traditional IRA, Roth, and 401(k). This would allow you to carefully consider the circumstances at the time funds were needed for college to determine which account(s) it made the most sense to access.

Another consideration is that the federal financial aid form (FAFSA) does not require parents to list retirement accounts as an asset. In other words, retirement account balances do not negatively impact your chances of receiving financial aid, whereas 529 accounts of which the parent is the owner must be listed as an asset on the FAFSA application. Funds received by the student from any 529 plan must also be listed on the FAFSA application.

The possibility you won't need the funds for college at all is an important consideration. In that case, you obviously just leave the money in the respective retirement accounts growing for your retirement. Your children may receive scholarships or qualify for financial aid, they may not go to college, you may decide to get loans, or you may let the child pay their college expenses. Also, a number of our elected officials have promoted the idea of having free college for all.

529 EDUCATION SAVINGS PLAN HIGHLIGHTS

$ No tax deduction for contributions to the 529 account.

$ Earnings accumulate without being taxed.

$ Distributions are tax free if used for qualified educational expenses (QEEs).

$ Can be used for K-12 tuition up to $10,000 per year.

$ Can be used for college and post-graduate QEEs.

$ Schools can be public, private, or religious-based.

$ Postsecondary (college) schools must be on the U.S. Department of Education's DAPIP list.

$ Anyone can establish a 529 for a designated beneficiary.

$ The beneficiary (student) can be changed at the account owner's discretion.

$ There is no limit on the amount of contributions.

$ Contributions are not allowed if the beneficiary's account balances exceed a designated level.

$ Federal law treats contributions to a 529 as a gift to the beneficiary; therefore, contributors should be mindful of gift tax considerations.

$ Most plans offer an array of mutual funds to invest in.

$ Non-qualified withdrawals are subject to taxation on the earnings.

$ Non-qualified withdrawals are also subject to a 10% penalty. The penalty is not imposed for certain exceptions.

$ Having a 529 could negatively impact eligibility for financial aid.

UNIFORM TRANSFERS TO MINORS ACT (UTMA)

Almost every state has passed a statute referred to as the Uniform Transfers to Minors Act (UTMA). The general purpose of a UTMA law is to provide rules and structure for how an adult (the custodian) can act as the fiduciary to control and manage assets owned by a minor under the age of 21. Even though age 18 is considered an adult in most legal settings, for purposes of UTMA laws, 21 is the age most states use.

Practically speaking, UTMA accounts are most often established by parents or grandparents who act as the custodian to gift money to a child as a nest egg to build for the child's future needs. UTMAs are also a convenient way to invest money a child has saved up or earned from a job.

A UTMA account is a simple and effective way to invest relatively small amounts of money that belong to a minor. There are several considerations that often make it unattractive to gift large amounts of money to be placed in a UTMA account. In my opinion, there are generally more potential negatives than positives to putting more than about $20,000 in UTMAs for any one child (more on that below).

Eligibility

There are no eligibility rules to having a UTMA account other than there must be one adult age 21 or older who is listed as the custodian of the account, and there is one minor who is under the age of 21 who is the beneficiary (owner) of the account.

Ownership and Registration

When assets are transferred to a minor via a UTMA account, it is an irrevocable gift; the money belongs to the minor. The typical titling of a UTMA account would be "Kurt Reid as custodian for Morgan Reid, under the North Carolina Uniform Transfers to Minors Act," which is usually abbreviated by the financial institution to "Kurt Reid cust. for Morgan Reid, NCUTMA."

Although there may only be one custodian and one minor per account, there could be multiple accounts for the same minor (for example, Mom is the custodian on one account, and Grandpa is custodian for another account for the same minor). Also, one person could provide the funds (Grandma) and another person could be the custodian (Mom).

Custodian Responsibility

The custodian has the legal responsibility to act as the fiduciary to manage the funds in the best interest of the minor. Those duties include how to invest and manage the assets, as well as when and how to distribute assets for the benefit of the minor.

Investment Options

UTMA accounts can be established at virtually any financial institution, including banks, credit unions, investment brokers, and mutual fund companies. The earnings of the account are obviously determined by how the assets are invested.

Tax Treatment

There is no tax deduction for gifting to a minor or adding to a UTMA account. However, to ensure people don't use UTMAs or other accounts as a scheme to dodge taxes, the federal government has enacted the often bemoaned so-called *kiddie tax* on unearned income.

The kiddie tax doesn't apply to the child's *earned* income (wages); it only applies to *unearned* income, such as interest income, dividends, and capital gains. For 2022, the kiddie tax generally applies to dependent children under age 19, or up to age 23 if a full-time student (with some other exceptions). The first $1,150 per year of unearned income is tax free, and the next $1,150 is taxed at the child's tax rate. Unearned income by the child in excess of $2,300 is taxed at the marginal tax rate of the parent of the child; hence, the term kiddie tax.

The kiddie tax is one of the reasons why it may not be advisable to put much more than about $20,000 into UTMA accounts for any one child. In essence, large amounts of money in a UTMA are likely to produce earnings in excess of $2,300 per year and will therefore be taxed at the parent's tax bracket, meaning there is likely no income tax incentive to make large transfers. However, some high-net-worth individuals may still choose to do so for estate planning purposes.

Contribution Limits and Gift Tax Consideration

There are no legal limits on how much may be given to a minor or placed in a UTMA account. However, as of 2022, gifts from one person to another in excess of $16,000 a year are subject to gift tax laws. Gifting more than $16,000 doesn't necessarily mean any gift taxes will be due, but a gift tax return would be required. Consult with a competent tax professional.

Transfer of Control to the Child

When the minor reaches age 21, the UTMA account should be transferred into the child's name as the sole owner. There are no tax consequences for changing the title, and the investments do not have to be liquidated, but legally, the child is then in control of the account.

UTMA laws are on a state-by-state basis. For the vast majority of states, the age of majority is 21, but in Florida, for example, the account can be set up to stipulate that the custodian can maintain control until the child is 25. Also, Uniform Gifts to Minors Act (UGMA) laws were common prior to the UTMA laws, and the age of majority for UGMA accounts was generally 18.

Impact on College Financial Aid

When completing the federal financial aid form (FAFSA) for potential college aid, UTMA account balances must be listed as an asset. The more money in a UTMA, the more it could negatively impact the chances of receiving financial aid.

Babies Grow Up

It's natural for parents and grandparents to believe their children will grow up to be good decision-makers and handle money in a wise and prudent manner. Somebody else's child will be the train wreck, not theirs. But remember, when the child reaches majority age (21), any money in their UTMA belongs to them. Unless there is some type of court order or ongoing guardianship in place, the child will have full legal access and control to do what they please with the account.

At the beginning of the UTMA section, I stated that it may be unadvisable to have more than $20,000 or so in UTMAs for a child. The following are the three primary reasons for that view:

1. Due to the kiddie tax, there is generally no tax benefit in having amounts in UTMA accounts that will produce more than $2,300 in annual earnings, since the excess will be taxed at the parent's marginal tax bracket rate.

2. Large balances in UTMAs could reduce the amount of college financial aid.

3. At age 21, the child is entitled to legal control of the account. Since nobody knows what a child's decision-making capacity will be at that time, there is an inherent risk in having large sums in UTMA accounts.

529s Rather than UTMAs to Save for College

If the primary purpose is to establish an account to accumulate funds to pay for future college expenses, a 529 education savings plan account may be a better option than a UTMA account. As discussed in detail in the previous section, a 529 offers the following advantages as compared to a UTMA for a college savings account: tax-free earnings accumulation and tax-free withdrawals for education expenses; the account is not owned by the child, and there is never a point when the child is legally entitled to the money; and the account beneficiary can be changed to another child at the fiduciary's discretion.

A UTMA is certainly the appropriate choice instead of a 529 when the money is already the property of the child, the child earned it by working, or it is money that was given to the child. A UTMA is also a good option vs. a 529 for smaller amounts in which the potential kiddie tax is not an issue, or when the money may be used for the child's benefit for expenses other than education.

Estate Planning and Wealth Transfer

Individuals with a high net worth often have a desire to transfer money to their children or grandchildren for estate planning purposes. Specialized trust accounts, rather than UTMAs, are generally more appropriate for such individuals.

Ideal UTMA Scenarios

Here are a few situations ideal for utilizing UTMA accounts.

- $ **The Child Earned the Money:** UTMAs are logical when the child made money from a job, since the money already belongs to them. Putting the money in a UTMA account in their name can have several positive impacts, such as encouraging them to save more as they see the account grow, learning about the financial world of making deposits and account statements, taking pride in the personal ownership and accumulation, safety and retention of the money, and many others.
- $ **Seasonal Gifts from Family:** Some family members may like the idea of being able to donate into a dedicated UTMA account for a child for future needs rather than giving cash for birthdays or holidays.
- $ **Earmarked for Specific Expenses:** UTMAs are a convenient way for a child to accumulate money over time for a major expense in the future for which they will be responsible, such as their first car or a new phone. Parents may provide an incentive for the child to save by making matching deposits to the child's UTMA account.
- $ **Learning Tool:** A UTMA account can be an excellent way for a child to learn about investing from a legitimate ownership perspective. For example, if a child's UTMA account is invested in an equity mutual fund, the child can learn about the stock market by reviewing the mutual fund's quarterly report (Mom and Dad may learn too). They will be able to see exactly which companies they own stock in and how much they earned in dividends and capital gains on those holdings. A child could further develop their math skills by calculating precisely how much of their money is in each different stock—"Wow, Dad. I own $6.71 worth of Amazon, and $3.09 of Apple!"

ANNUITIES

An annuity is an investment contract with an insurance company often purchased with the objective of providing a guaranteed income for life during retirement. Investors also use annuities in a more traditional investment sense as a long-term wealth-building option, whereby earnings accumulate on a tax-deferred basis until withdrawals are made years later.

With trillions of dollars invested in annuities, they have had wide appeal over the decades. Since there are numerous contractual differences from one annuity to the next, it is important to fully understand the applicable features and terms before purchasing or investing in any particular annuity.

Simply stated, annuities are not all created equal. Once purchased, the terms are often irrevocable. Due to these reasons and others, it is important to receive competent advice to ensure a particular annuity is a good choice in light of your personal circumstances and that you properly understand the key terms and features before purchasing.

TAX TERMINOLOGY

Tax free, tax credit, pre-tax, after-tax, tax this, tax that, tax what? Okay, here's what all those tax terms mean.

Tax Bracket: When reference is made to being in a high or low *tax bracket*, it refers to the percentage of your last taxable dollar of income that you paid in income taxes. Federal taxes have *progressive* brackets, meaning the percentage paid in taxes gradually rises as you reach certain income thresholds. The higher tax rate is only paid on the next dollars earned above each threshold. In accounting vernacular, it is called your *marginal tax bracket*, meaning what rate you paid on your last/highest dollar earned.

For example, for 2022, the highest personal tax bracket is 37%. For joint tax returns, the 37% threshold is reached at $647,850 of taxable income. For all ordinary taxable income over $647,850, tax is paid at a 37% rate. But the income earned below $647,850 is taxed at lower rates for each threshold level. There are currently seven personal tax brackets: 10%, 12%, 22%, 24%, 32%, 35%, and 37%. Everyone pays the same tax rate of 10% on all income up to the first threshold. Everyone pays tax at the rate of 12% up to the next threshold, and so on.

Pre-Tax: If an employee has $100 withheld from their paycheck and contributed to their FSA or 401(k) plan, no income tax is withheld or payable on the $100. Hence, the $100 contribution is pre-tax.

After-Tax (Post-Tax): An after-tax investment means you didn't get any tax benefit from making the investment, and there is no reduction in your taxable income or your taxes paid due to the investment. Roth contributions are made with *after-tax* money. For example, if you invest $6,000 in a Roth, there is no tax deduction for the contribution.

Tax Deductible: This term is frequently misunderstood. Tax deductible means a reduction to your taxable income, not to your tax owed. For example, if you made a tax-deductible contribution of $1,000 to an IRA, your taxable income is reduced by $1,000 when you file your tax return. If you are in a 22% marginal tax bracket, you would save $220 in income taxes from making a $1,000 tax-deductible contribution. Pre-tax and tax deductible result in the same tax liability, but they get there differently.

Tax Credit: A tax *credit* means a dollar-for-dollar reduction in the amount of tax owed. A credit is substantially more valuable than a deduction. For example, a $1,000 credit means your tax owed is reduced by $1,000, or your refund is increased by $1,000, whereas a deduction of $1,000 would save at most $370 for someone in the highest marginal tax bracket of 37%. There are numerous tax credits available, such as the earned income tax credit, lifetime learning credit, child and dependent care credit, solar investment tax credit, and others.

Tax Free (Tax Exempt): You do not have to pay income taxes on the receipt of the money. Interest earned on municipal bonds is tax free or exempt from taxation. Distributions from Roth accounts are tax free as long as certain conditions are met.

Tax Deferred: Earnings on various accounts are tax deferred, meaning that until a distribution is made from the account, earnings are not taxed. A tax-deferred investment means you pay taxes on earnings in the future rather than paying now. The benefit of tax deferred is that you can earn money on the money that you would have paid in taxes. It's sort of like using an interest-free loan to make money.

Tax Advantaged (Tax Favored or Tax Preferred): The descriptors *advantaged*, *favored*, and *preferred* are not unique to any one specific tax benefit. They are just non-specific adjectives to indicate you benefit in some fashion from a tax perspective. Tax free, tax deductible, tax credit, etc., are all examples of various tax advantages.

Capital Gains Tax: A gain from the sale of assets, such as stocks or real estate is a *capital gain*. If the asset was held for longer than one year, taxes are computed using capital gains tax rates, which are lower than normal income tax rates. For 2022, there are only three capital gains tax rates: 0%, 15%, and 20%. Someone in the maximum ordinary income tax bracket of 37% would pay a maximum of 20% in tax on any capital gains from the sale of assets held longer than one year. Gains on assets held for one year or less are considered short-term capital gains and are taxed based on ordinary income tax brackets.

Fully Taxable: Fully taxable means the income is taxed as ordinary income per the published tax rates, meaning capital gains tax rates don't apply, and there is no deductibility or exemption from tax.

Tax Shelter: The term *tax shelter* often has a negative stigma from a bygone era. Various types of tax shelters were popular investments for high-income earners in the mid-1980s and prior. Before 1981, the top marginal ordinary income tax rate was a staggering 70%. Tax laws also allowed for many creative investments in that era that were designed to *shelter* an investor's income in some pretty extraordinary and creative ways. It was not uncommon for investors in certain types of investment partnerships to be able to take income tax deductions that exceeded the amount of money they invested. The Tax Reform Act of 1986 changed all that, and many of these tax shelters ended badly for the investors.

In more recent years, tax shelter has taken on a much more positive connotation, as it generally alludes to any investment that allows the sheltering of income or investment earnings from taxation, such as IRAs, Roths, and 401(k)s.

Tack's Shelter: This is a tiny wooden shelter in which thumbtacks can hide to stay dry when it rains. I know, that's a really bad dad joke, but hey, I'm just trying to lighten the mood a little bit here.

Tax Avoidance: Tax avoidance means using legal means to avoid paying taxes. To take advantage of tax laws to reduce taxes, such as investing in tax-advantaged retirement accounts or tax-exempt bonds.

Tax Evasion: Tax evasion means using illegal methods to deliberately not pay taxes that are due. To conceal, falsify, or hide income or information from the taxing authorities. Intentionally not reporting earnings or wages that were paid in cash is a common form of tax evasion.

Using legal ways to *avoid* taxes may result in years of financial freedom.

Using illegal ways to *evade* taxes may result in years of no freedom.
Be an avoider, not an evader.

SUMMARY

Health savings accounts (HSAs) and flexible spending accounts (FSAs) are the two most widely used tax-advantaged accounts designed to pay qualified medical expenses (QMEs). The tax benefits of these two accounts are hands down the best of any tax-advantaged accounts. Like a traditional IRA, their contributions are tax deductible, **and** like a Roth, distributions are tax free when used for QMEs. It borderlines on being too good to be true.

A key difference between an FSA and an HSA is that FSA contributions must be spent each year, whereas HSA contributions can remain in the account indefinitely and be used at the owner's discretion in later years for QMEs.

Most HSA providers now allow account balances to be invested in mutual funds. If someone doesn't incur QMEs or simply decides not to use their HSA to pay for QMEs, their HSA could grow tax free to a sizable amount. After age 65, funds can be withdrawn penalty free for non-QME purposes, and the distribution would simply become taxable income. In effect, an HSA can be the equivalent of another IRA account—contributions are tax deductible and taxes are paid when a non-QME distribution is made.

For 529 education savings plans, there is no deduction for contributions, earnings grow without taxation, and distributions are tax free if used for qualified education expenses (QEEs). For parents who are contributing the maximum to their tax-advantaged retirement accounts and have additional funds to invest, 529s may be a great option. However, many middle-class families find it more appealing to invest in some combination of an IRA, a Roth, or a 401(k) for the most flexibility with the dual considerations of retirement savings and potential college costs for children.

Uniform Transfers to Minors Act (UTMA) accounts are often a good choice for relatively small amounts belonging to a minor child from work or gifts. When the child reaches age 21, they have the legal rights to the money.

CHAPTER 16

Bonds

B onds, which are commonly referred to as *fixed income*, are loans or indebt-edness. They have a stated maturity date, which is when the bond issuer (borrower) is obligated to pay back the face amount to the bond owner (lender). Most bonds have a fixed interest rate that does not change for the life of the bond, and interest payments are typically made every six months.

For example, assume a company needs capital to expand their business, so they sell $100 million of bonds to investors with a 10-year maturity and a 5% fixed annual interest rate, and the bonds can be purchased in $10,000 increments. If an investor purchased a $10,000 bond, they would receive $250 in interest every six months, and in 10 years, the company would repay the $10,000 to the bondholder.

Similar to the way stocks can be bought and sold on the secondary market, the bondholder could sell the bond prior to the maturity date, and the price they receive could be more or less than the $10,000 they originally paid. A subse-quent purchaser of the bond would continue to receive the same $250 interest payments every six months and receive the $10,000 at maturity, regardless of what price they may have paid for the bond.

INTEREST RATE RISK

Many retail investors (individuals) don't fully understand interest rate risk. Some people have the overly simplistic perception that, "stocks are risky and okay for young people, while bonds are safe, and therefore I should allocate more money to bonds as I near retirement age."

In my years as a broker, interest rate risk was one of the most difficult concepts for many clients to grasp. A bond default (bankruptcy), when it occurs, is the ultimate calamity for a bond owner. However, the percentage of bonds that actually default is very small. Interest rate risk, on the other hand, is not nearly as catastrophic as default, but it occurs for 100% of the bonds issued. Default would be the equivalent of the risk of being struck by lightning, while interest rate risk is the equivalent of daily changes in the weather.

Assuming the issuer's credit quality (default risk) has not changed, fluctuation in market interest rates is the primary factor causing the price (value) of fixed-rate bonds to move up or down. Bond prices have an inverse correlation with market interest rates, meaning when market interest rates rise, the value of existing bonds will decline.

For example, if a bond with a $10,000 face amount has 10 years until maturity and has a fixed rate of 5%, it will pay $500 per year to the bondholder. If current market interest rates for similar quality 10-year bonds had gone down to 4%, then new bonds being issued would only pay $400 per year in interest, therefore investors would find the 5% bond more appealing because it would pay them $100 more interest per year for the next 10 years. Hence, the market price of the 5% would increase, and the bondholder could sell at a *premium* (sell for more than the face amount of $10,000).

In this scenario, the 5% bond would trade somewhere around a price of 108 in the secondary market, which is 108% of the face, or $10,800. A buyer of the 5% bond at a price of 108 would receive $1,000 more in interest than the 4% bond would pay, but the holder would only receive $10,000 at maturity, even though they paid $10,800 for it in the secondary market. If the original bondholder keeps the bond until maturity, the gyrations in market price in which they *could have* sold at previously are irrelevant—they will get back exactly $10,000 at maturity regardless of the price fluctuation over the 10 years.

Conversely, if market rates for similar quality 10-year fixed-rate bonds had risen to 6%, then the 5% bond would be priced close to 92.5 ($9,250) because investors could receive $100 more interest per year by buying a new 6% bond. So in this instance, the buyer at $9,250 would not only get the $500 interest per year, but they would also make a $750 profit when they receive the $10,000 face amount at maturity, which would make their average annual return about 6%. The impact of bond prices fluctuating based on current market interest rates is that the effective yield is close to the same for all bonds with similar terms and quality.

HISTORICALLY LOW INTEREST RATES—THE LURKING DANGER OF OWNING BONDS

Interest rates peaked just over 40 years ago in October 1981 with the 30-year US Treasury bond yield reaching an all-time high of 15.21% and the 10-year US Treasury reaching 15.84%. As of the time of this writing in March 2022, the 30-year Treasury is yielding 2.46%, and the 10-year is yielding 2.19%. In other words, we have experienced an enormous and unprecedented, enduring decline in interest rates. This is enormous from both the perspective of time (40-year downtrend) and the amount of the change from the all-time high reached in 1981, to the low interest rate levels we are now experiencing.

There has been plenty of volatility in interest rates over that 40-year period in which rates temporarily moved up and down, but the long-term direction of rates has been an ongoing downtrend. Forty years ago, rates were at their all-time highs, and today rates hover near their all-time lows. We have literally gone from one extreme to the other during the last 40 years.

An owner of a 10-year Treasury today (March 2022) with a 2.19% interest rate would receive $219 per year in interest from a $10,000 bond. At the peak of interest rates in 1981 when the 10-year bond yield was 15.84%, the owner of a $10,000 bond would have received $1,584 per year in interest.

With interest rates currently near all-time lows, bonds have lost considerable appeal for investors seeking income.

The extremely low level of current interest rates presents two problems/ risks for bond investors. First, over the last four decades, the bond investor has seen their interest income steadily decline, while also experiencing a continual increase in the cost of living (inflation). The second problem for bond investors is the potential decline in the price of their bonds if or when interest rates rise. As described above, when interest rates increase, bond prices fall. With rates near their all-time lows, it is quite possible interest rates may eventually move significantly higher.

Many current investors have never personally experienced a prolonged period of rising interest rates and, therefore, have never endured a significant period of declining bond prices. With rates currently at unprecedented low levels, I think there is far more risk in owning bonds than what many retail investors understand.

From a risk vs. reward perspective, the dynamics have changed considerably in terms of owning bonds as a safe and conservative way to earn income and preserve capital. Clearly, the appeal of bonds to earn income has greatly diminished over the last 40 years, while at the same time, the risk is much greater of bond prices declining substantially in value due to an eventual increase in interest rates. Currently (March 2022), I find owning fixed-rate, long-term bonds less appealing than at any other time in my adult life.

One way many investors who are close to retirement may unwittingly be accepting substantially more risk than they are aware of is opting for so-called *target-date* funds in their 401(k) plans or in other retirement accounts. Target-date funds typically allocate an increasingly larger percentage to bonds, and a lesser percentage to stocks as the *target date* of the fund nears.

It is important for investors to understand if interest rates
rise, the market value of existing fixed-rate bonds will decline.
The more rates increase, the more bond prices fall.

THE FOUR MOST COMMON TYPES OF BONDS

United States Government Obligations

These are bonds issued by the US Treasury and other federal entities. For
the convenience of terms, the primary debt instruments issued by the US
Treasury are divided into three categories, and the letter T is used to indicate the
debt is issued by the Treasury. (1) T-bills have the shortest term of one year or
less, (2) T-notes are as long as 10 years, (3) and T-bonds are as long as 30 years.
Interest earned on Treasuries is exempt from state income taxes but is fully
taxable at the federal level. US Treasury obligations have long been considered
to be the safest debt obligations in the world in terms of timely payment of
interest and principal when due.

Various debt instruments issued by the Treasury may be purchased on
the Treasury Department's website, treasurydirect.gov. The website provides
a description of the various debt instruments available for direct purchase,
along with helpful videos. Individuals can set up a personal account on the
website and transfer funds electronically to make purchases. There are no fees
or commissions to invest directly on their website.

In addition to offering the aforementioned bills, notes, and bonds on their
website, investors may also purchase *floating-rate notes* (FRNs), *series I savings
bonds, series EE savings bonds, series HH savings bonds*, and *Treasury Inflation-
Protected Securities* (TIPS). All of those instruments are explained on the trea-
surydirect.gov website.

The series I bonds became dramatically more appealing in late 2021 when
inflation surged. The "I" in I bond stands for inflation. The interest rate on I
bonds is adjusted every six months in May and November based on the inflation

rate. The new interest rate for I bonds purchased from November 2021 through April 2022 was 7.12%, which is a substantially higher rate than what other government bonds and most corporate bonds were paying.

Series I bonds have a number of unique features, including the following:

- $ Interest can be tax deferred until the bond is redeemed—in effect, they are like a nondeductible IRA or a tax-deferred annuity.
- $ Interest is exempt from state income taxes (even when the bond is redeemed).
- $ The interest is compounded semiannually.
- $ A bond may not be redeemed until one year after purchase.
- $ If a bond is redeemed within five years of purchase, three months of interest is forfeited.
- $ I bonds may be held for as long as 30 years.
- $ The principal value never fluctuates.
- $ Purchases are limited to $10,000 per calendar year per individual.
- $ They are not available for IRAs or other retirement accounts.
- $ The interest rate earned is the sum of a fixed rate and the inflation rate. The fixed rate is set at the time the bond is purchased and remains constant for the life of the bond. The inflation portion of the interest rate is adjusted every six months. Historical I bond rates and the rate formula are detailed on the Treasury's website.

The interest rate on US government series I bonds jumped to 7.12% in November 2021 due to surging inflation—immediately making I bonds very appealing to risk-averse investors.

Municipal Bonds

These bonds are commonly referred to as munis or tax-free bonds because the interest earned is exempt from federal income taxes. Common issuers of municipal bonds are states, cities, counties, and nonprofit entities, such as hospitals, schools, and housing authorities. Munis typically pay interest to the bondholder every six months and often have maturities as long as 30 years.

The logic behind munis being exempt from federal tax is to reduce the interest cost for the nonprofit issuer because bond investors will accept a lower interest rate for the benefit of not being taxed on that interest. Interest is also generally exempt from state income taxes when the investor resides in the same state as the bond issuer. For example, if a North Carolina resident owns a muni from an issuer in North Carolina, the interest would be exempt from state income tax as well as federal income tax. The financial strength of the issuer and hence, the bond rating should be a major consideration for an investor when selecting a bond to purchase. Bond ratings and default risk are discussed later in this chapter.

Corporate Bonds

As the name implies, these are bonds issued by corporations (businesses). Corporations issue stocks and/or bonds when they need additional capital to operate or grow. When a bond is backed purely by the general credit of the corporation, it is called a debenture. Alternatively, corporate bonds may have specific corporate assets backing the bond, which is the case with collateralized debt obligations (CDOs). CDOs are one type of asset-backed security (ABS).

An example of an ABS would be if a company was in the business of making auto loans, they might package 1,000 auto loans as the collateral for an ABS. The only collateral and sole source of revenue to make the interest and principal payments to the ABS investors are the payments received on those specific 1,000 auto loans.

As is the case with muni bonds, it is important for corporate bond investors to have a comprehensive understanding of the credit quality of the issuing company or the underlying collateral backing the bond. There can be wide variation among different bonds in terms of safety and default risk.

Convertible bonds are a unique type of corporate bond. No, they are not bonds to finance cars that have removable tops! They are corporate bonds that can be exchanged (converted) into a specific number of shares of the issuer's stock at the bondholder's discretion. The benefit for the company is investors will accept a lower rate of interest on the bond for the upside opportunity on the stock. Likewise, investors may benefit if the stock price increases enough, so it is possible to convert the bond for the predetermined number of shares of stock, and then sell the stock for more than they paid for the bond.

Mortgage Bonds

The term mortgage means the title to a property (most commonly a home) is held as collateral until the loan against the property is paid in full. Many institutions offering mortgage loans are primarily or entirely in the business of originating mortgage loans rather than holding them long term. Those companies are merely conduits feeding (selling) newly originated mortgages into the mortgage-backed securities (MBS) market, or the collateralized mortgage obligation (CMO) market. The home loans are then packaged in bulk into MBS or CMO bonds and sold to investors. It is a huge market, amounting to trillions of dollars in size, that provides great liquidity for the system.

The first MBS bonds originated when the federal government formed the Government National Mortgage Association (GNMA), popularly known as Ginnie Mae in 1968. Since the founding of Ginnie Mae, numerous other mortgage-facilitating entities have been formed. Over the years, secondary market participants have been creative in developing clever and ingenious ways to convert simple home loans into securitized investments. These bonds can have complex structures when they have been repackaged and ultimately sold to investors.

ADDITIONAL BOND CHARACTERISTICS AND CONSIDERATIONS

Bond Denominations

Bonds are generally sold in increments of no less than $1,000 face value. Municipal bonds are usually sold in $5,000 increments. On the stated maturity date, the bond issuer (the company, municipality, etc.) is obligated to pay the bond owner (the investor) the stated face value of the bond.

Fixed Rate

Traditionally, most bonds have a fixed interest rate for the life of the bond. For example, a $10,000 bond with a fixed rate of 5% would pay the bondholder exactly $500 per year in interest until maturity. However, there are some bonds that carry a floating rate that may change periodically based on some prescribed index or formula.

Interest Payments

Municipal and Treasury bonds generally pay interest to the bondholders every six months. Corporate bonds generally pay interest every three or six months. Mortgage bonds generally pay interest monthly because the underlying home mortgages are paid monthly. *Zero-coupon* bonds pay all the interest at maturity.

Principal Payments

The principal amount (the face value) is generally repaid in one lump sum on the maturity date. Mortgage bonds are an exception to that since they are collateralized by home loans. As the homeowners pay back principal each month on their amortized home mortgages, those payments are in turn paid to the bondholders.

Default Risk

Default occurs when the bond issuer fails to make a timely payment of interest or principal when due. The risk of default is a consideration for all bond types. Bonds backed by the United States Government have never defaulted; however, many corporations have defaulted over the years, as well as municipal bond issuers and non-government-backed mortgage bonds. When default occurs, bondholders could experience a total loss in the worst-case scenario, or they could ultimately receive everything that was due to them in the best case. However, quite often, bondholders receive something in between those two extremes in the form of a partial payment. Many factors come into play during legal proceedings following a default that impact the ultimate payout to bondholders.

Bond Ratings

There are several independent companies that rate bonds in terms of their risk of default. Such ratings can be of great assistance to bond investors to assess the safety of a particular bond. S&P, Moody's, and Fitch are the most well-known rating agencies.

S&P has 10 different bond ratings as follows: AAA, AA, A, BBB, BB, B, CCC, CC, C, and D. AAA is the highest rating and therefore considered the least likely to default. Each successive rating level is considered incrementally more likely to default. Few corporate bonds receive a AAA rating. Bonds rated D have already defaulted. Bonds rated BBB and higher are referred to as *investment grade* (unlikely to default), while bonds in the next lowest category of BB are often referred to as *junk bonds* or *high-yield bonds*. As the issuer's financial condition changes over the life of the bond, the bond's rating may change. For example, many mortgage bonds eventually defaulted that were initially rated AAA in the period just before the collapse of the housing market in 2008.

Liquidity (Ability to Sell)

Retail investors are sometimes scared away from bond investing because bonds are often issued with maturities of 10, 20, or 30 years. A common retort I routinely received from clients when I was a broker relative to long-term bonds was, "30 years! I'll be dead before then! I can't tie my money up for that long!" Although clients seemed to understand bonds can be sold prior to maturity, the fact the bond had a maturity of 30 years in the future was unsettling to some. I would point out they owned a home and held stocks that never "mature." Like stocks, bonds can be sold in the secondary market at any time. The stated maturity is simply the longest you can own it; absent default, you'll get your money back at maturity whether you want it back or not.

Bond Pricing

Whereas stock shares are quoted and sold in dollars per share, bonds are quoted as a percentage of face value. Generally, bonds are sold for face value when issued, meaning a $10,000 bond priced at 100 (100%) would cost $10,000. Like all marketable securities, the price of bonds in the secondary market can fluctuate up and down. For example, if a bond with a face value of $10,000 traded at 95, it would cost $9,500.

Call Risk

Call risk doesn't mean the chances you will receive a robocall for a condo vacation package because you bought a bond. *Callable* means the issuer can pay off the bondholder prior to the stated maturity at the issuer's discretion. Hence, they can call the bond away from you. A premium of 3% or so must commonly be paid to the bondholder if the issuer calls the bond prior to maturity. Issuers are most likely to call a bond when interest rates have declined, as they are able to sell new bonds at a lower annual interest cost to the issuer. Corporate and municipal bonds often have call features, whereas Treasury bonds do not.

Inflation Risk

Bonds generally pay the same amount back at maturity as what was paid for the bond when issued. If the cost of living increases (inflation) during the holding period of a bond, the investor has lost purchasing power. Unlike bonds, some investments tend to appreciate in value when there is inflation. Inflation is the silent killer of true wealth.

SUMMARY

Bonds have traditionally been appealing to low-risk investors who want income. With interest rates now near their all-time lows, bonds have lost much of their appeal. Besides producing less income than they once did, fixed-rate bonds also have the risk of a decline in their principal value if interest rates rise. However, if a bond is held until its maturity date, the bondholder will receive the stated face value regardless of interest levels.

Bonds are issued by various entities, including corporations, state and local government authorities, the United States government and its agencies, as well as mortgage bonds that are collateralized by home mortgages. Bondholders typically receive the interest payments at least semiannually, and bonds can be sold prior to maturity in the secondary market. If a bond is sold prior to maturity, it could be at a premium or at a discount to its face value. Although a very small percentage of bonds default, investors should be aware of the credit quality of the issuer. Most bonds are rated by independent agencies, with the ratings indicating the perceived level of risk a bond may default.

DISCO BOND HUMOR

In 1984, I was a fledgling young stockbroker and still learning the industry terminology. On a phone call with Bob Sheets, the broker who trained me in Muscatine, Iowa, I asked what investments he liked currently that might be good for me to present to potential clients. The conversation went like this:

Bob: "I've been selling a lot of *disco* bonds lately. Check out the discos in inventory."

Kurt: "Disco bonds? Really? I didn't know they were still building discotheques."

Bob: (with an amused laugh) "No, no, Kurt. Discounted bonds. Bonds selling at a discount. No, we are not underwriting any bonds for discotheques."

I certainly understood all about discounted bonds, but I was so new in the business I had never heard them referred to as disco bonds before. Considering my poor dancing skills, I was very relieved to know my employer wasn't promoting discotheques.

THE OWEN REID STORY

Travel the world and stay involved with baseball—those were the two primary goals of my nephew, Owen Reid, when he graduated from college in 2009. Since his tee-ball years, Owen had been an outstanding baseball player, and the game was his passion.

At age 15, Owen's talents earned him a spot on an elite showcase team, which entailed a summer of travel throughout the Midwest. This is when he first became hooked on the cocktail of constant travel and baseball.

The norm that summer and in the following years was a 150-mile drive from his home to catch the team bus in St. Louis each Thursday morning, followed by an all-day bus ride to Texas, Arkansas, Oklahoma, or Nebraska to play games against other elite teams on college campuses Friday through Sunday, then arrive home on Monday and repeat the process again on Thursday.

After playing baseball in college and graduating from Winthrop University, Owen was at a crossroads. The timeline of maturing into adulthood and getting a *real job* had arrived, but his heart yearned for more travel and more baseball. Following his dream, Owen spent the summer after graduation as a player/coach for an adult league in Vienna, Austria. Thirteen years later in 2022, Owen is a full-time, self-employed international baseball consultant and instructor living in Singapore. Over the years, baseball has allowed Owen to make a comfortable living and has taken him to over 50 countries on five continents. During one baseball stint in Australia, he met his future bride.

His journey around the globe with baseball didn't happen by random chance. It occurred because of his deliberate actions. He did a great job connecting and networking with people worldwide in pursuit of opportunities related to baseball. Just as important, Owen also does a great job providing customer satisfaction in his baseball endeavors. For example, he has been repeatedly engaged to return to Saudi Arabia to provide lessons and coach teams, and he has a stable base of young customers on multiple continents to whom he provides lessons by Zoom.

Owen's story is not about enormous wealth accumulation but rather an example of how it is possible to make a good living while doing what you love to do.

OWEN'S LESSON: There are amazing possibilities when you combine the dream of an unconventional career path with creativity and resourcefulness while also delivering excellent performance.

CHAPTER 17

Working with an Investment Professional ... or Not

The landscape for investing assistance can be a bit confusing. The services provided and related costs can vary substantially between different investment firms. Some investors may prefer having an account with a *discount broker* in which no advice is offered, and the customer enters their own trades via an internet portal. Others may prefer having an investment professional they can sit down with who provides personalized investment advice and enters all trades for them. The information in this chapter is aimed at helping readers decide what services and which type of company suits their needs the best.

BROAD OVERVIEW

Although they are still commonly referred to as *stockbrokers*, the modern brokerage industry does far more than just execute stock trades. Brokerage firms that are registered with the Securities and Exchange Commission (SEC) are officially called *broker-dealers*. Acting as *brokers*, they execute trades for their clients. When they trade for the firm's account, they're acting as *dealers*.

Brokerages are generally referred to as either *full-service* or *discount* brokers. Full-service usually means there is a designated person (your broker) assigned to your account, who acts as your advisor and executes your investment trades only after a verbal conversation between the two of you. Most full-service firms do not accept orders electronically (for example, email or text), nor do they allow customers to physically place their own trades. Conversely, customers of discount firms generally don't have a specific broker assigned to them, and most customers enter their own trades electronically via an internet portal or a phone app.

There are also investment firms called registered investment advisers (RIAs) who are not broker-dealers. From the customer's perspective, RIAs and full-service brokers may appear to be one and the same, as they both provide personalized investment advice and services. RIAs generally don't charge commissions but instead, charge a fee that is a percentage of the value of the customer's account. However, most full-service and discount brokers now offer fee-based accounts as well as traditional commission-based accounts.

There are also financial planners who may charge either hourly rates or a flat fee to develop a financial plan for you that may address investing as well as other areas, such as budgeting, insurance, estate planning, retirement planning, or tax planning. You may then need to go to some other firm of your choice to actually execute the plan. But some planners are also licensed to offer products (investments and insurance), and they will receive additional compensation for steering you into those products. Some planners may have credentials, such as the Certified Financial Planner designation for taking educational courses and passing exams.

Insurance companies and their agents also offer investment products such as annuities, mutual funds, and IRAs. Many banks have licensed brokers with offices onsite to whom the bank will refer customers who are interested in investment products.

A level of investing that is beyond the scope of this book is the domain of *accredited investors*, who are individuals with either a net worth of $1 million or a $200,000 annual income or they meet other requirements based on experience and knowledge. Accredited investors legally qualify to invest in more sophisticated investments, such as securities that have *not* been *registered* with the SEC. Conduits for such investments are commonly referred to as hedge funds, private equity, private placements, and venture capital.

Apology: For simplicity, I will commonly refer to the universe of brokers and other professionals who assist the public with investing as investment professionals (IPs). Many IPs prefer other titles. No offense is intended.

WHAT CAN AN INVESTMENT PROFESSIONAL (IP) DO FOR YOU?

Providing investment advice and investing your money are obvious reasons investors engage with an IP, but there could be (and should be) other ways to benefit from the relationship as well. The following are a few examples:

Source of Calming Wisdom

Some clients need this more than others. Besides actually advising clients how to invest money, perhaps the most important role an IP can play is to provide a calming and balanced perspective when markets are volatile. When investors are making hurried and irrational decisions because markets are declining and the news of the day is bleak is when an IP can be most valuable to some investors. Simply reminding them of why they invested in the first place can be a valuable service. The stock market is one of the few markets where everybody gets nervous when prices are reduced. Conversely, IPs can also serve as a voice of reason when a client is overly exuberant about the hot trend of the day.

Periodic Account Reviews

The client/IP relationship should include periodic account reviews to discuss portfolio performance and make any appropriate adjustments. Reviews are also a good time for the IP to be made aware of any potential life changes, such as pending retirement or major changes in finances.

Education and Research

IPs can be a great source of general knowledge via educational seminars, webinars, research reports, and regular emails with commentary about economic and market conditions from their corporate experts. Most IPs have access to research and analysis from multiple sources they can pass along to their clients. Virtually all investment companies have a lot of information available on their websites on a wide range of financial and investing topics.

Introduction to Other Professionals

By having a holistic understanding of a client's situation, a diligent IP can be in a pivotal position to refer you to other professionals to address issues outside the IP's professional realm. For example, making sure the client has a current will, discussing generalities of a power of attorney (POA) and a living will, pointing out when a client may need more sophisticated estate planning, making clients aware of potential insurance needs, and sometimes helping clients connect with the right accountant. Also, an IP should be willing to review a client's 401(k) or other employer plans to make sure there is a cohesive overall investment strategy.

"Stockbroker" was once the ubiquitous title for anyone that assisted the public with investing. Regulators officially call licensed brokers "registered representatives." However, just about every firm has their own unique title for their investment professionals, such as:

financial advisor — wealth advisor — wealth manager — account executive
financial consultant — investment consultant — wealth professional
investment advisor (with an o) — investment adviser (with an e)
investment adviser representative — investment representative
financial manager — financial planner

THE ADVENT AND MATURATION OF DISCOUNT BROKERS

May 1, 1975, is the date the ***discount*** brokerage industry was born. Prior to that time, all brokers had the same commission rates as set by the regulators. After deregulation occurred, the existing traditional firms that continued to provide personalized advice for their clients became known colloquially as *full-service* brokers. The numerous new firms that quickly opened became known as *discount brokers* because they charged dramatically lower fees. The new discount firms only took unsolicited orders from their customers, and therefore they didn't have to employ IPs to offer advice, provide personalized service, or meet with clients in person.

Today, the labels full-service and discount broker still exist, but much has changed over the last five decades. Aggressive competition caused commissions to be continually reduced over the years, finally resulting in virtually all of the discount brokers going to commission-free trading a few years ago. Full-service brokers still charge commissions for stock trades but generally at much lower levels than in previous decades.

One of the biggest impacts on the discount brokerage industry was the advent of the internet. Unlike the early days when discounters relied on phone conversations and the US Postal Service, today's discounters efficiently offer a wide array of financial products and services on their websites. Their customers can now enter their own trades on a PC or on their phone, and money generally flows to and from client accounts by next-day (or same-day) electronic transfer, rather than physical checks being mailed, which was previously the norm.

The obvious question is, how do discounters make money if they execute trades for free? The modern-day mega-sized discount broker looks nothing like the discounters of yore who existed for the sole purpose of executing trades. Today's firms have many sources of revenue, such as fees for managing their proprietary family of mutual funds, commissions for options trades, fees on managed accounts, profits from subsidiary banks they own, fees for administering retirement plans, fees for assorted other services they provide, and a major source of revenue is the spread between what they pay customers on their cash balances and what they earn by loaning or by investing those balances. In effect, commission-free trading is simply a loss leader to attract customers so they can profit in other ways from the relationship.

The entire brokerage industry has become more consolidated due to mergers over the years. The remaining large discount brokers include Fidelity Investments, Charles Schwab, Vanguard, Robinhood, TD Ameritrade (which is now a subsidiary of Schwab), and E-Trade (a subsidiary of Morgan Stanley). Some of the largest full-service firms include Wells Fargo Advisors, Edward Jones, Morgan Stanley, Merrill, JP Morgan, Raymond James Financial, RBC, and LPL Financial. There are also hundreds of smaller firms.

The modern brokerage industry offers a wide range of services. Investors can opt to make their own decisions and execute transactions via the internet, or they can work closely with a designated professional who provides personalized advice.

COMMISSION-BASED VS. FEE-BASED

Traditionally, brokers made a living by charging commissions when buy or sell transactions occurred, similar to the way real estate agents only get paid when a property is bought or sold. Back in the 1980s, brokerage firms started offering *wrap* accounts, so-called because the entire account was wrapped into one annualized fee, which was a percentage of the total account value rather than charging commissions on each transaction. Firms now generally prefer using the term fee-based account instead of a wrap account.

Over the last 30+ years, such fee-based accounts have steadily grown in popularity in the brokerage industry as opposed to the traditional commission-based model. Most brokers now offer both structures for clients to select from. Supporters of fee-based accounts are quick to point out that by eliminating commissions for each transaction, the broker and client's objectives are better aligned.

HOW DO FEE-BASED ACCOUNTS WORK?

Let's say you invest $100,000 into a fee-based account with an annualized fee of 1.20%. You and your IP talk and decide to invest the $100,000 in an assortment of different mutual funds, ETFs, and one stock you really want to own. No commissions are charged to make the initial investments, but, each month, 0.10% of the account value will be deducted for the fee (0.10% x 12 months = 1.20% annually). At any time, you can buy and sell assets in the account, and there are no transactional charges. You can move money in or out of the account at any time, and the monthly fee is automatically adjusted based on the account value.

Some fee-based accounts are limited to a large selection of mutual funds or accounts managed by third-party money managers. Most firms now offer fee-based accounts that allow customers to own any type of investment the firm would normally offer, such as individual stocks, bonds, and ETFs, as well as mutual funds.

Philosophically, I like the concept of a fee-based account. It removes any incentive for the IP to recommend trades just to generate fees, which is a practice referred to as *churning* and is a major taboo for IPs, similar to a doctor performing unnecessary surgeries. Fee-based accounts align the objective of the IP and the client very well in that the more the client's account increases in value, the more money the IP will make. Also, I like the concept of pay-as-you-go rather than a larger single fee upfront and/or a fee to get out. Pay-as-you-go can make it easier and less costly if you are unsatisfied and decide to change investment strategies or firms.

However, quite candidly, I think the current level of fees for fee-based accounts for the industry, in general, is somewhat high and will likely gradually come down in the future. Annual fees somewhere in the 1.0% to 1.5% range are now typical. The norm is to have a fee schedule with breakpoints where the fee declines as the account size increases, with the annual fee getting down to the 0.50% range for multi-million-dollar accounts. Although the company sets the standard fees, the IP often has the discretion to reduce the fee, or the IP has a range in which they can charge.

If the account is invested in mutual funds, then there is normally another layer of fees that the mutual fund managers receive for managing the fund.

Like all mutual funds, the fees charged by the fund managers often go unseen by the customer (fees are disclosed in the fund's prospectus) since those fees are deducted before earnings are reported. Adding both layers of fees together, the total cost can often approach or exceed 2% a year. Although there are many different structures of how brokers and RIAs charge fees and commissions, one thing neither of them are allowed to do is take a share of the profits from a client's account.

Fee-based accounts have steadily become more common over the last few decades where a percentage of the account value is charged rather than a commission for each transaction.

UPFRONT QUESTIONS TO ASK AN INVESTMENT PROFESSIONAL

Before getting hip surgery, I met with four surgeons and asked each one of them the same extensive list of questions I had prepared in advance. I selected my surgeon based on their answers as well as other research I conducted. Just like surgery, investing your money is a serious matter, and I would encourage investors to do some due diligence prior to selecting an IP. If an IP provides unsatisfactory answers to your questions or doesn't have time to answer them, I would look for someone else.

The following are some potential questions that might be good to ask before opening an account with an IP. Depending on the complexity and sophistication of your situation, some of these questions may not be relevant, and there may be other questions you need to ask based on your personal situation.

1. Minimum account size: Many brokers don't have an account minimum, while other firms require as much as $500,000 to open an account as they work exclusively with high net worth individuals. If you are below their account size minimum, then the rest of the questions are mute.

2. Professional history: How long have you been an IP? How many years have you been with your current company? How many other investment companies have you worked for? Why did you change firms? Did you graduate from college? Do you have other professional experience besides being an IP?
   a. Changing firms five times in 10 years is a warning sign. You can also see the IP's employment history in the industry at finra.org.
3. What products and services do you deal with the most?
   a. For example, do they only handle investments, or do they also sell insurance? Do they mainly sell mutual funds, or do they invest in individual stocks? If half of the IP's business is options trading and you are primarily interested in mutual funds, they may not be the IP for you.
4. What is your investment philosophy?
   a. How do they diversify and allocate assets? Do they take a long-term approach, or do they move money around frequently, looking for short-term trends and opportunities?
5. If the IP handles mutual funds, what mutual fund families do they invest in and why, and which specific funds within the family?
   a. Ask for literature on the fund family(s) the IP uses.
6. Ask about the office team. Will I deal with you exclusively for investing, or with others too? For administrative issues, who will I deal with, and how many assistants do you have?
   a. Some IPs work alone, and others have a team approach with multiple IPs working together.
7. What if I have an investment question/issue and you are on vacation? Are other members of your team licensed and able to execute orders?
8. What is your preferred method for communicating with me? Phone, in person, email, etc.?
   a. This question may give you some insights into the role of the IP's assistants as well.
9. How many active clients do you have?
   a. The point of this question is to gauge how much time they

reasonably have for each client relative to how much attention you need. 500 clients vs. 100 may be relevant to you.

10. How often should I typically expect to hear from you, and how often do you have account reviews?

11. What do you do in terms of providing ongoing education and investment information?

    a. Do they send a weekly email from their analysts, do they offer online tools and calculators, do they have periodic in-person seminars or webcasts, is there a database of research reports customers have access to, etc.?

12. What is your typical client's age and investment experience?

    a. The point of this question is to determine if you are a good fit with the IP's business mix.

13. Do you offer both commission-based accounts and fee-based accounts? Which does the IP prefer, and approximately what percentage of their customers are in each?

14. Explain what I pay and how you get paid.

    a. Cost of commission-based vs. fee-based, if they offer a choice. Are there other fees?

15. If they recommend fee-based accounts, explain how their accounts work in terms of investment options, the process for deciding on the specific investments and for making changes in the future, and fee details.

16. Are their fee-based accounts discretionary, where the IP or the managers makes changes without talking to the client, or does the client have to authorize each investment/trade (non-discretionary)?

17. Can you provide a published schedule of your firm's fees?

    a. Most brokers publish a schedule of their fee-based percentages.

18. Are the fees for fee-based accounts within a range set by your company in which you have the discretion to charge more or less within that range, or is the fee a fixed amount to which you must adhere?

    a. Sometimes the fee range can be quite large (for example, 1% to 3% per year).

Candidly, the more money you potentially have to invest, the more time and patience you will likely receive from most IPs. Depending on whether you have $500,000 vs. $5,000 to invest may impact the questions you decide to ask and what you consider acceptable responses.

Be aware that during the first meeting with a potential client, many IPs will focus more on gathering information to qualify you as a client rather than telling you about their business. They will be keenly interested in knowing your investment background, where your investments are currently, the value of your accounts, what you currently need to invest, whether you have an IRA or 401(k), where you work, etc.

Answers to some of your questions may organically get addressed during your conversation. However, it may be good to tell the IP at the start of the meeting that you are happy to provide information about yourself, but you also have a number of questions about their business you want answered. They may then prefer to address your list of questions first, which is fine.

The ultimate objective of asking all the questions during the initial meeting with an IP is simply to determine if this is the right company and if they are the right IP you should do business with. Is their investment philosophy and their business structure a good fit for you? Are you comfortable with their answers to your questions, and are you comfortable with them as an IP?

Finally, don't feel pressured to make a decision at the first meeting. It's probably best to sleep on the information that was provided. Additional questions may come to mind the next day that warrant a follow-up conversation or meeting. Selecting an IP should be an important issue in your life, so treat the decision-making process accordingly.

If an investment professional's answers to your questions are unsatisfactory at your initial meeting, it may be wise to find another IP.

SUGGESTIONS FOR YOUNGER/NEWER INVESTORS

When You Don't Need an IP

For the typical young person out on their own and just starting to accumulate money, the logical first step is probably not to locate an IP. Step 1A is to establish an emergency fund equal to at least a couple of months' worth of expenses. Step 1B is to get educated about investing: read articles online, talk to mentors with investment experience, view investment websites, start developing goals and good financial habits, and maybe read a book or two about investing and personal finances. Prepare yourself to have an intelligent conversation with an IP in the future. There are also numerous innovative phone apps related to investing and finance that generally appeal more to younger investors that may provide education and helpful financial tools.

After completing steps 1A and 1B, step 2 would generally be to start making investments focused on the long term. Contributing to a 401(k) plan is often a great choice if that is an available option, particularly if the employer makes a matching contribution. Working with an IP to establish a Roth or an IRA is another attractive alternative. Splitting regular monthly investments into both a retirement account and a regular account often makes sense in the early accumulation years. This will help balance potential liquidity needs and tax benefits.

When to Start with an IP

A logical time to establish a relationship with an IP is when you have a lump sum to invest—even if it's a small sum—or if you have funds to invest regularly from your wages. For example, If you feel $10,000 is an adequate amount to keep in your emergency fund that you now have $15,000 in, you could establish a brokerage account to invest the excess $5,000. That account could be set up with either an IP at a full-service firm or with a discount brokerage.

Another example would be if you are regularly saving $500 a month, you could work with an IP to develop a monthly investment plan. Or you could do both by investing a lump sum initially and adding to the account monthly or quarterly going forward.

How to Connect with an IP

One way to locate an IP is to ask people you respect and trust, such as a parent or a close friend, who have experience investing, which IP they would refer you to. Credentials alone don't mean a particular IP is good or the right person for you. Many IPs spend the majority of their time helping rich people get richer, not spending an hour explaining what a mutual fund is to someone wanting to invest $1,000. However, if a rich person says to their IP, "Hey, I want you to take my grandchild under your wing and help them out," then you may get more attention.

Another viable option is to simply reach out to brokerage firms and request an appointment—see the list of some of the major full-service and discount brokers listed earlier in this chapter. Virtually all firms now have excellent websites that provide search tools to connect you with the nearest offices to your location. If they have an office that is convenient, an in-person appointment would be ideal. However, a phone appointment or video call will work fine as well. I have had a satisfactory relationship with brokers on a few occasions in which I didn't meet them in person until several years after I began working with them.

The discount firms often have IPs on salary who are there to work with clients regardless of their account size, and therefore new investors with smaller amounts to invest may find them more accommodating. Regardless of which type of IP you meet with and whether you meet with them in person or by phone, be sure to have your questions prepared, and be candid with them about your situation.

Resources

$ **Finra.org** has a wealth of helpful information on their website, particularly the *For Investors* tab, which has a wide range of educational, investing, and finance information. The *Brokercheck* tab provides information on registered brokers, such as which firms they have worked for, what licenses they have, and disclosures related to customer complaints or disciplinary action. FINRA is the self-regulatory body for the securities industry.

$ **Sec.gov** is the Securities and Exchange Commission website. The *Education* tab has numerous excellent subsections, including *Understanding Fees, Investment Products, Tools and Calculators*, and more.

$ Virtually all brokerage firms have volumes of information on their websites on a broad array of investment topics.

DO-IT-YOURSELF INVESTING

For reasons already stated in this chapter, I believe most investors would be better off working with an IP. But as previously stated, for those who prefer to invest without the assistance of an IP, there are plenty of discount brokerages to choose from with user friendly platforms. With the aid of the internet and detailed websites, it is now fairly easy to do everything yourself online. The new account forms are online, money can easily be transferred electronically, and the do-it-yourself order entry screens are simple and easy to use. Now all the major firms have well-staffed help desks that are excellent resources if you do need help with anything.

The real issue is not simply whether someone has the ability to make their own investment decisions unassisted; the real issue is, with all things considered, are they better off doing it alone or with the assistance of an IP?

SUMMARY

Every person has their own unique level of experience, knowledge, and comfort relative to investing and making investment decisions. Some investors have large and diverse investment portfolios, while others are just getting started in the wealth accumulation process. Some investors actively trade individual stocks and are comfortable making their own decisions, whereas other investors prefer mutual funds and want the guidance of an IP.

With those factors and others in mind, each investor should take the time to seek out which firm or IP is the right fit for them. There are many excellent full-service investment firms for those who want and need ongoing advice and management. Likewise, many of the discount brokers now provide licensed IPs who are available to provide investment advice as well. For investors who prefer less assistance and reduced fees, there are a number of discount brokers with excellent platforms and services to do so.

The two primary ways IPs are paid for their assistance are either commissions when transactions occur or an annualized percentage fee, which is based on the value of your account. Investors should not be shy about asking questions, and they should fully understand the applicable fee structure for their personal accounts.

CHAPTER 18

Author's Letter to a 63-Year-Old Retiring Couple

This chapter contains a letter from the author written to a couple retiring at the end of the year who did an excellent job managing their finances while raising a family. Readers may find this an inspirational example of how it is possible for middle-class wage earners to have a comfortable level of financial well-being and accumulate wealth by following the EARN+SAVE+INVEST+REPEAT steps.

Dear Retiring Couple,

Congratulations on your decision to retire at the end of the year, and happy 63rd birthday to both of you! I'm honored you asked for my thoughts relative to your overall finances and your plans for the future.

First, it appears you're in excellent financial shape heading into retirement, and you've obviously done a fantastic job of handling your affairs. It's great you've done an annual budget for so many years. Budgeting, no doubt, helped make you judicious consumers, which in turn allowed you to maximize your retirement account contributions. You clearly have a good handle on what your expenses will be in retirement.

It is impressive how much you have accumulated in your investment accounts, even though neither of you had high-paying jobs. You raised four children, supported charities, and were able to travel and take numerous family vacations. Job well done all the way around!

The following is a summary of your finances as you explained them to me, as well as my responses to questions you asked, and a few comments on other topics you may want to consider.

SUMMARY OF CURRENT SITUATION

1. **Debt free**: You own your home and two cars outright, and you are completely debt free.

2. **Annual expenses**: Per your budget projections, expenses in your first year of retirement will be $48,000 ($4,000 average per month). This includes $6,000 for travel during the year but does not include any charitable giving or any assistance to your children or grandchildren.

3. **Retirement accounts**: You have a total of $1,050,000 in your IRAs and 401(k) accounts, which are invested 100% in stock mutual funds.

4. **Rental houses**: You own three rental houses debt free, which net you about $18,000 per year ($1,500 average per month) after all expenses. You plan to keep the rentals.

5. **Brokerage and bank accounts**: You keep about $30,000 in your checking account, and you have approximately $200,000 in a regular brokerage account invested in stock mutual funds.

6. **Social Security**: You are leaning toward both of you starting to draw Social Security in January of next year. Your combined amount will be just over $4,000 per month. You are not sure whether you should start drawing next year or not, since the longer you wait up to age 70, the larger your social security check will be.

7. **Retirement accounts**: You are not sure when to start taking distributions from your retirement accounts or how much to withdraw. Also,

you are not sure if you should roll your 401(k) accounts into an IRA when you retire or if it makes more sense to leave the money in your companies' 401(k) plans, which both of your employers allow.

8. **Liquidity**: You are concerned you may not have adequate liquidity if you incur multiple expenses at the same time, such as if you have to buy a new car, a large expense related to your rental homes occurs, a health issue arises, or one of your children needs financial assistance.

9. **Health insurance**: The COBRA law entitles you to continue with your employer's health insurance for 18 months, which will coincide with your eligibility for Medicare.

10. **Not moving**: You don't plan to move or trade houses.

RETIREMENT GOALS

1. **Travel**: You plan to travel in your camper for a couple of months a year visiting national parks.

2. **Live modestly**: You plan to live on less than you are making, and you have no plans to take on any new significant expenses.

3. **Charity and grandchildren**: You would like to start giving more to charity each year, and you also believe you may want to provide some financial assistance for the needs of your grandchildren.

KURT'S COMMENTS

You are in excellent financial shape to be able to meet your desired goals. You are debt free, have a good handle on what your cost of living will be in retirement, and have plenty of options and resources to easily draw as much income as you need. The following are my comments on specific areas.

1. **Social Security**: I agree you should both start drawing Social Security in January after you retire. Your candid acknowledgment that both of you have an overwhelming family history of not living beyond age 80 makes drawing immediately the best choice, in my opinion.

2. **Income**: Annualized, you will draw $48,000 in Social Security benefits, and your rental units are producing $18,000 for a combined income of $66,000 from only those two sources, which is $18,000 more than your anticipated annual expenses of $48,000.

3. **Retirement account distributions**: Since you will have adequate income from Social Security and the rental units, I would not take withdrawals from your retirement accounts yet. Let them continue to grow tax deferred until withdrawals are required at age 72, or until you need some of the funds.

4. **Tax planning**: You have some unique circumstances for which I would suggest you seek out tax advice. You have depreciation on your rental units, you plan to do annual charitable giving, up to 85% of your Social Security may be taxable, and you have a relatively large balance in retirement accounts that will be taxable when distributed. With all that being said, it may be appropriate to convert a small portion of your IRAs each year to a Roth, depending on your overall tax situation.

5. **Investment philosophy**: You commented you have always invested your retirement accounts 100% in stock funds, and that you plan to continue to do so after retirement because you believe that diversified stock portfolios will continue to outperform bonds and interest-bearing accounts over the long haul. I couldn't agree more.

6. **401(k)**: There's no clear-cut answer as to whether you should leave your 401(k)s as is or roll them to an IRA. I would suggest you compare the fees for each; your level of comfort with your financial advisor that would handle the IRAs is also a factor, and the investment choices in the 401(k) vs. what you might roll the money into should be considered. Either way, you plan to keep the money invested in diversified stock funds, so the rate of return should be comparable for both.

7. **HELOC to increase liquidity**: I agree that having access to more cash would be a good idea for the reasons you cited, and I think it would give you peace of mind as well. Of course, you can always sell investments to raise cash, but that could create unnecessary income taxes. A home equity line of credit (HELOC) is the perfect solution. With a HELOC,

you can get approved for a line of credit for about 80% of the value of your home that you can access anytime by simply writing a check.

8. **Increasing income**: You asked for my opinion on what the hypothetical conservative maximum amount of income is you could draw using all of your assets. The rationale for your question relates to if you decided to substantially increase your charitable giving or assistance for your children, while still being comfortable that you can always provide for yourselves.

   a. Historically, stock portfolios have averaged more than 9% total return per annum. A 5% annual withdrawal from your retirement accounts would equal $52,500 the first year. Doing the same with your brokerage account would produce another $10,000. Adding in your Social Security of $48,000 and your net rental income of $18,000, your total annual income would be $128,500. Of course, you would need to budget more for income taxes as well.

   b. Your income should increase each year as well, since Social Security benefits are frequently increased, and your rental income will likely increase over time. Also, assuming your mutual funds and retirement accounts grow at a higher rate than what you withdraw, you will be able to increase your distributions in later years, since the account values would then be larger. Having rising income over time is the best way to protect yourselves from inflation and rising costs.

The two of you are an exemplary story in terms of your money management and decision-making over the years. How you accumulated more than $1 million in your retirement accounts is particularly inspiring and is a model others could learn from.

You said the two of you agreed 40 years ago as newlyweds, you would endeavor to contribute to your retirement accounts every year. The first year, you were only able to contribute $1,500; a few years later, you bumped it to $2,000, then $3,000, and so on, but the most you ever contributed for any year was $6,000 over the last few years. In fact, your total contributions are well under $200,000, whereas your earnings have amounted to over $800,000! You were wise beyond your years to invest your savings in diversified stock funds all this time.

It was so nice to catch up with both of you again, and congratulations on your upcoming retirement and the excellent job you have done preparing for this transition.

Your friend and former schoolmate. Go Spartans!
Kurt

PART IV

REPEAT

CHAPTER 19

Personal Financial Documents

Chapter Abbreviations

IS:	Income Statement
NW:	Net Worth
NWS:	Net Worth Statement

The net worth statement (NWS), income statement (IS), and budget are the three primary personal financial documents. Completing and adhering to one, two, or all three of these documents can serve as a valuable tool for money management and the wealth accumulation process.

The NWS shows what you own and what you owe as of a point in time and your resulting *net worth* (NW). Doing the NWS at regular intervals allows you to monitor your progress toward accumulating wealth. The IS and budget are basically the same document, each showing income and expenses. The difference between the two is that the IS shows income and expenses over a *previous* time period, whereas the budget provides a game plan or forecast of what you anticipate for the *future* in terms of your income and expenses. Simply stated, the IS shows what already happened, while the budget is a projection of what you plan to do.

There are many inexpensive ready-to-go personal financial document templates from software providers like Quicken.com, personalcapital.com, templatelab.com, and numerous others that could be located with a simple internet search. Many of these software packages offer integrated software that can link your investment accounts and bank statements to their financial statement templates, so you don't have to manually input the data. Some people may prefer using an excel spreadsheet for their financial documents as they can be easily customized. Free excel templates can be found online for each of the financial documents. This chapter provides examples and discussion on how to complete and analyze each of the three personal financial documents.

THE NET WORTH STATEMENT (NWS)

The NWS section is positioned first in the chapter because I believe it would be beneficial for most individuals to complete it before preparing the IS or budget. It provides the starting point showing what you are worth. This is the equivalent of weighing in before starting a physical training program designed to build size and muscle, or like a growth chart on the wall to record a child's height as they grow up. In essence, you are documenting your starting point before making your action plan for the future.

The NWS is appropriately named. It's a statement that tells you what you are worth after netting (subtracting) your liabilities (debts) from your assets (what you own). Your NW is simply the sum of your assets minus the sum of your liabilities. An NWS always has a single date, such as "Net Worth Statement as of December 31, 2021," because it indicates your assets and liabilities as of a specific point in time.

If your goal is to accumulate wealth, completing an NWS at least once a year is a great idea. It's the ongoing scorecard for life to monitor your advancement toward financial freedom and to show how your NW is progressing. This serves as confirmation things are going well and positive progress is being made or, conversely, that your NW is not growing as desired and perhaps adjustments to spending habits or investment strategies need to be considered.

Completing a net worth statement at least once a year is a great idea for anyone serious about accumulating wealth. It's the ongoing scorecard to monitor your financial progress.

Especially as your NW grows and thus becomes more complex, the NWS can serve as a valuable tool for a periodic review of your overall financial situation. It can graphically reveal useful information on various financial issues, such as the following:

$ **Retirement Planning:** How much, in terms of dollars and percentage, has your NW grown compared to previous points in time? Are you saving enough for retirement? At what age can you likely retire and have enough money to live in the manner you desire?

$ **Asset Diversification:** The NWS categorizes assets by type. What percent is in cash, real estate, stocks, private businesses, retirement accounts, etc?

$ **Liquidity:** Liquidity means how quickly and easily an asset can be converted to cash. For example, money in a checking account is extremely liquid. Real estate is at the other end of the spectrum and much less liquid. The NWS can indicate if you have adequate liquidity. Are you prepared if extraordinary expenses arise?

$ **Total Liabilities:** Even if your NW is growing nicely, excessive debt can be a risk.

$ **Overall Financial Well-Being:** Are you where you need to be to accomplish your goals? Are you satisfied with your overall financial situation? How easily could you survive a decrease in wages?

A person's NWS should be categorized and personalized, so it is specific to their circumstances. For example, if someone has a valuable coin collection worth 30% of their total assets, it should definitely be a separate line item on their NWS.

I'm generally not in favor of listing depreciating consumer assets on the NWS. In other words, those items, that even though they have current value and could be sold, will eventually become virtually worthless in all likelihood, such as a new $5,000 riding lawn mower. You didn't buy a lawn mower to sell it in six months; you bought it to mow grass for the next 10 years. If you ever sell it, you will likely receive a small fraction of what you paid.

A jet ski purchased for $10,000 might be different. If your plan is to enjoy it for the summer and then sell it, you should get some significant value for it. But I would still encourage inputting a conservative value on your NWS, as it will likely depreciate in value.

The fundamental reason I discourage listing depreciating assets on the NWS is it keeps people from listing items as investments or as assets when, in fact, they are really expenditures. Including such items as an asset on the NWS could encourage excessive spending. "I can feel better about buying a new fishing boat if I list it at full cost on the NWS, yeah, that's the ticket. I didn't spend; I invested!"

I've never listed jewelry on our NWS. No question, we could get some money for my wife's wedding ring, but it's not happening! Certainly, don't list clothes, electronic devices, household appliances, tools, furniture, most artwork, most jewelry, workout equipment, hobby equipment, or any other items you're tempted to mischaracterize as investments.

There are various ways to lay out an NWS, but regardless of the format, all the software programs have formulas embedded to do the math. The following are two personal NWS examples: one simple and one a little more complex. Some explanations are given below the samples.

Jack Greenback Net Worth Statement		
As of December 31, 2021		
ASSETS		
Cash Equivalents		
Cash on hand	$1,400	
Checking accounts	$5,200	
Total Cash	$6,600	
Investments (Intangibles)		
ABC Mutual Fund	$3,700	
XYZ Mutual Fund	$2,950	
401k (work)	$6,200	
Roth IRA	$6,000	
Total Investments	$18,850	
Property (Tangible)		
1 acre lot	$12,000	
Car	$22,000	
Total Property	$34,000	
Total Assets		$59,450
LIABILITIES		
Credit card	$700	
Car loan	$11,400	
Student loan	$18,000	
Lot loan	$4,950	
Total Liabilities		$35,050
Net Worth		$24,400
Unvalued Assets: Jewelry, shop tools, snowboards		

Table 19.1

Comments on Jack Greenback NWS

$ This is a simple yet meaningful NWS. Easy and fast to complete.

$ Certain assets were listed below the Net Worth line, but are unvalued since they will likely never be sold for a meaningful amount, and they are not a significant portion of his NW.

$ The car is valued at the low end of the wholesale price, and the one-acre lot is valued at Jack's best estimate of market value less 15%.

Chris Doe Net Worth Statement as of December 31, 2021		
ASSETS		
Cash Equivalents	Cash on hand	$20,000
	Checking accounts	$18,000
	Money Market Fund	$46,000
	CDs (Certificates of Deposit)	$415,000
	Total Cash Equivalents	**$499,000**
Investments, Liquid	TD Ameritrade Account	$687,000
	E-Trade Account	$2,449,000
	Robinhood Account	$97,000
	Total Liquid Investments	**$3,233,000**
Retirement Accounts	401(k)	$912,000
	Roth IRA	$253,000
	IRA, traditional	$690,000
	Total Retirement Accounts	**$1,855,000**
Illiquid Investments	Loan to Uncle Buster	$12,000
	Loan to I.C. Gold Enterprises	$150,000
	7 come 11 Opportunity Fund	$150,000
	Ben Dover Inc. (20% ownership)	$200,000
	Total Illiquid Investments	**$512,000**
Tangible Property	Primary Residence	$680,000

	Ski condo	$240,000
	Strip mall (25% ownership)	$450,000
	Total Tangible Property	**$1,370,000**
	Total Assets	**$7,469,000**
LIABILITIES		
	Taxes due	$28,000
	Home Loan	$402,000
	Ski condo loan	$137,000
	Total Liabilities	**$567,000**
	Net Worth	**$6,902,000**

Table 19.2

Comments on Chris Doe NWS

$ Mr. Doe has a more diverse portfolio of assets than Jack Greenback; therefore, he listed five asset categories instead of three like on Jack's NWS. Specific categories and line items on the NWS should always be based on the individual's unique assets and liabilities.

$ Autos are not listed since they would represent a small percentage of total assets, and their value will steadily depreciate each year.

$ Values are rounded to the nearest thousand, which makes for easier reading, and the odd numbers are not meaningful for a NW of this size.

THE INCOME STATEMENT (IS)

The income statement (IS), like the NWS, is appropriately named. However, an even more descriptive name for it would be income and expense statement, but nobody calls it that. While the NWS is a snapshot at a specific point in time, the IS covers a period of time—a month, a quarter, or a year.

The IS details all income/revenue and all expenses over the designated previous time period. In simple terms, the IS shows the amount of money that came in and its source, as well as how much money went out and for what purpose.

> The income statement is an excellent tool to understand
> how money was spent over the previous month or year,
> which aids in identifying ways to reduce expenses
> and therefore improve financial well-being.

To complete an IS for the entire previous year would be a time-consuming and perhaps unnecessary task. The main IS purpose is to gain an understanding of how your money has been spent in the past so you can make a reasonable budget for the future. Perhaps an IS of just the last month or two would be ambitious enough to allow you to complete a solid budget for the year ahead.

Constructing the Income Statement

For most people, the top portion (income) of the IS can be fast and easy to complete. It is often a single line—wages. Some people may have multiple sources of income, such as pensions, Social Security, interest, dividends, rent, IRA distributions, business income, and royalties.

The lower portion (expenses) of the IS will certainly have more categories and line items than the income section. It will also be more time-consuming to complete. This IS can be difficult to complete as accurately as you would like initially because it is a documentation of what you did in the past. Especially, if you pay in cash (green money) for some expenditures, it may be difficult to remember how much you paid for each particular line item unless you were keeping track of it.

The IS should be detailed and specific to your situation. A miscellaneous category is sometimes needed, but use it sparingly. Only put an expenditure in this category if it is a one-off item that seldom or never recurs and doesn't belong to another category (for example, the cost of a speeding ticket). A brief description of all items in the miscellaneous section should be made—noting the reason for the expense will assist when doing the budget for the next period.

If you are concerned you are living it up too much, rather than having one line titled *entertainment*, it might be more helpful to have separate lines for movies, concerts, sporting events, mud wrestling, etc. "Maybe I could have skipped my third Vanilla Ice tribute concert that cost $300. Hmm …"

If done well, the IS can graphically enlighten you as to precisely how much money is coming in and where the outflows of money are going. This will hopefully result in making better spending decisions in the future, which should lead to greater wealth accumulation. BOOM!

The following is an example of a personal income statement. Some comments are provided after the table.

Morgan Cash Personal Income Statement				
Income	Oct 2019	Nov 2019	Dec 2019	Q4 2019
Gross Salary (A)	$5,000	$5,000	$5,000	$15,000
Deductions from gross salary				
Federal income tax	$550	$550	$550	$1,650
State income tax	$200	$200	$200	$600
Medicare and Social security tax	$383	$383	$383	$1,148
Health insurance	$180	$180	$180	$540
401k contribution	$250	$250	$250	$750
Total deductions from salary (B)	$1,563	$1,563	$1,563	$4,688
Take home salary (A-B=C) (C)	$3,438	$3,438	$3,438	$10,313
Interest on bank accounts	$10	$10	$10	$30
Total Income (D)	**$3,448**	**$3,448**	**$3,448**	**$10,343**
Expenses				
Housing				
Rent	$500	$500	$500	$1,500
Renters insurance	$75	$0	$0	$75
Utilities	$82	$90	$115	$287
Internet and TV	$55	$55	$55	$165
Total Housing (E)	**$712**	**$645**	**$670**	**$2,027**
Auto				
Car payment	$308	$308	$308	$924
Car insurance	$0	$0	$350	$350

Oil change & car maintenance	$24	$42	$0	$66
Gas	$184	$158	$290	$632
Total Auto (F)	**$516**	**$508**	**$948**	**$1,972**
Food & Beverage				
Groceries	$450	$360	$210	$1,020
Eating Out	$120	$204	$310	$634
Alcohol	$40	$95	$220	$355
Total Food & Beverage (G)	**$610**	**$659**	**$740**	**$2,009**
Snowboarding				
Season pass	$348	$0	$0	$348
New snowboard gear	$0	$400	$0	$400
Total Snowboarding (H)	**$348**	**$400**	**$0**	**$748**
Other Living Expenses				
Cell phone service	$80	$80	$80	$240
Household consumables	$30	$40	$53	$123
Clothes	$150	$150	$150	$450
Entertainment	$100	$100	$100	$300
Vacation escrow fund	$150	$150	$150	$450
Miscellaneous	$90	$0	$0	$90
Total Other Living Expenses (I)	**$520**	**$440**	**$453**	**$1,413**
Total Expenses (E+F+G+H+I=J) (J)	**$2,706**	**$2,652**	**$2,811**	**$8,169**
Net Cash Flow (D-J=K) (K)	**$742**	**$796**	**$637**	**$2,174**

Table 19.3

Comments on Ms. Cash's IS:

$ Letters were added next to items to provide a graphic explanation for the computations. Such as the (A) next to *Gross Salary*. Such symbols would never appear on an income statement, but they were added here to ensure readers understand how the final numbers were derived. For example, the figure for the last line, *Net Cash Flow* (K), was derived by subtracting *Total Expenses* (J) from *Total Income* (D).

$ Deductions made by the employer from gross salary are listed in the Income section of the IS. Those deductions could alternatively be listed in the Expenses section. I prefer to show them as a *contra* expense to gross salary because Ms. Cash never receives that money. Showing those deductions in the Income section gives her the net take-home amount she actually has available for her personal expenses.

$ In accounting lingo, a contra expense is an expense directly against an income item. This is done when the income and the expense are directly related. For example, the amount of taxes Morgan has withheld is directly related to and deducted from her gross salary.

$ Data is shown for three months: October, November, and December. The fourth column totals those three months to show the sum for the quarter (Q4 = fourth quarter).

$ Snowboarding has its own expense category because it is her main hobby, and she has significant, related expenses. It will provide her with the data to answer the question, "Am I spending too much on snowboarding?" If snowboarding expenses were simply lumped into the *Entertainment* category, she wouldn't know how much she is spending specifically on snowboarding.

$ In the Other Living Expenses section, there is a category for *Vacation Escrow Fund*. Escrow means to segregate money for a specific future expense. She could simply add $150 each month to an envelope labeled *vacation money*, or she could establish a separate savings account with her bank.

$ The last line, *Net Cash Flow*, is the excess she is accumulating each month after all expenses are paid. This excess is the money Morgan needs to make plans for—should she increase her 401(k) contributions or start a Roth IRA, or maybe she should use it to pay off her car loan more quickly.

Effective Ways to Track Expenditures

Using credit/debit cards, paying by check, using peer-to-peer (P2P) transfer apps, or doing automated electronic funds transfers (EFT) can be helpful to document expenses. At the end of each month, you can review your statements or account records and allocate every expenditure to the appropriate line item— Taco Bell purchases to the food category.

Utilizing software programs, such as Quicken and others, that link your service providers with your financial documents have grown in popularity as an effective way to streamline the entire process. P2P payment phone apps such as Venmo, Paypal, and Zelle have become very popular with young adults. Such apps are useful for documenting and reviewing expenses to complete the IS.

However, for some situations and for some people, it is preferred or necessary to use cash for payments. One way to keep track of cash would be to purposely start a point or a period of time with a specific amount of cash, and then count the cash left over at the end of the period. If you are going out for a night on the town, take exactly $80 with you. If you have $30 left at the end of the night, you can then log $50 spent on your IS statement under the *Entertainment* category.

As long as your cash source is withdrawals from your bank account, you can also see exactly how much cash you spent by comparing the withdrawals on your bank statement to the remaining cash on hand. But you still have to keep up with it consistently to know where the cash went. Making notes on your cell phone, using an app, or sending a text to yourself are easy ways to keep track of cash until you can enter the data on your IS.

The Consolidated Income Statement (CIS)

A CIS provides only the category totals for a condensed overview of the IS. Once the first CIS is set up, it's very convenient because no data has to be added going forward. It is built entirely with embedded formulas from the unconsolidated IS, so data automatically appears in the appropriate CIS lines. Also, notice that a column was added to the right of the expense categories showing what percentage of the total expenses each expense category comprised. The following is the CIS version of Ms. Cash's IS.

Ms. Morgan Cash Personal Income Statement (Consolidated)					
Income	**Oct 21**	**Nov 21**	**Dec 21**	**Q4 2021**	
Gross Salary	$5,000	$5,000	$5,000	$15,000	
Deductions from gross salary	$1,563	$1,563	$1,563	$4,688	
Take-home salary	$3,438	$3,438	$3,438	$10,313	
Interest on bank accounts	$10	$10	$10	$30	
Gifts from family members	$0	$0	$300	$300	
Total Income	**$3,448**	**$3,448**	**$3,748**	**$10,643**	
Expenses					
Housing	$712	$645	$670	$2,027	22.2%
Auto	$516	$508	$948	$1,972	21.6%
Food & beverage	$678	$759	$885	$2,322	25.4%
Snowboarding	$348	$400	$0	$748	8.2%
Other living expenses	$528	$708	$835	$2,071	22.7%
Total Expenses	**$2,782**	**$3,020**	**$3,338**	**$9,140**	**100.0%**
Net Cash Flow	**$666**	**$428**	**$410**	**$1,503**	

Table 19.4

Supplemental Support Page for the Income Statement

A supplemental support page is helpful when compiling the actual numbers after the fact to produce the final IS, as well as to keep up with expenses going forward. For example, assume you are going to produce an IS for last month, and you purchased groceries three times during the month. In some way, you will have to total those three purchases and enter the sum in the groceries category on the IS.

If you have a support page to enter each of the three purchases, then those purchases can automatically be summed and put onto the IS. Going forward, you will have each month's historical data saved (in case you need to refer to it), and you will have a template you can use month after month, for which you only had to build the framework once.

Basically, the support page would have all the IS categories. Then, from time to time, you would input every expense you incur as a line item in the appropriate category. Some data you may enter daily, such as any cash purchases made that day. Other data you may enter monthly when you review your bank statement, credit card bill, or Venmo account.

THE BUDGET

The NWS is a snapshot of where you are at a point in time. The IS shows what you did in the past. The budget details what you forecast doing in the future. Hence, a budget is a specific plan for an upcoming time period indicating how much income you believe you will have coming in and how much you plan to spend and save.

There are some people who are more in need of budgeting than others. First, there are those who have a history of outspending their income and getting into debt, perhaps because they struggle to control their impulse to spend. They need a system to balance how much they are earning vs. how much they are spending.

Another group that would benefit from completing a budget are young adults who are just entering the workforce with little or no experience in balancing income and expenses. The entire process of making a budget and then keeping up with their actual performance going forward can be an informative and helpful endeavor. It can answer questions such as:

$ Where is my money going?
$ Am I spending more than I'm making?
$ How much did I spend on various activities/items?
$ Do I need to change or reduce any of my spending habits?
$ Can I currently afford to invest in my company's 401(k) plan?

A third group that might be keenly interested in budgeting are those who don't necessarily have any serious spending problems but who simply want to manage their financial affairs as well as possible. Maybe there is only a small difference between their income and their fixed expenses, and they need to be as judicious as possible.

I previously stated that anyone who is serious about accumulating wealth should do an NWS at least once a year. However, I don't believe everyone necessarily needs to do an IS or a budget. If someone is a good earner and a mindful spender, budgeting may be overkill. For some people, it can be an unnecessary task aimed at fixing a problem when there really isn't a problem to begin with.

A budget lists how much income you anticipate will come in and your plans for how much will go out for expenses over a given time period. It is an excellent tool for both planning and monitoring your cash flow.

Constructing the Budget

There are numerous ways to prepare a budget. The correct approach is whichever one works best for you. Following are four different ways to consider. Method #1 requires the least amount of time upfront, and method #4 requires the most initial time. Methods #2 and #3 are in the middle time wise.

Method #1, Build it as you go: Build the budget as you complete an IS one month at a time for a year. Start with a blank budget template and then record what your actual expenses are month by month as you go through the year. At the end of the year, use those numbers for next year's budget—making appropriate adjustments for any numbers that you think will change. This is an accurate and methodical way to do it, but you have to go through an entire year of recording your actual expenses to then develop a budget for the upcoming year.

Method #2, Best estimate: Start with a blank budget template and input your best estimates for everything. Some items, such as monthly loan payments and phone bills, are very easy to estimate as they tend to stay the same. Estimates for expenses such as food, gas, and entertainment may be less precise. Most people could complete a 12-month budget in a few hours with this method. The following year, you will have the numbers dialed in much better as you record the actual numbers throughout the year.

Method #3, Hybrid: Do a blend of methods #1 and #2. Instead of logging actual expenses for an entire year before preparing a budget, as described in method #1, just do it for a month or two and then estimate the other months as described in method #2.

Method #4, Do the IS first: Complete an IS for the entire previous period (month, quarter, or year) and then build the budget using those prior period actual numbers as a guide. Although this method is very accurate, it is considerably more time-consuming and therefore not the preferred method for most people.

An annual budget can be completed in a few hours for most households. It doesn't have to be a long precise endeavor to get started. Budgets are working documents that should be fine tuned as you go along.

Budget vs. Actual

Ultimately, after completing the budget with numbers for all 12 months, you will add a blank column for each month next to the budget column to record the current year *actual* numbers as they occur during the upcoming year.[5] What you are putting in place is an active working tool to help manage your finances that shows all income and expenses. Ideally, the document will have three columns for each month as follows from left to right: *previous year actual*, *budget*, and the *current year actual* column.

The IS and budget are basically the same document—the IS shows the past, and the budget shows the forecast for the future. After inputting the actual

---

5   The term "actual" is accounting lingo for what occurred. It means exactly what it implies—these are the actual numbers as opposed to what was budgeted (forecasted). Side-by-side columns titled "Budget" and "Actual" are used when accountants do "budget vs. actual" analysis.

numbers for a full year on the budget, that document will then serve as the prior year's IS. Just like that, you will never have to do another IS from scratch.

Variance Analysis

After completing a budget and then inputting the actual numbers month by month, the next step would be to compare the variance between the two. The practical aspect of this entire accounting process is to examine what you intended to do vs. what you actually did and learn from it as a tool to improve or maintain your money management decisions in the future. To do so, you would add a fourth column called *variance from budget* and a fifth column called *variance from prior*. These two columns have some of the most valuable pieces of information in terms of keeping you on track with your objectives.

The *variance* column shows the difference between the *actual* column and the *budget* column. For example, if you budgeted $500 for food but the actual was $700, then the variance would be negative $200. A negative number would draw your attention to considering why you spent more than you budgeted. A negative variance doesn't automatically mean anything is wrong, but it draws your attention so you can take a closer look.

The following is an example for one month of only the expenses with columns for budget, actual, and variance. The *prior year actual* and *variance from prior* are not shown, but they would be presented in the same manner.

Budget Variance Report			
	Budget	**Actual**	**Variance**
Expenses	**January**	**January**	**January**
Housing			
Rent	$900	$900	$0
Renters insurance	$80	$100	-$20
Utilities	$90	$120	-$30
Internet and TV	$30	$30	$0

Total Housing	$820	$870	-$50
Auto			
Car payment	$300	$300	$0
Car insurance	$40	$40	$0
Oil change & car maintenance	$30	$270	-$240
Gas	$210	$187	$23
Total Auto	**$240**	**$457**	**-$217**
Food & Beverage			
Groceries	$350	$295	$55
Eating out	$110	$170	-$60
Alcohol	$70	$90	-$20
Total Food & Beverage	**$530**	**$555**	**-$25**
Snowboarding			
Season pass	$0	$0	$0
New snowboard gear	$300	$0	$300
Total Snowboarding	**$300**	**$0**	**$300**
Other Living Expenses			
Cell phone service	$85	$89	-$4
Household consumables	$40	$88	-$48
Clothes	$150	$390	-$240
Entertainment	$100	$180	-$80
Vacation escrow fund	$100	$100	$0
Miscellaneous	$60	$0	$60
Total Other Living Expenses	**$450**	**$758**	**-$308**
Total Expenses	$2,960	$3,260	-$300

Table 19.5

> Understanding past behavior is the first step to improving future behavior. Resist spending money you have and need on things you don't have and don't need.

IMPLEMENTATION OF THE FINANCIAL DOCUMENTS

Let's think of the logical sequence for a person who has never completed financial documents, and who has never really focused on improving their financial well-being. They have never attempted to assess their net worth, analyze their expenditures, or make plans for how to improve the management of their finances. How does this person best use the financial documents covered in this chapter?

Step one would be to complete the NWS, as discussed earlier in the chapter. This gives them a starting point by documenting precisely all of their relevant assets and liabilities, and their beginning net worth.

I would encourage everyone to complete an NWS on a regular basis. I have personally done so at least twice each year since graduating from college in 1983. If someone has a desire and focus to accumulate wealth, doing an NWS regularly is your scorecard. It is sort of like a baseball player knowing their lifetime batting average or their total hits. Personally, *not* completing an NWS on a regular basis would add stress to my life. It would be like driving down the financial highway of life with a blindfold on, just hoping everything is okay.

There are some people who probably don't really need to do the other two documents—the IS or budget. If your income is high enough and you are naturally a conscientious spender, you may not need a budget or an IS as a management tool. It may be more effort than it is worth.

For those people for whom making a budget and adhering to it would be helpful or needed, the next step could be to construct an IS covering the last few months or so. Alternatively, you could forgo doing an IS and just make a budget using your best estimates.

Skipping the IS step may take a few months of living the budget to develop more realistic numbers. After tracking your income and expenses for a few months, you'll be well on your way to being knowledgeable of and in control of your financial life. You will be able to accurately produce an annual NWS made easy by using the previous year's NWS as a template. You will have completed the previous year's IS by virtue of entering the actual numbers on the budget month by month. Armed with accurate monthly income and expense numbers for the last year, it will be a quick and easy process to develop a budget for the upcoming year.

With the above steps working in unison, it should not be too onerous to routinely keep up with those financial documents. Hopefully, the end result will be that you are doing a great job managing your financial affairs and improving your overall financial well-being as you progress with the wealth accumulation process.

Routinely completing personal financial documents can be a powerful tool for improving financial well-being. Usually good things don't *just happen—we make them happen.* Effort and work come first and rewards come later.

SUMMARY

The income statement is your past *history*, the budget is your target for the *future*, and the net worth statement shows where you are *presently.* Using and analyzing these three documents can be a powerful tool to improve your overall financial well-being.

The net worth statement (NWS) lists all of your assets and all of your liabilities, with the difference between the two being your net worth. Preparing your NWS annually is a great idea to serve as a lifetime scorecard, showing how you are progressing with the wealth accumulation process.

The income statement lists your income and your expenses for a past period, such as the previous month or year. The budget lists the exact same information, except it is a forecast of what you anticipate your income and expenses will be for a future time period, such as the upcoming year. Preparing an income statement and/or a budget is of great assistance for some people to understand precisely how they are spending their money and to aid them in making positive steps with their money management in the future.

CHAPTER 20

Social Security: Rules, Choices, Decisions

Chapter Abbreviations

AIME:	Average Indexed Monthly Earnings
BENEFITS:	Social Security payments
COLA:	Cost of Living Adjustment
FRA:	Full Retirement Age
PIA:	Primary Insurance Amount
SSA:	Social Security Administration

What is the best age to start drawing Social Security retirement benefits? It depends on your personal circumstances.

This is a major financial decision for most people, as making the wrong decision could easily be a $200,000+ lifetime mistake. It seems like it should be a fairly easy question to answer but, unfortunately it's somewhat difficult and confusing.

There are a surprisingly large number of considerations that impact the decision, such as the need for immediate income, health status, family life-span history, employment and tax status, investing and money management abilities, marital status, and whether your spouse qualifies for benefits on their own.

The big dilemma is if you start drawing benefits at an early age, your benefit amount will be smaller permanently than if you delay the start date. Unfortunately, different considerations may lead to opposite conclusions. For example, your personal health may make drawing early seem like the logical choice, but your employment and income status may indicate that delaying benefits would be wiser.

Many articles written about Social Security refrain from giving a conclusive answer, as this is clearly not a one-size-fits-all situation. However, the common theme of many of those articles is that it is generally advantageous to delay receiving benefits until age 70 if possible, since doing so results in receiving the maximum monthly check, and if you live to a ripe old age, you will draw substantially more in total than if you started drawing at the youngest possible age of 62.

For some individuals (not everyone) with the appropriate circumstances, I have a completely different opinion due to the enormous impact of long-term compound earnings. Simply put, by drawing at age 62 and investing it well, it is quite possible to accumulate $500,000 or even $1 million more compared to drawing at age 70—the following section details how this could be done.

THE HYPOTHETICAL PERFECT STORM TO START DRAWING AT AGE 62

Let's assume someone is 62 and no longer working. They don't *need* Social Security income, and they probably never will. They have adequate investments and income from other sources to easily cover all of their expenses. They are a disciplined, long-term investor, and the bulk of their assets are positioned in a well-managed portfolio of equity investments.

The income from Social Security, whenever they start receiving it, will simply be added into their investment portfolio and increase the total value of their estate. The true beneficiaries of the decision of when to draw benefits are their heirs (the people or charities to whom they bequeath their estate).

For such a person, as described above, the dilemma of when to start Social

Security becomes purely a matter of number crunching to predict the best mathematical outcome—a calculation involving an assumed rate of return on investments and assumed income tax rates, resulting in various ending values that are dependent on the expiration date of their will (when they die).

The numbers below are based on my actual benefits as estimated for me by the SSA on their website as of July 2020. The calculations don't factor in any potential increases in the monthly benefit from cost-of-living adjustments (COLA) the SSA may make in future years, and no consideration is made relative to potential spousal benefits. I reached age 62 in September 2021.

$ My estimated monthly benefit if I start drawing at age 62: $1,712.

$ My estimated monthly benefit if I start drawing at age 70: $3,012.

$ If I start drawing at age 62, I will receive $164,352 total benefits by age 70. So, if I plan to start drawing at age 70, but I die the month I turn age 70, I missed out on receiving $164,352 in benefits.

$ If I start drawing at age 62, I will receive $380,064 by age 80 years and six months.

$ If I start drawing at age 70, I will receive $379,512 by age 80 years and six months. In other words, ignoring taxes and investment earnings, age 80½ is the age when delaying benefits until age 70 finally catches up with drawing at age 62.

So, if I die at any time before age 80½, it was better to draw early even without assuming any investment earnings on the benefits.

A Long-Term View With Tax and Earnings Assumptions as follows:

$ Your personal tax rates may be higher or lower than these numbers.

$ All benefits are invested monthly when received, and all earnings are reinvested.

$ Income taxes are paid on 85% (the maximum) of all benefits at a rate of 22%.

$ Income taxes are paid on all investment earnings at the qualified dividend and long-term capital gains rate of 15%.

$ Age 62 benefits invested monthly are $1,391.86 ($1,712 monthly benefit less taxes on the benefit).

$ Age 70 benefits invested monthly are $2,448.76 ($3,012 monthly benefit less taxes on the benefit).

$ The three tables below each assume a different investment earnings rate as follows:

- The first table assumes a pre-tax annual earnings rate of 6%, less 15% for income taxes, resulting in a 5.1% net after-tax compound rate.

- The second table assumes a pre-tax annual earnings rate of 8.4%, less 15% for income taxes, resulting in a 7.14% net after-tax compound rate.

- The third table assumes a pre-tax annual earnings rate of 11.1%, less 15% for income taxes, resulting in a 9.435% net after-tax compound rate.

5.1% Compound After-Tax Growth Rate			
Age	Draw at Age 62 Value	Draw at Age 70 Value	Draw at Age 62 Cumulative Advantage
70	$164,569	$0	$164,569
80	$491,051	$382,290	$108,761
90	$1,034,151	$1,018,227	$15,924
91yrs, 3mos	$1,123,587	$1,122,951	$636
100	$1,937,595	$2,076,104	($138,508)

Table 20.1

7.14% Compound After-Tax Growth Rate			
Age	Draw at Age 62 Value	Draw at Age 70 Value	Draw at Age 62 Cumulative Advantage
70	$179,513	$0	$179,513
80	$608,593	$427,124	$181,468
90	$1,482,983	$1,297,530	$185,452
100	$3,264,838	$3,071,267	$193,571

Table 20.2

9.435% Compound After-Tax Growth Rate			
Age	Draw at Age 62 Value	Draw at Age 70 Value	Draw at Age 62 Cumulative Advantage
70	$198,430	$0	$198,430
80	$783,951	$485,701	$298,249
90	$2,282,590	$1,728,853	$553,736
100	$6,118,349	$4,910,694	$1,207,654

Table 20.3

Comments on the Tables Above

$ The first table assumes a 5.1% compound after-tax growth rate. At that rate, drawing early will be a $164,569 advantage at age 70. Gradually, each year after 70, the *draw at age 70* column gains on the *draw at age 62* strategy, where the age 70 amount finally catches up if I live to 91 years and three months. If I live to be 100, I would have accumulated $138,508 more by waiting until age 70 to draw.

$ The second table assumes a 7.14% compound after-tax growth rate. That rate is just about the sweet spot where the additional accumulated earnings by drawing early makes it impossible for the draw at age 70 strategy to ever catch up. The longer I live, the greater the cumulative advantage of drawing early.

$ The third table assumes a 9.435% compound after-tax growth rate. I am using that rate because that is about 1% less than the average return produced by the first mutual fund I ever purchased (a large-cap equity fund), since its inception on January 1, 1934. Obviously, there is no assurance what the earnings from equity funds will be in the future, but I like the risk vs. reward trade-off, and, if it does repeat and I can just make it to 100, my heirs will have *over a million* reasons to thank me.

MAJOR SOCIAL SECURITY RULES AND OTHER INFORMATION

Warning: A lot of data will be thrown at you in the next few pages. It can be a bit complicated and confusing.

The ssa.gov website is a helpful resource—it has volumes of information and explanations about all things related to Social Security. Also, many well-written and informative articles explaining the rules, laws, and practical implications of Social Security are available on the internet. Such articles may serve as a convenient tool to assist in interpreting the sometimes overwhelming amount of information on the ssa.gov website. Seeking the advice of a competent professional with expertise on all aspects of Social Security may also be appropriate for some people.

You Don't Have to Retire to Draw

Although the SSA calls it *retirement* benefits, you don't have to retire to receive benefits. You may continue to earn wages (with certain conditions as described below) while receiving benefits.

Full Retirement Age

Although benefits can be started as early as age 62, it is important to understand when you reach what the SSA refers to as *full retirement age* (FRA). As shown in the chart below, your FRA is determined by the year you were born. Your FRA serves as the baseline to determine your benefits, as described below.

| Full Retirement Age (FRA) Based on Year of Birth ||
Year of Birth	Full Retirement Age (FRA)
1943–1954	66
1955	66 and 2 months
1956	66 and 4 months
1957	66 and 6 months
1958	66 and 8 months
1959	66 and 10 months
1960 or later	67

Table 20.4

How Your Starting Age Affects Your Benefit Amount

The benefit increases 8% per year, for each year you delay the start of benefits after your FRA up to age 70. For example, everyone born in 1960 or later has an FRA of age 67, so if they wait three years after their FRA until age 70 to start drawing, they will receive 24% (8% x 3 years) more per month than if they started at age 67.

Although benefits can be started as early as age 62, if you start drawing prior to your FRA, the benefit is reduced 6.66% per year for the three years just prior to your FRA, which equals a total 20% reduction for the three years. So, if someone with an FRA of 67 started drawing at 64, they would receive 20% less than their FRA amount.

If you start drawing more than three years prior to your FRA, your benefit is reduced by 5% per year for all other years. For example, if your FRA is 67 and you start drawing at 62, your benefit will be 30% less than if you had waited until 67, which is a 20% total decrease for three years, plus a 5% reduction for each of the other two years.

An example: Let's assume your benefit would be $1,000 per month if you start drawing at your FRA of 67. If you waited to start drawing at age 70 your benefit would be $1,240 (24% more than $1,000). Or if you started drawing at 62, your benefit would be $700 (30% less than $1,000). If you started drawing at 64, your benefit would be $800 (20% less than $1,000). This hypothetical person would draw $540 more per month by delaying benefits until 70 vs. starting at 62, which is a 77% increase.

For simplicity, the numbers above are on an annual basis. However, the SSA actually calculates your benefit based on the exact month you start drawing. For example, your benefit will be slightly higher if you start benefits at 63 and five months rather than at 63 and four months.

How Your Benefits Are Determined

Your monthly benefit is based on your highest-earning 35 years of employment. For example, if you worked 48 years, your lowest 13 earning years are not considered in your benefit calculation by the SSA. The calculation adjusts each year's earnings for inflation. In other words, a dollar you paid in social security tax 30 years ago is more beneficial than a dollar paid last year in terms of increasing your benefit amount.

After running your past earnings through the calculation, it results in a single number the SSA refers to as your *average indexed monthly earnings* (AIME). In other words, your AIME represents your average monthly earnings for your 35 highest-earning years in today's inflation-adjusted dollars. (Note: the calculation only takes into account earnings you paid social security tax on.) Also, you must work at least 10 years to draw any benefits.

Your AIME amount is put through another calculation by the SSA to determine your *primary insurance amount* (PIA). The PIA is the amount your monthly benefit would be if you started drawing at your FRA (age 67 for those born in 1960 or later). The PIA formula is the sum of three separate percentages of portions of your AIME. The PIA formula for 2022 is:

1. 90% of the first $1,024 of AIME, plus
2. 32% of AIME from $1,025 through $6,172, plus
3. 15% of AIME over $6,172

For example, if your AIME was $8,172, your PIA calculation would be as follows:

1. 90% x $1,024 = $922, plus
2. 32% x $5,148 = $1,647, plus
3. 15% x $2,000 = $300
4. the sum of a), b), and c) = $2,869

The PIA of $2,869 would be the monthly benefit amount if you started drawing at your FRA. As previously discussed in this chapter, if you started drawing at age 62 your monthly benefit would be 30% less than the PIA amount, and if you started benefits at age 70, the benefit would be 24% higher than the PIA.

The calculation is skewed to favor the lower portion of your AIME as you get 90% of the first earnings, then 32% of the next portion, and then only 15% of the highest earnings. The logic for this formula is that those who earned less, and paid less into the system, are probably in greater need of benefits, so the payout percentage is higher for the lower levels paid in. In other words, those who pay the most social security taxes do not get the same pro rata amount in benefits.

Workers should create an account on the ssa.gov website. Periodically check your account to ensure you were credited for all SS taxes paid on your behalf because benefits in retirement are based on the amount of taxes paid in.

Your Benefits on the SSA Website

For young and old, it's a good idea to create your personal account on the ssa.gov website to ensure they have correctly credited all payments to your account. In the *My Social Security* section it shows all of your employment wages and all contributions made to your account by your employers and the amounts you personally paid in Social Security tax (deductions from your paychecks). Notify the SSA if you believe you have not been credited with everything you should have as this could reduce the amount of your benefits when you start drawing. For example, once a year check to make sure the amount credited to your social security account is the same amount that your W-2 tax form indicates was withheld from your checks.

Your account will also indicate what the SSA currently estimates your monthly retirement benefits would be if you start drawing at three different ages, which are your FRA, age 70 (which is the latest anyone should start), and age 62 (the earliest you can draw). For example, as of July 2020, my estimated benefits were the following:

$ $2,403 a month if I start drawing at my FRA age of 66 years and 10 months (I was born in 1959)

$ $3,012 a month if I start drawing at age 70

$ $1,712 a month if I start drawing at age 62

Spousal Benefits

$ After being married for at least one year, a spouse who did not work enough to qualify for benefits themself is generally entitled to benefits based on the earned benefits of their spouse.

$ Spousal benefits may not be drawn until the spouse that earned the benefits starts drawing.

$ If the nonworking spouse begins receiving benefits at their FRA, they are entitled to receive 50% of the amount their spouse is receiving. For example, if the spouse who earned the benefits is receiving $2,000 per month, their spouse is entitled to an additional $1,000 per month.

- Spousal benefits may be drawn as early as age 62, but it will be at a reduced rate below 50% based on how many months they start before their FRA.
- However, the benefit for a nonworking spouse does not continue to increase after their FRA for delaying benefits, as it does for the spouse who earned the benefits; therefore, it would be a mistake to wait until age 70 to draw spousal benefits.

$ A spouse who worked and is entitled to their own benefit is entitled to receive either the larger of their own benefit, or the spousal benefit, but not both.

$ A widow(er) is generally entitled to whatever benefit their deceased spouse would have been entitled to, or their own benefit, whichever is greater.

$ If a widow(er) remarries after age 60, they may be entitled to the greater of their deceased spouse's benefit, or their spousal benefit based on their new spouse's benefit. If a widow(er) remarries prior to age 60, they are no longer entitled to spousal benefits based on their deceased spouse.

$ If divorced, you can receive spousal benefits beginning at age 62 based on your ex-spouse's earnings as long as you were married for at least 10 years, and you have not remarried (even if your ex-spouse has remarried). If you have been divorced for at least two years and you are age 62 or older, you may draw spousal benefits based on your ex-spouse, even if they haven't started drawing yet.

Wages Can Impact Benefits

$ If you start drawing benefits prior to your FRA and you continue to receive employment wages, your monthly benefit could be reduced until you reach your FRA. For the year 2022, you can earn up to $19,560 in wages without reducing your benefit.

$ Once you reach your FRA, you can earn an unlimited amount of wages without affecting your benefit. Having benefits reduced due to wages is at most a five-year issue between the ages of 62 and 67. The earliest you can draw is 62, and by age 67 everyone has reached their FRA. Those born before 1960 reach their FRA before age 67. Refer to the chart earlier in this chapter for FRA ages based on the year of birth.

$ Prior to reaching your FRA, for every $2 above the limit someone earns wages their benefit is reduced by $1. However, the wage limit is much higher in the year you attain your FRA. For those reaching their FRA in 2022, they can earn wages of $51,960 without any benefit reduction, and benefits are reduced by $1 for every $3 in wages over the limit. The wage limit has historically been increased each year for inflation.

$ Other types of income other than wages do not impact your benefits. You can always receive unlimited amounts of interest, dividends, rental income, capital gains, etc. without it impacting your benefits.

$ Your benefits will not be reduced because of your spouse's wages.

Prior to reaching full retirement age (FRA), earned wages may cause benefits to be reduced or eliminated. After reaching FRA, wages no longer impact benefits.

Taxation of Benefits

All recipients are potentially subject to federal income tax on up to 85% of their retirement benefits. The calculation is somewhat complex and confusing. The following are a few of the main points:

$ The *combined income* threshold at which benefits start being taxed is $25,000 for individuals and $32,000 for married couples filing joint tax returns.

$ Combined income is calculated by totaling your adjusted gross income (AGI), nontaxable income (municipal bond interest), and 50% of your Social Security. Many people reach this threshold fairly quickly.

$ IRS Publication 915 provides a full explanation of the tax, as well as the form to compute the tax, which contains a whopping 19 lines of calculations to determine the taxable amount.

$ After determining how much of the benefit is taxed, the amount of tax owed is dependent on the person's marginal tax bracket.

$ For example, if someone received a total of $20,000 in benefits for the year, the most they would have to include in their taxable income would be $17,000 (85% of the benefit). If their marginal federal tax bracket was 22%, they would pay at most $3,740 in federal taxes on their benefit.

$ As of 2022, there are 12 states that also tax Social Security benefits in some fashion.

Cost-of-Living Adjustment (COLA)

$ Since 1975, as required by law, the SSA makes an annual cost-of-living adjustment (COLA) to the amount of benefits for all recipients. The COLA is based on an inflation index for the previous year.

$ Through 2021, the average benefit increase for the last 10 years has been 1.9% per year. For the last 20 years, the average has been 2.2%. Three of the last 13 years saw no increase in benefits as the inflation index was near 0%. The 2021 COLA increase was 5.9% which was the largest in 39 years. The ssa.gov website provides a list of all past COLAs by year.

$ Although benefits are permanently at a reduced level for those who start receiving benefits prior to their FRA age, everyone receives the same percentage increase when there is a COLA.

PERSONAL CONSIDERATIONS

Deciding what age to start receiving benefits should be made with an understanding of the rules and laws and consideration of an individual's personal circumstances. As a reminder, the earliest you can draw is age 62, and the latest you would ever want to start drawing is age 70. Every month you wait between age 62 and 70 to start drawing will increase the amount of your monthly benefit when you do start drawing. The following are examples of issues that may be important to consider when deciding what age to start your benefits.

Health Issues and Family History

Drawing benefits early may be a wise choice if you have poor health conditions that are life threatening and your family has a genetic history of dying young. If you die just before age 70, a month before you start receiving benefits, it was obviously a mistake to delay (ignoring any potential spousal benefits). You would have simply lost out on receiving eight years of benefits as compared to if you would have started drawing at age 62. Having a spouse who may rely on spousal benefits if you die first is also a consideration.

Drawing benefits later may be a wise choice if you are in excellent health and your ancestors have a history of living into their late 80s and 90s. By delaying until age 70 and receiving the larger benefit, you will have received more total benefits by age 81 than if you started drawing at age 62. If you live to age 90+, you will receive substantially more by delaying.

Employment Status

If you have not reached your FRA and you earn wages in excess of the allowed threshold ($19,560 in 2022), your benefits will be reduced. After reaching FRA, employment income does not impact benefits.

There is some good news. If you start drawing before your FRA and your benefits are reduced or withheld because of your wages, your monthly benefit will increase starting at your FRA to take into account those months in which benefits were withheld. In other words, if your benefits are reduced or withheld altogether because your income exceeds the threshold, you will receive a larger monthly benefit once you reach your FRA.

Personal Tax Considerations

If your taxable income will likely decrease within a few years such that your tax bracket will decline, it may be beneficial to delay benefits.

Need for Immediate Income

If you need the money to live and pay bills now, that may be the most important consideration.

Personal Money Management and Investing Abilities

Even if you don't need the benefits early to pay expenses and if you invest the benefits well, the earnings on the money potentially make drawing early a wise choice. However, if you tend to spend money frivolously simply because you have money, delaying benefits until you actually need the money may be a better choice.

Marital Status

You may want to draw early if you are single and you want to ensure you leave assets to your children or others. If an unmarried person delays benefits and then dies just before they were to start drawing at age 70, their heirs get nothing.

Conversely, if a married wage earner dies, their surviving spouse is entitled to draw the larger of the same benefit their deceased spouse was drawing or the amount based on their own earned benefits. Therefore, if the surviving spouse had relatively low earned benefits (didn't work), the decision when to draw would logically be based on what is in the best interest of both spouses.

Potential for Law or Rule Changes

If you think tax laws or Social Security rules will be changed in a negative way in the future, it may be advantageous to start receiving benefits before such changes. For example:

- $ Prior to 1984, Social Security benefits were not subject to federal income taxes. Currently, up to 85% of benefits may be subject to income tax. Congress could decide to tax 100% of benefits, as well as eliminate any wage threshold.
- $ Income tax rates, in general, could increase in the future.
- $ Social Security fund trustees have estimated the fund will be insolvent by 2034 or sooner. To deal with this issue, benefits could be reduced or altered for all recipients, or just for some recipients. Logically, if any group is going to be more heavily taxed or have their benefits reduced, it would be those with higher levels of income.

Deciding when to start drawing monthly benefits is a significant financial decision that should be determined after carefully considering all relevant personal factors.

SUMMARY

The earliest you can draw benefits is age 62, but you have the choice to delay benefits until age 70, or anywhere in between. By drawing at age 70 instead of 62, your monthly benefit would be more than 75% larger. However, there are many considerations that impact what the best age is to start drawing, such as the need for income, employment status, health status, marital status, money management abilities, and others.

One often overlooked consideration is the possibility of drawing early and investing those benefits wisely. The long-term average annual return produced by numerous stock mutual funds could make drawing early an excellent choice. Of course, there is no assurance of what rate such mutual funds will earn in the future.

Workers paying Social Security tax should set up their personal account on the Social Security Administration website and confirm their account has been correctly credited for all payments made on their behalf to the SSA by their employers and themselves. Doing so is a good idea because the monthly benefits you receive in retirement are determined by how much was paid into your account from social security taxes.

CHAPTER 21

Compound Earnings: Hypothetical Examples

Compound earnings are such an important and powerful force relative to wealth accumulation that this chapter is devoted entirely to providing nine hypothetical examples of compound earnings tables.

There are three mathematical variables to consider in a compound earnings table:

1. Amount of money contributed/invested
2. Earnings rate
3. Length of time invested

Each of the three variables can dramatically impact how much wealth someone accumulates.

Best case: contribute a lot of money + earn a high rate of return + do it for many years = great results

Worst case: contribute very little money + earn a low rate of return + do it for very few years = poor results

The examples depicted in this chapter represent various hypothetical circumstances. The two factors of *time* (years invested) and the *amount invested* are the differing variables between the nine examples. Each of the nine tables show various compound annual growth rates (CAGRs).

Many readers will be able to make a connection with their personal circumstances and at least one of the hypotheticals. By looking at the values in the tables, readers will gain an understanding of the impact on wealth accumulation caused by factors such as:

$ Starting to invest 10 or 20 years earlier vs. 10 or 20 years later.

$ Investing twice as much money vs. half as much.

$ Earning a higher rate of return vs. a lower rate of return.

$ The combination of time invested, amount invested, and the CAGR.

Often, capable wage earners are never compelled to become investors simply because they are not aware of the enormous power money has to make more money when invested wisely for many years. In each of the hypotheticals, the amount contributed eventually becomes a small fraction of what the earnings accumulate to. In other words, at some point in time, the earning power of your money becomes a much more important factor for wealth accumulation than the amount you invested.

The transition from *you working for the money* to *the money working for you* is the essence of the enormous wealth-building capacity of compound earnings.

As a youngster, I constructed handwritten compound earning tables similar to those in this chapter. It was inspiring for my young mind to realize the enormous capacity of compounding to produce wealth. The message was clear and powerful: the more I contribute + the higher the CAGR + the sooner I get started + the longer I do it = the more exponential the accumulation of wealth will be!

I encourage readers to look at the tables and let your mind wander and consider the possibilities. What if I invest x amount for x years and earn x percent? What if I invest twice as much? What if I start now instead of 10 years from now? If I have success in the wealth-building process, what opportunities will it create to help myself and to assist others? Hopefully, spending some time looking at the tables will have a positive impact on some readers' wealth accumulation efforts.

Note: The hypothetical examples make no consideration for income taxes or inflation. The amount of any applicable income tax is dependent on the type of account the money is invested in, as well as each individual's personal tax situation. Each example assumes all annual contributions are made at the start of each year. However, for many investors, it will be more practical and convenient to make monthly investment contributions.

It is fair to assume we will have inflation in the years ahead, and hence, the values in the tables won't have the same purchasing power in the future as they do today. However, it is also fair to assume wages will also increase in the future, and therefore the assumed annual contributions in the tables would increase in the future. If the inflation rate averages 3% per year, the value (purchasing power) of money would be cut in half in approximately 24 years. In other words, in 24 years, it would take twice as many dollars to have the same purchasing power as today.

CLASSIC MIDDLE CLASS
Hypothetical Example #1

The Scenario: Contributions (investments) of $10,000 are made each year for 38 years between the ages of 28 and 65. A total of $380,000 is contributed (38 years x $10,000/year = $380,000).

This hypothetical is very feasible for middle-class wage earners and a great example of how average-income workers can become multimillionaires. This example could be a married couple with a combined income of $100,000, and each spouse invests $5,000 a year in a tax-advantaged retirement account beginning at age 28. The table graphically shows the huge difference the rate of return can make over the long haul. For example, at age 65, the 12% CAGR column amounts to more than seven times as much as the 4% CAGR column.

The table also shows the benefit of starting the investment process early. For example, the accumulated value at age 65 in the 12% column is $6.8 million. If the hypothetical couple had waited 10 years longer to start investing at age 38 instead of age 28, they would only have $2.1 million at age 65 ($4.7 million less).

The table also demonstrates the awesome earning potential of compounded earnings when repeated for many years. A total of $380,000 was invested. At a 7% CAGR, the cumulative earnings at age 65 amounted to almost five times more than the amount invested by the wage earner. At a 12% CAGR, the compounded earnings were responsible for over 94% of the total account value at age 65—a great example of the money working for you instead of you working for the money.

Year	Age	Total Contributions	Compound Annual Growth Rate (CAGR)			
			4%	7%	10%	12%
1	28	$10,000	$10,400	$10,700	$11,000	$11,200
2	29	$20,000	$21,216	$22,149	$23,100	$23,744
3	30	$30,000	$32,465	$34,399	$36,410	$37,793
5	32	$50,000	$56,330	$61,533	$67,156	$71,152
8	35	$80,000	$95,828	$109,780	$125,795	$137,757
13	40	$130,000	$172,919	$215,505	$269,750	$313,926
23	50	$230,000	$380,826	$571,767	$874,973	$1,171,552
28	55	$280,000	$519,663	$863,465	$1,476,309	$2,135,828
33	60	$330,000	$688,579	$1,272,588	$2,444,767	$3,835,210
38	65	$380,000	$894,091	$1,846,403	$4,004,478	$6,830,102

The table title is: **$10,000 Annual Contribution from Age 28 to 65**

Table 21.1

LATE BLOOMER
Hypothetical Example #2

The Scenario: Contributions are made annually for 18 years from age 48 until age 65. For the first five years, contributions of $24,000 per year are made; then $30,000 contributions per year are made for five years; followed by $36,000 contributions per year for five years; and for the last three years, $40,000 is contributed per year. A total of $570,000 is contributed/invested during the 18 years.

This example depicts someone with a slightly above average income who didn't start saving until age 48. Perhaps they focused on paying off their home mortgage and the costs of raising a family. Once they did start investing, they contributed substantially more per year than the $10,000 in example #1. Even though they got a late start investing, they are still able to accumulate a sizeable retirement fund.

Comparing example #1 with example #2 underscores how beneficial it is to start investing early. Even though #1 invested only $380,000 vs. $570,000 for #2, the total accumulation was considerably higher for #1 because of all the extra years of compound earnings. For example, a CAGR of 10% would result in example #1 accumulating 2.7 times as much money as example #2.

All Contributions Made from Age 48 to 65							
Year	Age	Annual Contribution	Total Contributions	Compound Annual Growth Rate (CAGR)			
				4%	7%	10%	12%
1	48	$24,000	$24,000	$24,960	$25,680	$26,400	$26,880
2	49	$24,000	$48,000	$50,918	$53,158	$55,440	$56,986
3	50	$24,000	$72,000	$77,915	$82,559	$87,384	$90,704
5	52	$24,000	$120,000	$135,191	$147,679	$161,175	$170,765
6	53	$30,000	$150,000	$171,799	$190,117	$210,292	$224,856
8	55	$30,000	$210,000	$249,466	$284,111	$323,753	$353,292
10	57	$30,000	$270,000	$333,470	$391,726	$461,042	$514,401
11	58	$36,000	$306,000	$384,249	$457,667	$546,746	$616,449
13	60	$36,000	$378,000	$491,981	$603,719	$744,722	$858,752
15	62	$36,000	$450,000	$608,505	$770,935	$984,274	$1,162,697
16	63	$40,000	$490,000	$674,445	$867,700	$1,126,702	$1,347,021
18	65	$40,000	$570,000	$814,344	$1,082,026	$1,455,709	$1,784,679

Table 21.2

20/20 VISION
Hypothetical Example #3

The Scenario: Contributions of $20,000 per year are made for five years from age 21 to 25 for a total of $100,000 in contributions. No additional contributions are made after age 25.

Example #3 is rarely achieved, but is perhaps the easiest way for a young visionary wage earner to accumulate wealth. A more typical approach is when someone enjoys (spends) what money comes their way when they are young (early 20s), and then starts thinking seriously about investing in their 30s or 40s.

The hypothetical young person in this example essentially sets themself for life financially by the age of 25. Their total investment of $100,000 is capable of producing 50 to 100 times that amount in earnings over the 45-year time span until they reach 65 years of age. Even if someone started investing a couple of years later at age 23 or so, the results are still quite good.

How is a young person supposed to save $20,000 a year? That's for you to figure out based on your personal circumstances. The bottom line is—earn more and spend less. For example, find inexpensive (or free) housing, stop buying things you really don't need, buy a cheaper car or no car at all, don't buy a house quite yet, utilize no-cost recreation opportunities, work some overtime, delay starting a family for a few years, drink free water instead of expensive beverages, etc. The point of this example is not for me to tell young people how to live or what their goals should be, but rather to illustrate a path to wealth accumulation, if that is what they wish to pursue.

Contributions of $20,000 a Year for 5 Years from Age 21 to 25							
Year	Age	Annual Contribution	Total Contributions	Compound Annual Growth Rate (CAGR)			
				4%	7%	10%	12%
1	21	$20,000	$20,000	$20,800	$21,400	$22,000	$22,400
2	22	$20,000	$40,000	$42,432	$44,298	$46,200	$47,488
3	23	$20,000	$60,000	$64,929	$68,799	$72,820	$75,587
4	24	$20,000	$80,000	$88,326	$95,015	$102,102	$107,057
5	25	$20,000	$100,000	$112,660	$123,066	$134,312	$142,304
10	30	$0	$100,000	$137,068	$172,606	$216,311	$250,788
20	40	$0	$100,000	$202,893	$339,542	$561,055	$778,909
30	50	$0	$100,000	$300,332	$667,931	$1,455,233	$2,419,173
40	60	$0	$100,000	$444,564	$1,313,922	$3,774,500	$7,513,585
45	65	$0	$100,000	$540,881	$1,842,844	$6,078,870	$13,241,505

Table 21.3

HIGH-INCOME SAVER
Hypothetical Example #4

The Scenario: Contributions of $50,000 are made to the account each year for 40 years between the ages of 26 and 65. A total of $2,000,000 is contributed (40 years x $50,000/year = $2,000,000).

Example #4 may seem extraordinary for many wage earners, but it is quite feasible for someone commanding an annual income of about $200,000 or more. Being able to save and invest large amounts at a young age sets the stage for wealth accumulation amounts that very few investors obtain.

At a 12% CAGR, the total wealth accumulation, for this example, just about doubles every five years. Total contributions of $2 million is a significant amount to save over a 40-year period, but even more impressive is that the compound earnings can grow to 10 or 20 times the amount invested.

\$50,000 Annual Contribution for 30 Years						
Year	Age	Annual Contribution	Total Contributions	Compound Annual Growth Rate (CAGR)			
				4%	7%	10%	12%
1	26	$50,000	$50,000	$52,000	$53,500	$55,000	$56,000
2	27	$50,000	$100,000	$106,080	$110,745	$115,500	$118,720
5	30	$50,000	$250,000	$281,649	$307,665	$335,781	$355,759
10	35	$50,000	$500,000	$624,318	$739,180	$876,558	$982,729
15	40	$50,000	$750,000	$1,041,227	$1,344,403	$1,747,486	$2,087,664
20	45	$50,000	$1,000,000	$1,548,460	$2,193,259	$3,150,125	$4,034,937
25	50	$50,000	$1,250,000	$2,165,587	$3,383,824	$5,409,088	$7,466,697
30	55	$50,000	$1,500,000	$2,916,417	$5,053,652	$9,047,171	$13,514,630
35	60	$50,000	$1,750,000	$3,829,916	$7,395,673	$14,906,340	$24,173,156
40	65	$50,000	$2,000,000	$4,941,327	$13,989,052	$24,342,591	$42,957,120

Table 21.4

TEENAGER AND ADULT SAVER
Hypothetical Example #5

The Scenario: Contributions of $2,000 per year are made to the account for 50 years between the ages of 16 and 65. A total of $100,000 is contributed (50 years x $2,000/year = $100,000).

Example #5 is perhaps the easiest example to achieve of all the hypotheticals in the chapter. Investing $2,000 a year is feasible for the majority of wage earners. Commencing contributions at the young age of 16 is a significant factor in maximizing the total accumulation.

Convincing a teenager to invest a sizable portion of their hard-earned wages is usually easier said than done. However, if a teenager develops the discipline to always invest a certain portion of their wages, there is a good chance it will be a routine they will stick with in the future. That one habit has the potential to make a profound positive impact on the wealth accumulation process.

$2,000 Annual Contribution From Age 16 to 65						
Year	Age	Total Contributions	Compound Annual Growth Rate (CAGR)			
			4%	7%	10%	12%
1	16	$2,000	$2,080	$2,140	$2,200	$2,240
2	17	$4,000	$4,243	$4,430	$4,620	$4,749
5	20	$10,000	$11,266	$12,307	$13,431	$14,230
10	25	$20,000	$24,973	$29,567	$35,062	$39,309
15	30	$30,000	$41,649	$53,776	$69,899	$83,507
20	35	$40,000	$61,938	$87,730	$126,005	$161,397
25	40	$50,000	$86,623	$135,353	$216,364	$298,668
30	45	$60,000	$116,657	$202,146	$361,887	$540,585
40	55	$80,000	$197,653	$427,219	$973,704	$1,718,285
50	65	$100,000	$317,548	$869,972	$2,560,599	$5,376,041

Table 21.5

THE ROTH CHILD
Hypothetical Example #6

The Scenario: Contributions are made annually into a custodial Roth account for 11 years from age eight until age 18. No contributions are made after age 18. Contributions start at $500 in the first year and periodically increase during the 11 years as shown in the table. A total of $22,000 is contributed.

Example #6 is somewhat of a novelty. A child investing annually in a Roth beginning at age eight is rare. Most parents don't think about setting up a Roth for their children because most are not aware it can be done. The key benefit for establishing a custodial Roth is the earnings grow tax free. Numerous rules and laws apply to this scenario, so seek competent advice.

A few considerations for this scenario:

1. The child must have *earned income* (wages) to be eligible for Roth contributions.
2. Federal and state child labor laws should be obeyed.
3. Social Security taxes should generally be paid on the wages.
4. There are many jobs minor children can't legally have. However, there is no age limit for some jobs such as babysitting, delivering newspapers, minor chores around a private home, or doing certain types of jobs in a business owned by their parent, as well as some other jobs.

Annual Roth Contributions from Ages 8 to 18							
Year	Age	Annual Contribution	Total Contributions	Compound Annual Growth Rate (CAGR)			
				4%	7%	10%	12%
1	8	$500	$500	$520	$535	$594	$665
2	9	$500	$1,000	$1,061	$1,107	$1,203	$1,305
3	10	$1,000	$2,000	$2,143	$2,255	$2,424	$2,582
4	11	$1,000	$3,000	$3,269	$3,483	$3,766	$4,012
5	12	$1,000	$4,000	$4,440	$4,797	$5,243	$5,613
6	13	$2,000	$6,000	$6,697	$7,272	$7,967	$8,526
7	14	$2,000	$8,000	$9,045	$9,921	$10,964	$11,790
8	15	$2,000	$10,000	$11,487	$12,756	$14,260	$15,444
9	16	$3,000	$13,000	$15,066	$16,859	$18,986	$20,658
10	17	$3,000	$16,000	$18,789	$21,249	$24,185	$26,497
11	18	$6,000	$22,000	$25,781	$29,156	$33,203	$36,396
12	19	$0	$22,000	$26,812	$31,197	$36,523	$40,764
13	20	$0	$22,000	$27,884	$33,381	$40,176	$45,655
23	30	$0	$22,000	$41,276	$65,666	$104,206	$141,799
33	40	$0	$22,000	$61,098	$129,175	$270,283	$440,406
43	50	$0	$22,000	$90,440	$254,106	$701,044	$1,367,834
53	60	$0	$22,000	$133,874	$499,865	$1,818,327	$4,248,285
58	65	$0	$22,000	$162,878	$701,087	$2,928,434	$7,486,930

Table 21.6

THE ROTH CHILD AND ADULT SAVER
Hypothetical Example #7

The Scenario: Contributions identical to those in example #6 are made annually into a custodial Roth for 11 years from age 8 until age 18. However, in this example, $6,000 is also contributed each year from age 19 to age 65. A total of $304,000 is contributed.

Although the annual amount invested is not an extraordinary sum, the diligent effort to invest consistently year after year and the resulting wealth that can accumulate is quite extraordinary.

This table once again highlights the benefit of starting the investment process as young as possible. Only 7.2% ($22,000) of the total $304,000 was contributed by age 18. However, at a 10% CAGR, that 7.2% of the contributions was responsible for producing over 1/3 of the total account value at age 65 ($2,928,434 of the $8,683,468 total).

Annual Roth Contributions from Ages 8 to 65							
Year	Age	Annual Contribution	Total Contributions	Compound Annual Growth Rate (CAGR)			
				4%	7%	10%	12%
1	8	$500	$500	$520	$556	$594	$665
2	9	$500	$1,000	$1,061	$1,130	$1,203	$1,305
3	10	$1,000	$2,000	$2,143	$2,279	$2,424	$2,582
4	11	$1,000	$3,000	$3,269	$3,509	$3,766	$4,012
5	12	$1,000	$4,000	$4,440	$4,825	$5,243	$5,613
6	13	$2,000	$6,000	$6,697	$7,302	$7,967	$8,526
7	14	$2,000	$8,000	$9,045	$9,954	$10,964	$11,790
8	15	$2,000	$10,000	$11,487	$12,790	$14,260	$15,444
9	16	$3,000	$13,000	$15,066	$16,896	$18,986	$20,658
10	17	$3,000	$16,000	$18,789	$21,288	$24,185	$26,497
11	18	$6,000	$22,000	$25,781	$29,199	$33,203	$36,396
13	20	$6,000	$34,000	$40,614	$46,719	$54,036	$59,902
23	30	$6,000	$94,000	$135,037	$180,604	$245,342	$303,974
33	40	$6,000	$154,000	$274,806	$443,978	$741,541	$1,062,023
43	50	$6,000	$214,000	$481,697	$962,073	$2,028,553	$3,416,411
53	60	$6,000	$274,000	$787,948	$1,981,246	$5,366,731	$10,728,781
58	65	$6,000	$304,000	$992,457	$2,815,719	$8,683,468	$18,950,469

Table 21.7

SMALL INHERITANCE
Hypothetical Example #8

The Scenario: Resulting from an inheritance, a onetime contribution of $24,000 is made at age 21 with no contributions thereafter.

Example #8 is the simplest hypothetical in the chapter. A young person receiving such an inheritance may be tempted to buy that new car they always wanted or enjoy the money in some other way. But for a 21-year-old who takes a longer term view and invests the money instead, the wealth accumulation in the years ahead could be significant from a $24,000 inheritance.

Virtually all of the earnings could be tax free as well by investing the inheritance in a Roth over several years (assuming the inheritor also had earned income to qualify for a Roth contribution). This could be accomplished by shifting the maximum allowable amount of $6,000 per year into a Roth. After five years or so, all the money would then be in the Roth, and therefore all future earnings would be tax free.

$24,000 Onetime Contribution at Age 21						
Year	Age	Total Contributions	Compound Annual Growth Rate (CAGR)			
			4%	7%	10%	12%
1	21	$24,000	$24,960	$25,680	$26,400	$26,880
5	25	$0	$29,200	$33,661	$38,652	$42,296
10	30	$0	$35,526	$47,212	$62,250	$74,540
15	35	$0	$43,223	$66,217	$100,254	$131,366
20	40	$0	$52,587	$92,872	$161,460	$231,511
25	45	$0	$63,980	$130,258	$260,033	$408,002
30	50	$0	$77,842	$182,694	$418,786	$719,038
35	55	$0	$94,706	$256,238	$674,458	$1,267,191
40	60	$0	$115,224	$359,387	$1,086,222	$2,233,223
45	65	$0	$140,188	$504,059	$1,749,372	$3,935,702

Table 21.8

THE PATH TO $1 MILLION
Hypothetical Example #9

The Scenario: This table reflects the two variables of time and CAGR to reach a target value of $1 million by age 65. The values in each cell indicate the required annual contribution based on the age when the contributions start (and continue annually thereafter) and the CAGR.

The younger the age when contributions start and the higher the CAGR achieved, the smaller the required annual contribution is to obtain a $1 million value at age 65. Likewise, the older the age contributions start and the lower the CAGR achieved, the larger the required annual contribution has to be to obtain a $1 million value at age 65.

For example, at one extreme, if someone started contributions at age 20 and achieved a 12% CAGR, it would require an annual contribution of $658 to obtain $1 million by age 65. At the other extreme, if someone started contributions at age 60 and achieved a 4% CAGR, they would have to contribute $177,526 per year to obtain $1 million by age 65.

Annual Contribution Required to Amass $1 Million at Age 65					
Starting Age	4% CAGR Required Annual Contribution	7% CAGR Required Annual Contribution	10% CAGR Required Annual Contribution	12% CAGR Required Annual Contribution	Number of Contribution Years
20	$7,945	$3,271	$1,265	$658	45
25	$10,119	$4,682	$2,055	$1,164	40
30	$13,056	$6,761	$3,355	$2,069	35
35	$17,145	$9,894	$5,527	$3,700	30
40	$23,089	$14,777	$9,244	$6,697	25
45	$32,291	$22,798	$15,873	$12,392	20
50	$48,021	$37,192	$28,613	$23,951	15
55	$80,088	$67,643	$57,042	$50,879	10
60	$177,526	$162,515	$148,907	$140,545	5

Table 21.9

THE RULE OF 72

The Rule of 72 is an easy way to estimate how long it takes for investments to double in value. Divide 72 by the annual compound rate of return to get a close approximation of the number of years to double your money. For example, 72 divided by 8% equals nine years to double.

It is also a handy tool to estimate the impact of long-term inflation. Dividing 72 by an assumed annual inflation rate will indicate the approximate number of years when purchasing power will be cut in half, or in other words, when it will require twice as much money to purchase the same amount of goods and services as today. For example, 72 divided by 3% (inflation rate) means purchasing power would be cut in half in 24 years.

The Rule of 72 is a close approximation, however, it is not exact. The precise time period depends on the compounding frequency (annual, monthly, daily, etc.). Also, the higher the rate of return, the less accurate the calculation. Mathematicians would generally opt for using 70 or 69.3 as the dividend rather than 72 for a more precise answer, but 72 is divisible by more whole numbers and is, therefore, an easier benchmark to do quick calculations in your head.

THE JEFF KOTTKAMP STORY

Jeff Kottkamp is an example of someone with superior ability in a specific field who took full advantage of his natural gift. He was my roommate at Southern Illinois University (SIU) and had a truly exceptional talent in the field of accounting, in which he majored.

He was not the stereotypical nerdy and boring accountant type. He had a wonderful personality, and we thoroughly enjoyed ourselves on many occasions together. However, Jeff had the capacity and commitment to study and apply himself to learning in a way that set him apart from his peers. He knew he had a unique ability in his chosen field, but he also knew it was up to him to put in the time and effort to learn and obtain the vast amount of knowledge necessary to excel as an accountant.

During Jeff's senior year, he studied the entire spring semester for the Certified Public Accountant (CPA) exam in addition to his normal class load.

In May, he passed all four parts of the CPA exam and then proceeded to take and ace all of his final college exams the very next week. Those accomplishments basically put him in the enviable position of being able to choose which accounting firm he wanted to work for. He went on to have a distinguished career as a partner with the international accounting firm Deloitte & Touche, which was recognized by SIU when he was asked to give the commencement speech to the College of Business at our alma mater in 2011.

Jeff's intellect and innate accounting ability would have allowed him to still make good grades by putting in considerably less effort than he did; that was never a consideration for him. Some people have extraordinary talent, and other people are hard workers. When one person possesses both of those qualities, great things can happen. Jeff's story is a testimony to that.

JEFF'S LESSON: Hard work may beat talent when talent doesn't work hard. When you have talent and you work hard, phenomenal results can occur.

Concluding Thoughts

CHAPTER 22

Myths and Misconceptions That Could Cost You Money

1. AVERAGE WAGE EARNERS CAN'T BECOME MULTIMILLIONAIRES

I've upped the ante. Not only can average wage earners become millionaires, but they can also become multimillionaires without using farfetched or extraordinary hypotheticals. For example, investing $500 a month into a Roth IRA for 40 years at a compound annual earnings rate of 10% will grow to over $3 million. If a couple invested $12,000 (or $6,000 each) per year into a Roth for 35 years and achieved 10% average annual earnings, they would have just under $4 million. Incidentally, numerous stock mutual funds have averaged in excess of 10% annually for multiple decades. Past performance is no guarantee of future performance.

The reason so many people view becoming a millionaire as an unrealistic goal is because they never get started with a consistent save-and-invest pattern. Simply put, many people fail to accumulate significant wealth as a matter of choice. *Chapter 21 is a collection of various hypothetical compound earning examples.*

2. CREDIT CARDS ARE BAD

Yes, credit cards are bad if not used wisely, and certain people shouldn't have them for that reason. On the other hand, credit cards are an excellent financial tool with many good features and virtually no bad features for those who use them judiciously.

My wife and I use credit cards for virtually all of our consumer spending for the following reasons:

- \$ The credit card company (not us) is responsible for fraudulent charges, if they occur.
- \$ Since we pay our entire bill monthly, there is no interest cost, and our card has no annual fee.
- \$ They are much more convenient than paying with cash.
- \$ They help improve our credit score.
- \$ Our card has a 2% cash-back feature for purchases.

Chapter 5 is devoted entirely to a discussion of credit and debit cards.

3. YOU CAN'T ACCESS MONEY IN AN IRA UNTIL AGE 59½

One of the biggest investment myths is that IRA funds are tied up and can't be withdrawn until age 59½. In reality, distributions (withdrawals) can be made for any reason at any age from an IRA. But generally, if a distribution is made prior to age 59½, there is a 10% penalty imposed in addition to reporting the distribution as taxable income. However, there are about nine specific exceptions when the 10% penalty is waived for reasons such as death, disability, qualified educational expenses, etc. *IRAs are discussed in detail in Chapter 14.*

4. YOUR HOME IS A GREAT INVESTMENT

In general, home values have increased over the years, and in some areas, they have risen substantially. However, homes generally don't constitute good investments once all the costs of ownership are considered, such as annual property taxes, insurance, maintenance, repairs, and periodic updating, as well as costs to buy and sell the home. Home ownership generally resembles an expense more than an investment asset over the long haul. Purchasing a home should primarily be motivated by housing needs and desires.

Home price indexes show that home values have increased only about 1% more than the inflation rate long term, which is far less than the long-term appreciation for common stocks, for example. *You can read more about home ownership in Chapter 7.*

5. INVESTING IN STOCKS IS ALL JUST A BIG GAMBLE

History indicates this myth is fundamentally inaccurate. Stocks, on average, have actually provided better returns than all of the other major asset classes when looked at over generational time periods. Stocks certainly can and do fluctuate in value, but a broadly diversified portfolio of high-quality stocks has been the most effective way for most investors to accumulate wealth over the long term.

I agree that being involved with the speculative fringes of stock-related activities can be very high risk, such as day trading, options trading, futures trading, trading on margin, and a heavy concentration in speculative stocks. *Chapter 9 covers investing vs. speculating and gambling, and Chapter 11 is devoted to stocks.*

6. NEVER BUY A NEW CAR BECAUSE THEY LOSE VALUE IMMEDIATELY

We have all heard someone say, "When you buy a brand new car, you lose money because it depreciates thousands of dollars the minute you drive it off the dealer's lot." Guess what? The same thing happens when you buy a used car or virtually any other consumer retail product. It's called wholesale price vs. retail price.

Both new and used car dealers have various costs to cover to be profitable and to stay in business. The primary way they cover those costs is selling cars for a higher price than they paid for them. If you try to sell a car (new or used) back to the dealer the day after you bought it, you're going to take a haircut. They sold it to you at the retail price, and they will buy it back at the wholesale price.

7. HIGH RISK MEANS HIGH RETURN

Saying that high risk means high return suggests there is generally a commensurate potential for high return just because you take a high risk. However, quite frequently, higher risk simply means a higher likelihood you will lose some or all of your money, particularly when it comes to extremely high-risk ventures, activities of random chance, or high-frequency wagering in which a middle-man repeatedly gets a cut of the action.

I have spent my adult life trying to identify investments that actually have a disproportionately low risk vs. the potential for high return, which is considerably more appealing to me than trying to sort through high-risk opportunities to make high returns. *Chapter 9 provides a deeper discussion of this topic.*

8. IT'S BEST TO PAY OFF YOUR HOME LOAN AS QUICKLY AS POSSIBLE

Many knowledgeable and high-profile authors and financial gurus espouse that homeowners should pay off their mortgages as quickly as possible. Their most common talking point is that tens of thousands of dollars can be saved by having a 15-year mortgage instead of a 30-year mortgage. Their basic premise is that people lack the discipline to have a 30-year loan with a lower payment and to invest the difference. In other words, their belief is that people are better off with a high monthly mortgage payment because it is a de facto forced savings plan.

If someone has a fixed-rate mortgage at 8%, 7%, or even 6%, I would agree with this philosophy. But for the millions of homeowners with fixed-rate loans between 2% and 5% there is another worthy strategic consideration. They could keep their mortgage and invest the extra money in stock mutual funds or ETFs, which have produced returns in the 9% to 11% range over the long haul. In fact, I recently did exactly that when I refinanced our home loan at 2% in October 2021.

The gurus have solid logic behind their advice because they have seen so many people *spend the difference* instead of *invest the difference*. For those with low fixed-rate mortgages and the discipline to invest the difference, their low interest rate loan may provide a unique financial opportunity. *In Chapter 7, this issue is discussed in more detail.*

9. YOU ARE WASTING MONEY IF YOU RENT INSTEAD OF OWN

The common wisdom is that when you rent, you are not *building equity* like when you're a homeowner; therefore, you are wasting money if you rent. If the total costs of home ownership were the same as the total costs of renting, I would readily agree. Unfortunately, that is usually not the case after all the costs of home ownership are considered.

If you have a lower housing cost because you choose to rent rather than own, you can invest the money you saved in a tax-advantaged retirement account or a mutual fund to build equity. *Renting vs. owning is discussed in Chapter 7.*

10. ROTHS, IRAs, AND 401(k)s ARE THE MOST LUCRATIVE TAX-ADVANTAGED ACCOUNTS

This is a little bit of a trick statement because Roths, IRAs and 401(k)s are all excellent tax-advantaged opportunities to utilize. However, my favorite and the most lucrative tax-advantaged account is the Health Savings Account (HSA). Unfortunately, not everyone qualifies for an HSA, but for those who do, it is a terrific opportunity.

HSA contributions are tax deductible, the earnings grow tax free, and distributions are also tax free if made for a qualified medical expense (QME). To my knowledge, HSAs and related accounts, such as FSAs, are the only accounts in which contributions are tax deductible *and* distributions can be made tax free. *See Chapter 15 for more information on HSAs.*

11. 529 PLANS ARE THE BEST WAY TO SAVE FOR COLLEGE

Contributing to a 529 plan may be a great idea for wealthy grandparents or high-income parents who are already contributing the maximum to their tax-advantaged retirement accounts. But for most working parents, the tax benefits and withdrawal flexibilities of a Roth, a traditional IRA, a 401(k), or even a regular mutual fund or ETF are usually a better choice than a 529 plan.

Since there is no tax deduction for contributing to a 529 account, the only tax incentive is that the distributions of earnings from the account are not taxed if the money is used for a qualified education expense (QEE). However, earnings withdrawn for reasons other than QEEs are fully taxable and subject to a 10% penalty. There are exceptions in which the penalty is waived. *There is more information about 529 plans in Chapter 15.*

12. TARGET-DATE FUNDS ARE THE BEST CHOICE IF YOU ARE CLOSE TO RETIREMENT

The basic premise of target-date funds is simply to shift an increasing percentage of your account out of stocks and into bonds as you get closer to retirement. In previous years, when interest rates were higher, target-date funds made more sense. With bond interest rates currently near all-time lows, it's perplexing these funds are still popular and promoted as much as they are.

Being invested in a fund that *targets* the exact year you plan to retire sounds so perfect and logical. Investors should understand that we experienced an unprecedented 40-year decline in interest rates from 1981 to 2021, and the risk to bond prices if/when interest rates rise. *Target-date funds are also discussed near the end of Chapter 14.*

13. IT'S ALWAYS BEST TO WAIT UNTIL AGE 70 TO START DRAWING SOCIAL SECURITY

Article after article suggest it is best to wait until age 70 to start drawing Social Security because your monthly check will be larger by waiting. That advice is a bit reckless as a blanket statement. True, the check will be larger by waiting, but that doesn't necessarily mean it's wise to do so. In fact, there are some situations when waiting until age 70 to start drawing can cost an individual or their heirs a lot of money. *Chapter 20 is devoted entirely to Social Security.*

14. GETTING INTO A HIGHER TAX BRACKET TRIGGERS A LARGE TAX BILL

Some people are fearful of making more money because they believe it could result in them owing thousands of dollars more in taxes because they made one dollar too much and jumped up into a higher tax bracket. A higher tax bracket means you pay a higher rate only on earnings above the threshold for that bracket. *Tax brackets are explained in more detail at the end of Chapter 15 in the Tax Terminology section.*

MY PERSONAL STORY

By college graduation in 1983, I had decided to pursue a career as a financial advisor (stockbroker). I was keenly interested in investing and financial matters. It seemed like a perfect fit for me, but the problem was that my profile was not a perfect fit for the job. Hiring young people right out of college was rare in the industry, since providing advice on how to invest money is generally viewed as a domain for mature professionals with experience.

However, I decided the brokerage firm Edward D. Jones & Co. was where I wanted to work. When their hiring officer denied my request for an interview, I got creative and aggressive. I sent him a letter accepting the job he had refused to even interview me for; then I got him on the phone and told him I had to be in his area the following week (100 miles away), and I just wanted to come by and shake his hand. We shook hands, then we talked for two hours, and ultimately, I walked out with a job offer. I was stoked!

I think he hired me more out of amusement, curiosity, and appreciation for my original approach rather than me actually fitting the profile of a good candidate for the job. Over the years, in various meetings, he loved to tell the story of how he and his wife laughed as he read her the "acceptance letter" from this brazen and arrogant kid to whom he hadn't even offered a job.

Becoming a "financial advisor" sounds sort of prestigious and distinguished, but the harsh reality is that it's a 100% commission sales position. Until a new broker lands customers, they are providing financial advice to absolutely nobody. Therefore, my new career as a Jones broker was a bit daunting, as about 50% of new hires didn't survive the first year in those days, but it also was extremely appealing because of the enormous upside potential.

There I was, fresh out of college, no practical business skills, no sales experience, and certainly no wisdom or background worthy of advising people on how to invest their life savings. However, the opportunity and job description was like a dream-come-true situation for me. An occupation with no income limit and no capital investment required on my part, in which I set my own hours and I was my own boss, and working in the industry of my choice.

Candidly, when I started with Jones, I was scared. I wasn't afraid of the work or process; I was afraid I might fail. There was so much about the job I didn't know, and even though I was ready to give it my best shot, I really had no idea if I could succeed. I did have one quality that was paramount to my eventual success—one positive trait that dwarfed all the negatives—and that was an all-in 100% commitment to do everything I could do to not fail.

The first part of my formal training was spending two months under the mentorship of Bob Sheets in his Muscatine, Iowa, branch. Two weeks of the training was to make cold calls in the community, mimicking the process all new brokers went through when opening their office. It entailed knocking on doors, introducing myself and the firm, and asking questions to determine if people were prospective customers.

I actually enjoyed the cold calling process and consistently made more calls per day than was required. At the end of each day, I would sit down with Bob and go over every one of my calls. I always had thorough details such as what stocks they owned and how many shares, if they had an IRA and where, if they had CDs at the bank and when they matured, and sometimes how much was in the CDs.

At the culmination of my training with Bob, he was confident I was going to be a successful broker, which surprised me because I was still very unsure.

He confessed that after my first few days of cold calling, he thought I was the biggest BS artist he had ever met. He said, "When you came back with all this detailed information about what people owned, and how much, and where it's invested, I thought you were making it up. No way anybody can get that much information out of people on a cold call. Then, on your callbacks, you started setting appointments, and people came in and invested, and I realized you were real."

During the final week of group training with 30 other new brokers at headquarters in St. Louis, the training partners would give a short written analysis of each new broker. The only comment they made about me was, "Kurt asked more questions than the rest of the class combined." At this point, I was locked in and ready to go. I now knew what it took to be a successful broker.

When I arrived in Morganton, North Carolina, my newly assigned town, the one thing I was certain of was that I was not going to fail due to lack of effort. For the first two years, I didn't take a single day off unless I was out of town (Sundays were a half day). I made well over 1,000 cold calls in person in the first year, and I was following the Jones recipe for success, but what I really became proficient at was cold calling on the phone.

It quickly became obvious that developing a base of clients was just like football—it was a contact game! The more contacts I made, the more business I developed. There were approximately 5,000 residents listed in the county directory as being a homeowner, and I systematically cold-called every single one of them. I became a self-taught expert in the art of prospecting for customers on the phone.

After I left the brokerage business, a local bank president curiously asked me how I knew so much about their customers. Talking with other bankers, he said he confirmed they were having the same problem. At one point, they even hired a private detective to figure out if I had a mole employee inside their bank that was feeding me information. In reality, I was just really good at systematically gathering information as I talked with potential customers. For example, if someone told me their CD was renewed last week, it went on my calendar to call them back just before the next maturity. The banker's paranoid suspicion of me was perhaps the best validation I ever received that I was doing a great job.

There are many anecdotal stories I would love to share about the early years building the business, but what it really boils down to, using a highly technical term, I worked my ass off! But it didn't feel like work because I was passionate about the opportunity, and I enjoyed what I was doing. I would have been disgusted and miserable if I was taking days off early in the process.

Thankfully, my efforts were rewarded. By the end of my second year with Jones, I ranked in the top 20% in the firm in terms of business volume. By year seven of the firm's 1,000+ brokers, I had the highest production for 12 months.

In retrospect, my intensity and effort the first two years in the business were pivotal for how the rest of my life has played out. Some of my peers accused me of working too much back then, but I see it differently.

MY LESSON: If you live like few people will for a while, you may be able to live like few people can for the rest of your life.

CHAPTER 23

99 E+S+I+R Reminders

This final chapter is a collection of 99 brief reminders pertaining to key topics discussed throughout the book. You may want to use this list to flag items particularly relevant to your situation that you need to take action on or items you simply want to be more mindful of going forward. Like-kind items are generally clustered together in the list.

WEALTH ACCUMULATION AND INVESTING PHILOSOPHY

1. EARN+SAVE+INVEST+REPEAT are the four distinct steps to the wealth accumulation formula. When adopted as a way of life, they can lead to improving financial well-being, security, and freedom.

2. During step one (EARN) of the wealth accumulation formula, **you work for the money**. During step three (INVEST), the **money works for you**. Step two (SAVE) is the necessary bridge in the middle that allows *earners* to become *investors*. Step four (REPEAT) is doing the first three steps over and over for many years.

3. Many middle-class wage earners have become millionaires by simply investing on a regular basis in high-quality stock mutual funds in their retirement accounts.

4. Accumulating wealth doesn't mean living like a miser or always doing without, but rather living wisely and utilizing the various financial opportunities available to improve your financial well-being to live your best life.

5. One of the simplest ways to become a multimillionaire is to start investing at a young age (teens or 20s). Time is on your side when you are young—but only if you seize the opportunity and take action. *Time in the market* is more important than *timing the market.*

6. Wealth accumulation is a lifelong journey. Look for opportunities and be willing to assume some calculated risks, but don't take excessive risks hoping to get rich quick.

7. Wealth accumulation seldom happens by accident. It requires discipline, consistency, and specific, intentional actions.

8. A more accurate version of the old adage "money can't buy happiness" is "frivolous spending can't buy happiness." Wealth accumulation is about what you retain, not what you earn.

9. Compound earnings have been called the eighth wonder of the world for good reason. Earning just a few percentage points higher rate of return year after year can have an exponential effect on wealth accumulation.

10. The three components of compound earnings growth are: (1) the amount invested, (2) the earnings rate, and (3) the length of time invested. Each of the three are equally important to accumulate wealth.

11. Don't let every increase in pay be offset by an increase in spending. The price of short-term pleasure is often long-term pain.

12. A single investment of $22,095 compounded annually at 11% will grow to $1 million in 40 years. Of the $1 million total, 97.8% came from the earnings, only 2.2% was the original contribution—a graphic example of the power of compound earnings.

13. The Rule of 72: Divide 72 by the annual compound rate of return to get a close approximation of the number of years to double your money. For example, 72 divided by 8% equals nine years to double.

14. Inflation (rising prices) erodes the true value of money. If your investments are not growing as fast as inflation and your rate of taxation, then you are losing value.

15. Think and act like a long-term investor—not like a trader, speculator, or gambler. Don't get lured into taking excessive risks by visions of making fast money.

16. Don't mistake quick profits from a rising stock market as personal investing expertise.

17. Understand the risk and reward characteristics before making any investment. Make investment decisions based on prudence and objective rational thinking, not on greed and fear.

18. Investing with borrowed money is an easy way to add risk and stress. Many investors have gone bankrupt due to leveraged transactions.

SAVING AND SPENDING

19. When used judiciously, credit cards have numerous positive features that far outweigh the negatives, but they can lead to financial problems when used unwisely. Don't have a credit card at all if it will likely lead to unnecessary spending.

20. Credit card positives include: fraud protection, potential cash-back rebate for purchases, no fees or charges when balances are paid in full and on time, credit history growth, travel benefits, convenience, and a retrievable record of all charges.

21. Credit card negatives include: may encourage unnecessary spending, unwise use can create troublesome levels of debt, high interest rates charged on unpaid balances, fees charged for late payments, annual fees may be charged, and can create a bad credit history.

22. Promptly review your monthly credit and debit card statements and immediately notify the card company if there are any errors or fraudulent charges listed.

23. Pay off your entire credit card balance every month to avoid interest expenses. Only charge what you can pay in full each month. High-interest-rate credit card debt can be a major hindrance for wealth accumulation.

24. Debit cards can be an excellent alternative when parents need to monitor or manage spending for teens or young adult children. Moving specific amounts to children's debit accounts via a phone app or online transfer can control spending.

25. Most card fraud occurs when someone obtains your data, not your physical card. Protect the secrecy of all data related to your cards and your personal information.

26. The three primary reasons to buy insurance and warranties are: (1) when it is required (auto insurance for example), (2) when it could be a financial hardship if you did not have the insurance and a loss occurred (health insurance for example), and (3) when the cost of the insurance versus the likelihood of a claim is in your favor.

27. Don't waste money buying insurance or warranties to protect from relatively minor expenses. Buy insurance to protect from losses that would create a financial problem. Personal financial resources are often the determining factor of whether insurance is appropriate—a minor expense for one person is a hardship for someone else.

28. Every dollar spent unwisely on insurance premiums is a dollar that doesn't get invested to accumulate wealth.

29. The decision whether to own a home or rent should be made after careful consideration of financial and personal factors. Owning is a great choice for some people, while renting is the right choice for others.

30. The belief that renting is unwise because you are not *building equity* would be true if the all-in cost of home ownership was no greater than the cost to rent. However, that is seldom the case. Renters can effectively *build equity* by investing the money they saved by renting instead of owning.

31. From a financial perspective, homes are generally not good investments after all the related costs of ownership are considered. Particularly, buying a bigger house than needed as an *investment* strategy can be a costly mistake.

32. Taking advantage of the opportunity to refinance your home loan at a lower interest rate can have a profound impact on the wealth accumulation process. Refi and invest the savings!

33. With interest rates near all-time lows as of this writing, adjustable-rate mortgages (ARMs) don't have the appeal they once did. ARMs have more complex structures than fixed-rate loans, so be sure to understand the details if considering an ARM.

34. Having a Home Equity Line of Credit (HELOC) in place can act as an emergency line of credit to provide peace of mind, knowing money is available if a need arises. However, HELOCs can also lead to unwise spending that results in burdensome debt.

35. Trading cars frequently and owning expensive cars can be a major drag on wealth accumulation. Take care of your car and get a new one when you *need* it, not just because you *want* it.

36. Completing a net worth statement at least once a year is a great idea for anyone serious about accumulating wealth. It's the ongoing scorecard to monitor your wealth-building progress.

37. An income statement and a budget are basically the same document. An income statement shows actual income and expenses from a *prior period*, whereas a budget is a forecast of anticipated income and expenses for a *future period*.

38. The income statement is your past *history*, the budget is your target for the *future*, and the net worth statement shows where you are *presently*. Using and analyzing these three documents can be a powerful tool to improve your overall financial well-being.

39. Budgeting may be particularly helpful for the following groups: (1) those who have difficulty controlling their spending, (2) young adults with little experience balancing income and expenses, and (3) anyone with a small difference between their income and their fixed expenses, thus needing to be as judicious as possible.

40. Comparing your actual expenses with what was budgeted is one of the main reasons to do a budget. Doing so brings attention to potential overspending and identifies items where the budget may need to be adjusted.

41. Most people could construct a reasonably thorough personal budget in a few hours. The initial budget doesn't have to be precise. The budget can evolve and be tweaked as you go forward.

42. For those at mid-life who are not where they want to be financially, the "empty-nest" phase may be an opportune time for improvement—expenses are likely declining, and you are hopefully in the high-earning years—perhaps the perfect time to commit to the EARN+SAVE+INVEST+REPEAT formula for the years leading to retirement.

43. Understanding past money management behavior is the first step to improving future behavior. Resist spending money you have and need on things you don't have and don't need.

44. A *higher tax bracket* only affects the tax due on the income above the threshold for that bracket. Getting into a higher tax bracket doesn't mean a large tax bill is triggered because you earned one dollar too much.

45. *Tax-deductible* means your taxable income is reduced by the amount of the deduction. The reduction in your tax bill is the deduction amount times your tax bracket. If your marginal tax bracket is 22%, a $1,000 *deduction* would reduce your tax bill by $220.

46. A *tax credit* is a dollar-for-dollar reduction in your taxes owed or increase in your refund. A $1,000 tax credit reduces your taxes owed by $1,000. A tax *credit* is much more valuable than a tax *deduction*.

47. Deciding what age to start drawing Social Security retirement benefits is a major financial decision. The dilemma is that the younger you start drawing, the lower your benefit will permanently be. There are numerous issues to consider that often result in opposite conclusions.

48. Age 62 is the earliest you can start drawing Social Security, and 70 is the latest age anyone should start. If you start at 70 instead of 62, your monthly check would be more than 75% larger, but of course, you would miss out on eight years of monthly benefits. Drawing early and investing the money well could result in that option being substantially more lucrative.

49. Even though it is called *retirement* benefits by the SSA, you can continue working and still draw Social Security. However, there is a limit on the annual wages you can earn before you reach *full retirement age* (FRA), which is age 67 or sooner, depending on your year of birth. After reaching FRA, there is no limit on the wages you can earn and still draw Social Security.

INVESTING

50. Tax-advantaged retirement accounts such as 401(k)s, IRAs, and Roths are generally the most lucrative option for the vast majority of serious long-term investors to accumulate wealth.

51. If an employer offers a matching contribution with their 401(k) plan, employees should do everything possible to take advantage of the entire match.

52. There is no tax deduction for contributions made to a Roth, whereas there is a deduction for contributions to traditional IRAs. Conversely, distributions from a Roth are generally tax free, whereas distributions from traditional IRAs are fully taxable.

53. Employers can offer employees both traditional (pre-tax) and Roth (after-tax) options within 401(k) plans.

54. 401(k) plans may allow participants to borrow from their account balances, whereas borrowing is not allowed from IRAs or Roths.

55. You can withdraw up to the amount of your total Roth contributions without taxes or penalty at any age. Roth distributions are treated as contributions coming out first and earnings last.

56. Splitting contributions between a Roth, a traditional IRA, and a 401(k) has appeal because the rules for contribution limits, distributions, early withdrawal penalties, and taxation differ between them.

57. IRAs and Roths can be established at any institution of the wage earners choosing, whereas 401(k) plans are only available if the employer provides the plan for employees.

58. *Target-date* mutual funds are offered in many 401(k)s and other retirement accounts. The general concept of such funds is to shift an increasing percentage of the portfolio out of stocks and into bonds as the target date nears.

59. Minor children can have a Roth as long as they have earned income (wages). There is no minimum age limit.

60. Health savings accounts (HSAs) and flexible spending accounts (FSAs) are the absolute best of both worlds from a tax perspective. Contributions are tax deductible, and distributions for qualified medical expenses (QMEs) are tax free.

61. FSAs are only available if offered by an employer, whereas anyone (employed or unemployed) may establish an HSA as long as they qualify.

62. FSA contributions must generally be used (spent) each year or the unused portion is forfeited by the employee to the employer. HSA contributions may remain in the account indefinitely and grow tax free until needed for a QME, in later years. This is a significant advantage for an HSA over an FSA.

63. Most HSAs now allow investing in mutual funds, so HSAs can, in effect, be like having another IRA—contributions are tax deductible, and earnings can grow tax free for years or decades.

64. HSAs allow the choice of either taking tax-free distributions to pay for QMEs, or after age 65 distributions can be made for any reason without penalty, but the distribution is taxable if not used for a QME.

65. 529 plans may be a good option for high-income parents who have contributed the maximum to their retirement plans and have additional funds to invest for future college expenses.

66. For many parents, it may be more advantageous to contribute to their own retirement account rather than a 529 education savings plan account for the dual considerations of retirement planning and potential education costs for children.

67. UTMA accounts invested in stock mutual funds are a popular choice for investing money that belongs to a minor—money they earned working or that was a birthday gift, for example.

68. Be careful about gifting too much to a minor via a UTMA account since they have legal rights to the account when they reach age 21.

69. Stocks as a group have historically outperformed other asset classes. Choosing to invest in supposedly *safe*, interest-bearing assets to avoid the risk of investing in stocks has been to the detriment of many long-term savers.

70. Stock owners can profit in two ways—by receiving cash dividends, as well as having the potential for share price appreciation.

71. There are many companies that have consistently increased their dividend payout annually, thus providing a rising income for their shareholders.

72. A stock's price-to-earnings ratio (P/E ratio) is the most basic metric investors consider to decide if a stock is reasonably priced. When investing in stocks, be aware that a company's *value* (price) is eventually determined by its earnings.

73. Investing heavily in the stock of your employer can expose you to the dual risk of losing both your job and your investment assets if the company falters.

74. Investing in mutual funds, ETFs, and other managed accounts are a convenient way to own a diversified portfolio rather than buying individual stocks.

75. Each mutual fund and ETF has stated objectives and criteria for the way the fund is invested and managed. Investors should clearly understand that information before investing.

76. The main appeal of mutual funds and ETFs is not outperforming the stock market, but rather an easy and efficient way to simply be in the market.

77. Most mutual funds are *actively* managed, whereby the fund managers make discretionary stock selections, whereas most ETFs are *passively* managed, whereby stocks are selected by a computer model, which is often based on a market index. However, there are both *active* and *passive* mutual funds and ETFs.

78. The *prospectus* of a mutual fund or ETF provides information for investors, such as fees and expenses, historical rates of return, the objective of the fund, the fund's investment strategies, and much more.

79. In terms of sales charges (commissions), there are two basic types of mutual funds: *load* and *no-load*. Load means there is a fee paid to purchase the fund. No-load funds generally don't charge a fee because they don't compensate a broker for distributing the fund.

80. One of the best things for the overall financial well-being of American workers is that mutual funds are the predominant investment choice offered in most 401(k) plans.

81. Don't buy mutual funds or ETFs based solely on past performance. Funds with a narrow focus can have spectacular past performance for reasons that are unlikely to be repeated.

82. One appeal of ETFs is real-time order execution, whereby shares are bought and sold throughout the trading day, as opposed to traditional open-end mutual funds, where all orders receive the same end-of-day price.

83. Index ETFs and index mutual funds typically have annual expense ratios substantially lower than actively managed funds because they have eliminated many of the management expenses.

84. Investors should be careful when investing in *sector* funds, as being in the wrong sector can be almost as financially damaging as being too consolidated in a few poor-performing individual stocks.

85. When interest rates rise, the market price of existing fixed-rate bonds declines. With interest rates near all-time lows, bond investors need to understand the risk associated with rising interest rates.

86. Due to low current interest rates, bonds don't have the appeal for investors seeking income like they once did.

87. Full-service brokers may be the best choice for investors who want a relationship with an investment professional, who they can rely on to provide advice and guidance as their designated account representative, whereas discount brokers may be the best choice for someone who prefers to make their own investment decisions and enter their own trades online.

WORK ETHICS AND MINDSET

88. Always do your best at your job. Your performance in an entry-level position may be the pivotal point to launch a highly successful career.

89. Hone your personal skills and prepare yourself today so you are positioned to take advantage of opportunities tomorrow. Utilize ways to improve your skills, knowledge, experience, and education. Make yourself worthy of a promotion, a pay raise, or a positive career change.

90. A relatively small increase in wages has the potential to have an enormous impact on wealth accumulation, but only if that wage increase is saved and invested wisely.

91. Taking on a side hustle job doing something you enjoy could have significant benefits financially and mentally.

92. Learn from your mistakes. Making bad decisions is sometimes the best way to learn how to make good decisions.

93. Listen to and learn from others, but think for yourself. Just because someone else says it's so doesn't make it so.

94. Hard work may beat talent when talent doesn't work hard. When you have talent and you work hard, phenomenal results can occur.

95. Simply surviving difficult periods can be a victory in itself and can have rippling benefits far into the future in ways impossible to see during those challenging times.

96. High-performing team-oriented individuals who continue to seek personal growth and development throughout their careers are excellent candidates for upward mobility. Never stop learning.

97. The rewards can be enormous for those with the courage and follow-through who dare to take risks to pursue better opportunities.

98. If you live like few people *will* for a while, you may be able to live like few people *can* for the rest of your life.

99. Usually good things don't just happen—we make them happen. Effort and work come first—rewards come later.

Are you wondering why the list has 99 items and not 100? Actually, there is one more item, and #100 is whatever is most suitable for you based on your personal circumstances. Fill in your answer below.

100.

CHAPTER 24

Final Words

THE WHY

There are numerous reasons why people focus on financial well-being and wealth accumulation. Some examples include:

$ Freedom of choice and independence of lifestyle that wealth provides.

$ Financial security and mental comfort knowing money is available if needed to deal with potential expenses in the future.

$ The ability to assist others financially, such as charities, family, or others in need.

$ Leaving a legacy of wealth to heirs.

$ Wealth serves as an income replacement, hence the ability to no longer require a job. (For example, a $2 million portfolio equates to $80,000 in income if only 4% is withdrawn annually.)

As an author, my objective is not to convince people why, or if, they should focus on wealth accumulation—it is up to each individual to make that decision.

But rather, my perspective is simply to share useful information to help maximize success for those who have decided to do so.

THE WHAT

Improving financial well-being, wealth accumulation, and financial freedom are obtainable objectives for average Americans by following the steps of EARN+SAVE+INVEST+REPEAT.

Step 1: EARN

Step 2: SAVE

Step 3: INVEST

Step 4: REPEAT

The process is quite simple and intuitive for most people … (1) **Earn** as much as possible, (2) **Save** a portion of what you earn consistently, (3) **Invest** the money well that you save, (4) **Repeat** the first three steps for many years.

The process is simple and straightforward. There are no slick new strategies, no extraordinary investing wisdom, no revelational secrets from the author that will quickly change your life forever.

The most impressive thing about the EARN+SAVE+INVEST+REPEAT process is how well it works—extremely simple but highly effective! It worked for me, and it has worked for millions of ordinary wage earners.

THE HOW

The book is primarily devoted to providing information and insights on a wide range of financial-related topics to help readers understand how to succeed with the wealth accumulation process. Specific things to do as well as pitfalls to avoid are covered. EARN+SAVE+INVEST+REPEAT is a simple formula to understand, but a close look at ways to optimize wages as well as reduce personal expenditures are often critical considerations. Specific knowledge about various aspects of the investing step can play a significant role in maximizing wealth accumulation. Having recurring money management methods and monitoring tools are also key elements to developing good habits to ensure long-term success.

STARTING THE WEALTH ACCUMULATION PROCESS

The best time to start the wealth accumulation process is **now**. Time is a critical factor; the sooner you start and the more years your investment earnings compound, the more success you will have. Late teens or 20s is a great age to start the habit of saving and investing regularly, but it is certainly not too late in your 30s, 40s, 50s, or older to take action.

An elaborate plan is not required to get started, and it is not necessary to implement everything at once. Focusing on easy initial steps is a great start. For example, taking a few minutes to cancel a $100 monthly membership you are not using and start investing that $100 a month in a stock fund in your 401(k) plan or an IRA would be great initial moves.

For those who fully embrace the wealth accumulation process, it is a multi-faceted effort whereby all aspects of one's financial life are considered. It is my sincere hope this book will help many readers on their way to wealth accumulation and financial freedom. EARN+SAVE+INVEST+REPEAT.

Best wishes on your journey,

Kurt
kurtreid59@gmail.com

REQUEST FROM THE AUTHOR

I t would be a pleasure to receive your feedback about this book, such as ways to improve the book, topics that should be added, areas you found confusing or that you disagreed with, as well as what topics you found the most helpful and what areas you agreed with the most.

If you enjoyed the book and found it beneficial, I would appreciate you providing a positive review on my book page on Amazon as well as telling your friends about it. Feel free to post a picture of the book on your social media accounts.

Thank you for reading, and I hope you have much success in the future.

Kurt Reid
kurtreid59@gmail.com

ACKNOWLEDGMENTS

My *smokin-hot* wife, Ruthie, my comma queen, my paragraph princess, who spent nearly as many hours proofreading as I did writing this book. Fortunately, she paid attention in middle school English class (unlike her husband).

David Young, who provided much-needed critical feedback as I started the book and encouraged me to continue writing. David was also a valuable proofreader, chapter by chapter. Harrison Winter, for sharing his creative conceptual insights early on that helped me shape the book.

The volunteer proofreaders, who are first and foremost my friends and family. Many changes were made to the book as a result of their collective comments and critiques. A special thanks to each of them ... Tom Ballew, Cliff Cain, Eric Clark, Tonya Coates, Jerry Fireman, Jerry Fleming, Wyatt Fleming, Rick Franklin, Dennis Mehl, Larry Midler, Mark Miller, Morgan Reid, Nick Rodriguez, Jacob Rooks, Mark Smith, and Gwen Veazey.

Made in the USA
Las Vegas, NV
16 November 2022

59621167R00208